D0231644

THE FAITH OF THE SCOTS

GORDON DONALDSON

THE FAITH OF
THE SCOTS

B. T. Batsford Ltd · London

© Gordon Donaldson 1990
First published 1990

All rights reserved. No part of this publication
may be reproduced, in any form or by any means,
without permission from the Publisher

Typeset by Photosetting, Yeovil
and printed in Great Britain by
Courier International, Tiptree, Essex

Published by B T Batsford Ltd
4 Fitzhardinge Street, London W1H 0AH

A CIP catalogue record for this book is
available from the British Library

ISBN 0 7134 6052 0

The publishers gratefully acknowledge a grant from The
Drummond Trust towards publication of this book.

CONTENTS

LIST OF ILLUSTRATIONS

LIST OF
ABBREVIATIONS

APS	*Acts of the Parliaments of Scotland*
Baillie	Robert Baillie, *Letters and Journals* (Bannatyne Club)
Calderwood	David Calderwood, *History of the Kirk of Scotland*, (Wodrow Society)
E.S.	*Early Sources of Scottish History*, ed. A. O. Anderson
EUL	Edinburgh University Library
IR	*Innes Review*
Kirkton	James Kirkton, *Secret and True History of the Church of Scotland* (1817)
Knox	John Knox, *History of the Reformation in Scotland*, ed. W. Croft Dickinson
Larner	C J. Larner, *Enemies to God: The Witch Cult in Scotland* (1981)
Moorman	John Moorman, *Church Life in England in the Thirteenth Century*
NLS	National Library of Scotland
OSA	*Old Statistical Account of Scotland*
Patrick	David Patrick, *Statutes of the Scottish Church* (SHS)
PCM	*The Party-coloured Mind*, ed. David Reid
Pitcairn	Robert Pitcairn, *Ancient Criminal Trials* (Bannatyne Club)
PSAS	*Proceedings of the Society of Antiquaries of Scotland*
R. Hist. Soc.	Royal Historical Society
RSCHS	*Records of the Scottish Church History Society*
RSS	*Registrum Secreti Sigilli Regum Scotorum*
SA	*Scottish Annals from English Chroniclers*, ed. A. O. Anderson
SHR	*Scottish Historical Review*
SHS	Scottish History Society

SR	*Scottish Reformation,* by Gordon Donaldson
SRO	Scottish Record Office
SRS	Scottish Record Society
STS	Scottish Text Society
St A F	*St Andrews Formulare* (Stair Society)
St A KS Reg	*St Andrews Kirk Session Register* (SHS)
TRHS	*Transactions of the Royal Historical Society*
TA	*Treasurer's Accounts*
Wodrow	Robert Wodrow, *History of the Sufferings of the Church of Scotland,* 2 vols. 1721.

ACKNOWLEDGEMENTS

Mr Imlach Shearer and Mr John McLintock were so good as to read my typescript, and I profited greatly from discussions with them on various points. The text benefited further from the counsel of Mr Anthony Seward of Batsford after his expert eye had been over the typescript. For advice on illustrations I turned to Dr David Caldwell and Dr Richard Fawcett, who gave me ready help. I am grateful for the good offices of the Community of the Carmelite Convent at Dysart, whose grounds include St Serf's cave, to which no public access is permitted. The photograph of the 'Hermitage' from St Serf's Tower was taken by Mr Bob Paterson, who kindly lent me his transparency. The reproduction of a photograph of the Beaton panel has been authorised by the National Museums of Scotland.

PREFACE

Libraries of books have been written about ecclesiastical organisation and finance, church buildings, the careers of clerics and the relations of the Church with the government, but few attempts have been made to discover how widely and how deeply the Christian faith was held and how it influenced the lives of individuals and communities. The search must be not for men's actions, which are narrated in chronicles, but for their thoughts, which are related, if related at all, in private writings; not what was recorded in records or survives in tangible structures or artefacts, but what lurked invisibly in human minds. It must be said that the evidence is distinctly thin. For a thousand years and more after Christianity appeared in Scotland there is little in writing which professes to disclose men's thoughts about even secular affairs, never mind the more private matter of religious belief. A good deal of what men did may be seen, but their motives, if discernible at all, can be discerned only by inference from their deeds.

From about the middle of the sixteenth century there is a growing *corpus* of private correspondence, memoirs and diaries which furnish some understanding of thoughts as well as actions. Of course the personal letter may convey not the views of the writer, but rather the impression he wanted to give to his correspondent; and as for a journal, account must be taken of how far the writer intended it to be preserved for posterity and how far he was exaggerating his own importance. These are significant qualifications. It must be kept in mind, too, that few extant journals and letters came from the pens of people on the lower levels of society. G. G. Coulton, who wrote *Five Centuries of Religion*, criticised those who have 'blindly mistaken the most enthusiastic devotional writings of a few picked men for the real average man's religion in the middle ages',[1] and much the same continues to be true for some time after the middle ages. It is only for the last few generations that the correspondence columns of newspapers preserve the views and beliefs of 'the average man'.

With all the information which ultimately becomes available, it may still be impossible to form a complete and coherent picture of what Scots believed and what effect their faith had on their actions. The historian of *The Expansion of Christianity*, Latourette, wrote: 'The individual Christian, if he is both honest and intelligent, often finds it almost impossible to judge how far even the most decisive of his actions has been due to Him whom he calls Lord. If the individual is perplexed to apportion the sources of his own deeds, how much more at a loss must the historian be when he endeavours to discover the part that the influence of Jesus has played in the lives of millions of individuals and in the culture and institutions which both mould and are moulded by these individuals?'[2]

Theology should perhaps be left to the theologians (though they do not always reciprocate by leaving history to the historians). In any event, the quest is not necessarily for the theology of the professional theologians, because what they taught may not have been what ordinary men and women believed. It must also be said that it is not entirely inappropriate that most writing about the Scottish Church has been concerned very largely with its organisation, for over the centuries disputes seldom focussed on theology, and most of the divisions and secessions were the outcome of what were essentially questions of ecclesiastical politics.

In nearly half a century of teaching and writing about Scottish history, and not least church history, I was keenly aware of the gap in our studies. I sometimes remarked to my students that in my lectures they heard a great deal about the history of the Church but little about the history of Christianity. They were apt to titter at that, whereupon I assured them that my remark had not been a mere cynical gibe. I did sometimes observe – not specifically with reference to religion and before I had read Latourette's words – that it is sometimes difficult enough to be certain of our own motives in the twentieth century and I asked how we could even begin to know the motives of other people in some earlier century. In lecturing on the reformation period, when essentials of the faith for once predominated over ecclesiastical politics, and being aware that I had written little about faith in my books on that period, I used to give a little attention to that topic, in order to redress the somewhat materialistic interpretation which appeared in my writings. I tried to put across some understanding of the medieval concepts of the Mass and of the evangelical view of the Atonement and of Justification by Faith. And incidentally – it seems to me highly significant – of all the lectures I gave to undergraduates that lecture was listened to with keener attention than any other. Possibly in the mid-twentieth century it was all a novelty to most of my hearers.

When, in May 1985, I received from the University of Stirling an invitation to give the Drummond Lectures in March 1987 on the theme of 'Scottish History and Religion', it occurred to me that this was an opportunity to try to explore the general topic of the influence of Christianity on Scottish life and thought. This proposal proved acceptable to the University and the Drummond Trust, and as the lectures took shape it emerged that the subject was one appropriately associated with the name of Henry Drummond. This book deals at more length with the themes I discussed in the Lectures.

Dysart, Fife   G D
April 1989

1

THE CONVERSIONS

Those who have written confidently, and perhaps a little glibly, of how Ninian preached to the southern Picts, Columba to the northern Picts, and so on, have seldom stopped to ask exactly what the missionaries taught, how many heard them, what their teaching meant in bringing their hearers to a new outlook on their own lives and on the society in which they lived, and endowing them with new motives to shape their actions. And, granted that men's hearts were touched, what gave Christianity its appeal, why did it prevail and indeed how widely did it prevail?

Little is known in Scotland even about what may be called the externals of 'the conversions'. In other countries there are episodes among which there are such strong resemblances that it is almost tempting to dismiss them as pieces of folklore, in which tales so often conform to a type. Two or three elements recur: a marriage of a pagan ruler to a Christian princess, the working of some miracle – not infrequently a victory in battle after an appeal to the God of the Christians – the conversion and baptism of a ruler and then the mass baptism of his subjects.

The story is told in France, in Kent, in Northumbria, in Mercia. In Kent, Bede tells us, King Ethelbert feared that Augustine was bringing not a superior religion but more powerful magic and insisted on meeting him and his companions in the open air, 'lest, if they practised any magical arts, they might impose on him and get the better of him'. The visitors came 'with divine, not magic, virtue, bearing a cross, an image of Our Lord, and singing the Litany' – which might have seemed magical enough to the pagans of Kent – and the king was persuaded to baptism not only by 'the innocent life' of the missionaries but also by promises 'which by many miracles they proved most certain'. Augustine boasted of his 'outward miracles' by which the English were 'drawn to inward grace', and was rebuked by Pope Gregory for bragging. An example of success by miracle-working is related in Denmark, where a German priest called Poppo, about 960, persuaded King Harald Bluetooth to accept Christianity by carrying red-hot iron in his bare hands without suffering injury.

Conversion could take place as a result of the defeat of pagans by Christians or as part of a military or political bargain. Charlemagne's campaigns against the Saxons and the Avars forced them to accept Christianity. When King Alfred acquiesced in the Danish occupation of part of England, the treaty provided that the Danish leader should be baptized. According to rather late evidence, the viking Erik Bloodaxe, who had harried Northumbria, was allowed by King Athelstan to hold his conquest on condition that he accepted baptism, with his wife, his children and his army. A marriage could be thrown in as part of the bargain: when the settlement in France of the viking Rolf the Ganger, *alias* Rollo, first Duke of Normandy, was recognised by the French king, Rollo received a French princess in marriage, did homage and agreed to be baptized.

As the conversion of the Scandinavian countries came about later than the conversion of the peoples of Britain, one element there was the influence not of imported queens but of cosmopolitan rulers who had themselves encountered Christianity in foreign lands. Among Norwegian kings, Haakon the Good (934–61) had become a Christian in England, Olaf Trygvasson (995–1000) was baptized in the Scilly Isles, St Olaf (1015–28) was baptized at Rouen. Each of them returned home to urge his compatriots to follow his example. There often had to be recourse to force. In Denmark there is a proclamation of almost arrogant autocracy in the Jellinge stone which was erected by Harald Bluetooth (d. 985) as a memorial to his father Gorm and his mother Thyra: Harald, it states, 'made himself master of the whole of Denmark and Norway and made the Danes Christian'. Harald also 'compelled' Earl Haakon, who ruled in the Trondheim area of Norway, to be baptized. Although the issue might be discussed in the *things* or assemblies, it was not necessarily decided by a vote, for the king could dictate that the alternative to baptism was combat or even death.

Marriage, miracles, conquest and compulsion seem, wherever we look, to have been the recurring factors. We have little positive evidence about similar events in Scotland, but it would at any rate be unreasonable to doubt that missionaries there would do their best to win the support of rulers, as was their strategy in every century and in every continent. The little we know of the social structure of Dark Age Scotland, its landscape peppered with hill forts, suggests that there were warring tribes and concentrations of population, which postulate leadership at one level or another. Columba's visit to a Pictish king, perhaps at Inverness, is related in an early source, but it may be as significant that the relations of Ninian with a local ruler, Tudwall, whom he is supposed to have cured from sickness and converted, and also the relations of Kentigern or Mungo with his local king, were recounted in sources composed long after their day as if such events were typical and to be expected.

If marriage figured in the conversions of sovereigns in Scotland, it is conceivable that it was not Christian brides, but Christian bridegrooms, who played their parts. As the Pictish rule of succession was matrilinear, a Pictish princess might marry a foreign prince whose son she would bear as heir to the throne. We can say with a good deal of confidence that among the fathers of Pictish kings were one or two princes from Wales, which had been Christian since the fourth century, a king of the Britons of Strathclyde, which had been Christian since the fifth or sixth century, and a scion of the Christian royal house of Northumbria. If a Christian prince from another land fathered a king of Pictland, the offspring may have been Christian too.

There is little evidence of any part played by conquest in the expansion of Christianity within Scotland, though some of the military successes of the Christian Irish settlers ('the Scots') against the Picts may have meant at least a temporary penetration of Christianity into central Scotland before the Picts were in general converted. When a king was converted he would put pressure on his people to follow him, but the only specific example of coercion comes from the north, where Scandinavian practice prevailed: Olaf Trygvasson, on his way home to Norway in 995, inveigled Earl Sigurd of Orkney on to his ship off South Ronaldsay and commanded him on pain of death to receive baptism and make his people follow his example.

Leaving aside such fortuitous elements as marriage, conquest and compulsion, none of which had anything specifically Christian about it, what appeal, what attraction, did Christianity have? It is rare to find evidence of the issues which were debated between the advocates of the new faith and the upholders of the old. The best-known instance is Bede's story of what happened in Northumbria among King Edwin's advisers. After Coife, the chief priest, proposed to assess Christianity in the light of the success it would confer in worldly affairs, he declared his lack of confidence in the old religion even by that standard, and the account goes on:

> Another of the king's chief men ... presently added: 'The present life of man, O king, seems to me, in comparison of that time which is unknown to us, like the swift flight of a sparrow through the room wherein you sit at supper in winter, with your commanders and ministers and a good fire in the midst, while the storms of rain and snow prevail abroad; the sparrow, I say, flying in at one door, and immediately out at another, whilst he is within is safe from the wintry storm; but after a short space of fair weather he immediately vanishes out of your sight, into the dark winter from which he had emerged. So this life of man appears for a short space, but of what went before or what is to follow we are utterly ignorant. If, therefore, this new doctrine contains something more certain, it seems justly to deserve to be followed'. The other elders and the king's councillors, by divine inspiration, spoke to the same effect.

The chief priest spoke again: 'I have long since been sensible that there was nothing in that which we worshipped, because the more diligently I sought after truth in that worship the less I found it. But now I freely confess that such truth evidently appears in this preaching as can confer on us the gifts of life, of salvation and of eternal happiness'. He also returned to the practical argument that Christianity was 'more efficacious'.

That incident indicates the appeal which Christianity could make to people who were concerned about the immortality of the soul. The discussion in the *things* or assemblies of the hard-headed Scandinavians turned to more mundane matters. When Haakon the Good put the issue to the *thing* the opposition was based partly on the ground that if they abstained from labour on Sundays and fasted on Fridays they would lose the benefit of their labour and would be weakened by lack of food: 'they could not work if they did not get meat'. There was serious discussion among the Scandinavians, conversion was reluctant and it took place largely at the dictate of the king, but there is little indication of profound examination of the meaning of Christianity.

We know nothing of discussions in Scotland on either the Northumbrian or the Scandinavian model. What we do know is that when Columba encountered the

Pictish druids they did not talk theology. Instead they had a competition in miracle-working, like those between the Hebrew and Egyptian priests in Exodus vii and between Elijah and the priests of Baal in 1 Kings xviii:

'On the third day', says the Saint, '. . . we propose to begin our voyage'. 'Thou wilt not be able to do so', says Broichan in reply, 'for I can make the wind contrary for thee'. The Saint says, 'The omnipotence of God rules over all things'. . . . Our Columba, therefore, seeing the furious elements stirred up against him, calls upon Christ the Lord, and, entering the boat while the sailors are hesitating, he, with all the more confidence, orders the sails to be rigged against the wind. Which being done, the whole crowd looking on meanwhile, the boat is borne along against contrary winds with amazing velocity.

Columba turned out to be almost the miracle-worker *par excellence*. He calmed the sea, he made stones float, he drove off the Loch Ness monster, he opened the locked gates of Inverness, he turned water into wine, he foretold the future and he raised the dead. The miracles attributed to him must have conveyed the message that belief in the Christian God had practical advantages. For people who constantly travelled by water and were so often afloat in those narrow Highland lochs, where the wind invariably blows along the valley in either one direction or the other and never across it, Columba's ability to sail into the wind must have been immensely impressive. Then there is the story that without collating a copy which had been made of a psalter he was able to pronounce that in the entire transcript there was only one scribal error, and the story that a wheeled vehicle which had been blessed by the saint travelled safely although the lynch pins to secure the wheels to the axles were not in place. It must have seemed that Columba was a very useful chap to have around, and some have found the idea attractive that he was introducing people to new technology, as we should say now.

Very similar stories are told of Cuthbert's miracles, in an account written not long after his time. There are also the miracles (related very much later) of Ninian and of Mungo (some of the latter remembered because they figure in the armorial bearings of Glasgow). Perhaps the late 'Lives' tell us more about the beliefs of the twelfth century, when they were written, than of the fifth or sixth, when the heroes flourished, but the point is that later writers were apt to attribute the success of missionaries more to their skill as miracle-workers than to the content of their sermons. The Christian narrators presented it all in the context of the proclamation, 'As for all the gods of the heathen, they are but idols; but it is the Lord that made the heavens' (Ps. xcvi, 7), and much scripture could have been cited to the effect that God bore witness with signs and wonders and divers miracles. It would be more difficult to take to heart Our Lord's rebuke, 'Except ye see signs and wonders, ye will not believe' or to remember His warning that 'false prophets' would 'show great signs and wonders' (John, iv, 48; Matthew, xxiv, 24).

Granted the 'conversions' and baptisms, what happened next? Collective emotion can carry a host of people into deeds, good or evil, which they would never have committed as individuals, but often the emotion has no lasting results and can even be followed by a reaction when reflection causes men to wonder why they had ever acted as they did. It is not surprising, therefore, that conversion could be followed by a speedy relapse into paganism. Besides, while leadership from a ruler might produce results, too much depended on a single life and personality, and there were many instances of relapse – in Kent, Northumbria, Norway, Denmark and, it has been suggested, Pictland.[1]

Some tried to combine the old faith and the new. In East Anglia King Redwald set up an altar for Christian worship but kept another for sacrifices to the old gods (or 'devils' as Bede called them). Egil's Saga[2] has it that Athelstan of England, who was 'a good Christian,' asked Egil and his brother Thorolf to 'let themselves be prime-signed' or baptized and goes on: 'that was then a great custom both with merchants and with those men who went for hire among Christian men, since those men that had been prime-signed had full intercourse with Christian men and heathens also, and kept that as their religion which they liked best'. It is believed, on the evidence of a mould which has survived, that a Scandinavian metal-worker supplied his customers, according to their preference, with either a cross or a Thor's hammer.

On the other hand, while there were reluctant and inconstant converts, the abruptness of some of the conversions can be exaggerated. A certain knowledge of Christianity must have filtered through in the course of communication between the pagans outside the Roman Empire and the Christians within it – which in the Scottish context meant outside and inside the province of Britain. Christianity may have made an appeal as part of Roman civilisation. One can understand the impression made on the Caledonians of the north and the Britons of southern Scotland by the marching legions, the purposeful roads, camps, forts, frontier walls – the impression of order, uniformity and efficiency. In the fourth century the Christian Church was seen as part and parcel of the imperial machine and part also of a culture which extended beyond the military frontier. Contemporaries were not aware that the imperial machine was shortly to come to an end. Peoples outside the Empire, who had not felt the weight of Roman arms for generations, did not view Christianity as a religion of their conquerors. Individual missionaries, who had themselves learned the faith within the Empire, could be bearers also of cultural and perhaps technical progress. Yet, if Christianity came with the Empire, it did not fade with the Empire.

The possibility that 'conversion' may not have been as abrupt as has been supposed has another aspect – the absorption by Christianity of pagan elements. It is well known that in general the Church adapted pagan festivals (especially those associated with the rhythm of the seasons), architecture, vestments, the deification of human beings, the attribution of human characteristics to divinities, attachment to relics and so on, and links have been traced between pagan beliefs and the reverence paid to the Blessed Virgin; this can all be seen in the east and the Mediterranean, where Christianity first developed. In Scotland as elsewhere the identification of Christmas with the turn of the day and of Easter with seed-time did not escape notice among people living off the soil. The heathen term 'Yule' was preferred to 'Christmas' (though 'Pasch' [Passover] was preferred to the pagan 'Easter'). It is likely that some churches were built on pagan sites.

But leaving aside the more or less fortuitous elements in the process of conversion, is it possible to discern what was expected from religion, on the part of those, whether few or many, who gave the matter serious thought? Christianity has always gained its massive numbers of converts from people who knew only primitive beliefs; it has had little success against more mature faiths like Islam or Buddhism. The native religions of Scotland and of most neighbours of the Roman Empire belonged to the primitive model. As there is evidence of a belief in the immortality of the soul and even of the body (which was thought to require material goods in the future life), people wanted to know where they were going after death, like the man who spoke of the sparrow at Edwin's court. If druids taught the prospect of life in the Happy Isles, if Norsemen believed in the pleasures of Valhalla, even if there were those who had been touched by the thought of philosophers with an image of rewards and punishments in a future life, Christianity and the Christian sacrifice offered the prospect of eternal bliss. A presentation of Christianity which presupposed a consciousness of sin and a need for redemption, a presentation of Christ as the Saviour, the reconciler of man and God, would have been more difficult had missionaries not been able to work on the idea of salvation or damnation in the next world. Without a base in belief in immortality, the Christian God could have been presented only as the all-powerful controller of nature, to pagans who had deified the natural phenomena on which they felt their dependence.

Miraculous victory in battle no doubt appealed to rulers, but their subjects, well aware that there were always losers, may have had their doubts, and in any event the Dark Age peoples did not spend all their time warring around their hill-forts. They were farming, fishing, hunting, and in that predominantly rural setting they would look not only for safety from acquisitive neighbours but for good weather and good harvests, the averting of storms and pestilence, natural disasters against which a supernatural being could protect them. The weather might make the difference not only between plenty and scarcity but between survival and starvation, and those whose life was precarious because of human as well as natural action sought a god who could control nature as well as man's passions. Echoes of this are still to be heard in the words of the Litany, which have come down through many centuries with little alteration: 'From lightning and tempest, from plague, pestilence and famine, from battle and murder and from sudden death, Good Lord deliver us' and 'That it may please thee to give and preserve to our use the kindly fruits of the earth, so as in due time we may enjoy them, we beseech thee to hear us, Good Lord'. These phrases are seldom used now with either the sense of need or the conviction our ancestors felt. The hazards from which man implored deliverance could be seen as indications of the wrath of a God who could be appeased. Whether there was a pre-Christian concept of such wrath as the consequence of wrongdoing is uncertain, but the missionaries, no doubt quoting Old Testament prophets, may have had something to say about this. Many centuries later natural disasters were unhesitatingly regarded as punishments for sin.

Christianity offered what people had been accustomed to look for from their deities. It taught the possibility of miracles, it taught not only an omnipotent (if remote) God but also the ever-present power of prayer. It presented in the Mass a sacrificial offering with the expectation of some kind of return – a *quid pro quo* – though the sacrifice could also be an act of thanksgiving. The Mass could be offered for any 'intention', and prospective converts may have found it hard to detect – perhaps they were not expected to detect – much difference in principle between this 'unbloody sacrifice' and the bloody sacrifices which they had made to pagan deities for this or that prospective benefit.

Whether the concept of a loving God rather than one of terror and judgment prevailed it is impossible to say. If the message of the fatherhood of God penetrated, it implied the brotherhood of man, and the notion that Christianity is not for solitaries but involves fellowship may have been potent in a tribal society which had undergone mass conversion – though it might not influence their attitude to those beyond the confines of their own territory, whom they loved no better than before.

A central question, no easier to answer than some of the others which confront us in that early period, is what happened after the initial 'conversion' if relapse was to be avoided. In the first phases of Christianity, when conversions had been mainly of individuals, families, small groups, who could be thoroughly instructed and tested in the faith, the Church had consisted of something like what would later be called 'gathered congregations' of fervent and instructed believers, with a uniform level of commitment, whose differentiation from the surrounding paganism was obvious and who could be commanded, 'Come out from among them and be ye separate' (II Corinthians vi, 14 – vii, 1). Catechumens, it seems, might spend two or three years in preparation. However, even Paul's epistles indicate an awareness of first and second class levels of Christian achievement and it was not long before a distinction developed between the perfectionist few and the more lax majority. With the mass conversions it was easier to become a Christian – of a kind – and unless the way of life of a whole people was to be changed there was danger of the emergence of nominal, socially conforming, Christians and the blurring of distinctions between them and pagans. The primitive catechumenate, the intensive preparation before baptism, may have been generally abandoned before Christianity reached Scotland, but there ought to have been adequate instruction, even if time pressed. There is a story of a Burgundian tribe who, threatened by the Huns in 428, decided to seek the help of the God of the Romans and went to a city in Gaul for baptism. The bishop prepared them for seven days, baptized them on the eighth and sent them off to victory.[3] Instruction on even this scale would have been impossible with mass baptisms. On Christmas day 597, so Pope Gregory (no doubt misinformed by a boastful Augustine) told the patriarch of Alexandria, 10,000 people were baptized in Kent.[4] For comparative purposes, it may be noted that a Franciscan in Mexico in the early sixteenth century said that he had personally baptised 14,000 in one day. One almost wonders how many minutes it took to baptize each – or was it all done by a single collective ducking and a single recital of the baptismal formula? The community was moving as a whole, sometimes at the bidding of a ruler. How many of the thousands understood what it was all about? And how was the instruction and shepherding provided by a handful of missionaries? How long did the new converts remain under instruction?

Inadequate pre-baptismal instruction could have been remedied by additional instruction before admission to Communion, and the circumstances suggest that this must have been so if there were to be instructed Christians at all. This would be the stage at which, as in mission fields in later centuries, those under instruction would be commanded to give up practices which the Church thought superstitious or immoral. Even for the most sincere converts there should have been a period of vigilant policing of conduct, with breakers of the moral law subjected to exposure to their brethren in sackcloth and ashes. At this stage pressure of numbers still presented obvious difficulties. Who gave instruction, examined the thousands of converts and imposed discipline? Who shepherded the flock? Amid the likelihood of compromise and imperfect conversions it is impossible to quantify the spread of Christianity in Scotland. We do know that Christian institutions, in the shape of monasteries and bishops' sees, soon came into existence, but there are few signs of anything like local churches to serve a scattered population, settled mainly on the fertile soil of the coastal plains and the river valleys. We do get a glimpse from Bede of what looks like a kind of itinerant ministry in Northumbria:

> Wherever any cleric or monk arrived, he was joyfully received as a servant of God. Yea, if he were discovered as he went upon the way, they ran to him, and, bowing their necks, rejoiced to be either signed by his hand or blessed by his mouth. And they diligently offered a hearing also to their exhortations ... And if any of the priests chanced to come into a village, straightway the villagers gathered together and endeavoured to learn of him the word of life.

The first missionaries, after all, had been either foreigners or natives trained abroad, and one is bound to ask the question, though one cannot answer it, how the first native pastors were trained in their own country, for without them there can hardly have been the pastoral care and the sacramental ministrations which were necessary if Christian life was to develop. Much of the missionary work was done, one hears, by monks, who were indeed full-time clerics, but in view of their duties within their own communities they were not full-time pastors, if indeed they were pastors at all. It has been argued ingeniously but cogently from the occurrence of place-names with the element *eccles* (British *egles*) that there were local churches of some kind in south-western and central Scotland in the fifth century and in south-eastern Scotland in the seventh.[5]

If it is to some extent vain to look to monks for the ministry that was necessary, it is even more vain to look for it to the hermits, for their lives were lived in a greater or lesser measure of seclusion or solitude, in a tradition extending back to the early fourth century at least. Scotland seems to have had a fair supply of such 'holy men'. Some of them lived in caves, for example on the coast of Fife, where the Irish word 'uamh', meaning a cave, has given us the place-names Wemyss and Pittenweem and where the names of Fillan and Serf are associated with particular caves. The name of Serf's hermitage was Dysart, a name which means a desert or place of solitude and which occurs also in Dalmally in Argyll, at Faskally, Pitlochry, and in the Angus parish of Maryton. There had in pagan religions been a similar association of sanctity with isolated spots.

Some would have us believe that hermits sought isolation more austere than a cave provided. On a number of rock-pinnacles in the northern isles, barely accessible except for expert cragsmen, there are vestigial remains indicating an early human use. It is difficult to accept that they were used for permanent occupation (unless the occupants had access – as hermits perhaps had, being holy men – to supernatural sources of food and fresh water, or perhaps ability to fly) and to envisage a number of individuals, each perched on his pinnacle amid stormy seas, in emulation perhaps of St Simeon Stylites, who in the early fifth century took up residence near Antioch on a pillar about 60 feet high. There were some more substantial peninsulas or islands which offered sufficient solitude for all but the most austere, yet were practicable for habitation. Baldred on the Bass, Adrian on the May, are well known, and some more isolated islands may have housed small communities – Eileach an Naoimh in the Garvellochs, the Shiant Islands, the Flannan Islands – while others may well have been no more than hermitages – North Rona and Sula Sgeir, for example. The purpose of hermits, and even of insular communities, was ascetic, not the provision of a ministry.

There is little evidence of the extent to which pagan beliefs and practices survived alongside Christianity in Scotland, but there is some knowledge of what happened elsewhere and some scope for inference. The fact that Christians continued to name days of the week after heathen deities may mean no more than the fact that non-Christians today number their years from the birth of Christ. Devotion to local shrines may well have preserved elements of pagan worship and contained a danger of polytheism. The fire rituals of the lengthening day and of the summer solstice survived through the centuries and must have remained meaningful for long after the 'conversions'. Standing stones testified to ancient beliefs and possibly fertility rites. Christian priests, who were often hardly more educated than their parishioners, may have been prevailed on to lead pagan ceremonies, and the repeated legislation against dancing in churches and their precincts may point to the survival of ancient rituals. There are one or two instances in Scotland – far fewer than in Ireland or Denmark – of the insertion into church walls of stones carved with fertility symbols. After all, the king-making rite which persisted under Christian auspices had its roots in pagan superstitions surrounding a magic stone.[6]

There is ample evidence of continued reverence for trees, rocks and wells (sometimes given the names of saints).[7] It has been suggested that Columba's love of animals, birds and trees reflected a survival of pre-Christian ideas, and if he did not shed such pagan elements his 'converts' can hardly have done so. Admittedly, it was possible to cite Old Testament references to something like a sacred character in oaks (Judges, vi, 11; 1 Kings, xiii, 14; Ezekiel, vi, 13; Hosea, iv, 13), but the sacred grove, a common feature in Aryan religion, appeared in Ireland as a druid sanctuary. Adamnan mentions how Columba remembered Derry (*Daire Calgach*, the oakwood of Calgach) as 'my little oak grove' and was unwilling to cut down the oaks. The first nunnery in Ireland is said to have been founded at Kildare, 'the church of the oak', by St Bride, and some would have it that she is nothing else than a thinly disguised pagan goddess.

The art-forms of the Celtic Church have sometimes little about them that speaks of Christianity. Attention has been drawn to the fact that the Brecbannoch, or Monymusk reliquary, which presumably contained a relic of Columba, has few signs of Christian symbolism; they may be there, but they have to be searched for.[8] Anything Christian is even less visible on 'Ranvaig's Shrine', a reliquary of form identical to the Monymusk reliquary and thought to have been of Pictish workmanship.[9] Similar casket-reliquaries elsewhere are contrasts, with conspicuous Christian symbolism: e.g. the example from Limoges in the Royal Museum of Scotland.[10] Of even the Ardach chalice it has been said that it could be 'the wine-cup of a pagan king but for a band inscribed with the names of the Apostles'.[11] It may well be that a lot of the intricate interlaced ornament which long survived in Celtic decoration had a quality which was magical rather than Christian, and it has been a matter of debate whether the circle joining the arms of a 'Celtic cross' derives from the nimbus or halo surrounding the head of the Crucified or represents the sun or is merely a structural device.

If it is difficult to assess the extent to which pagan elements survived alongside or even within Christianity, one can be more positive about the survival of unchristian conduct. The stern public discipline of earlier times, which compelled the adherence of church members to certain standards, is not likely to have long, if at all, survived the conversions. There may have been ways in which Christianity actually had a damaging effect on morality, for sanctions derived from ancient tribal structures and old religions vanished without effective replacement. Certainly some of the enthusiasts for the extension of Christianity did not reach high standards in their own lives. Charlemagne contributed to the identification of an earthly empire with Christianity, he imposed baptism on conquered enemies, he went to mass every morning, but he had several 'wives' and in his family the border between concubinage and marriage was not at all clear. The Church's teaching that the ministers of the sacrament of matrimony were not the priests but the parties themselves (by whose declaration a marriage could be validly contracted) may have had a relaxing effect. At any rate, a contemporary envisaged Charlemagne in torments after death 'because he defiled his good deeds with foul lust', though his punishment was temporary as he was on his way to 'the place of honour the Lord has set aside for him'.[12]

One gathers from Bede that in his own Northumbria, years after the 'conversion', people 'disgraced the faith by unholy deeds' and had recourse to idolatrous remedies and the use of 'charms or amulets or any other mysteries of the magical arts'. Many people had not been reached at all, discipline was weak, there was no systematic oversight or instruction in morals, some of the clergy did not know Latin (without which they could not understand, even if they could read, the services), and some were lazy and licentious.[13] The life of the community had not yet been permeated by Christianity.

2

THE DARK AND EARLY MIDDLE AGES

The 'Dark Ages' embrace a third of the whole span of Christianity in Scotland, beginning with the conversions and ending with a kind of twilight zone in the eleventh century. Even at the end of that period we have little in writing to show what was in men's minds. And among their actions, from which we might infer something about their beliefs, we know little save of 'battle, murder and sudden death'.

In the whole tenth century only some fifty events are known to have happened within what is now Scotland. The tally includes eight battles, seven Norse raids, five agreements with English kings, a dozen non-violent deaths of notables, chiefly ecclesiastical dignitaries. As ten kings met violent ends, we can hardly blame a king of Alba for abdicating and becoming a monk, or a king of Strathclyde for going to Rome to take the tonsure, even though they might be reproached for shirking their responsibilities. Leaving such headline events aside, there is some evidence that a number of religious houses were founded or further endowed and that a number of holy men sought their own salvation in greater or less solitude. There was, at the beginning of the century, some kind of formal recognition or proclamation by a king and a bishop of the rights of the Church and an acknowledgment of its discipline, but in cryptic terms.[1] A few years later the clergy asked for money to ransom captives.[2] Perhaps the most specific item is the conviction of the Scots in 918 that they won a victory because they prayed to Columba, fasted and chanted, performed charitable works and received Communion.[3] There was, then, benevolence to the Church, a disposition to charity and some recourse to religious exercises in the expectation of material rewards.

About the middle of the eleventh century we hear more about gifts to the Church and we catch glimpses of local churches, presumably served by resident priests. Royal personages cease to be mere names and for the first time look like creatures of flesh and blood. Macbeth and Gruoch, Malcolm Canmore and Margaret, pass before our eyes. We still know little or nothing about the actions, never mind the thoughts, of any inhabitants of Scotland except the royal family, indeed we know the names of only a handful of individuals outside that circle – half a dozen bishops, two or three lay magnates.

Within the royal family we can discern what looks like a strong dose of more than conventional piety – though to say that implies an assessment of previous generations of which we know so little. Macbeth gave endowments to the Church – that was nothing new – and was so far as we know the first (and apparently the only) ruler of Scotland to go on pilgrimage to Rome, where the papal court had just been rescued from degradation and was on the eve of a thoroughgoing reform at the hands of Hildebrand. Another visitor to Rome was Thorfinn, Earl of Orkney; perhaps he travelled with his ally Macbeth, perhaps, as Dorothy Dunnett suggested, he was Macbeth under an *alias*. Royal pilgrimages to Rome were then the fashion: Knut, the Danish king who had recently ruled England, had been to Rome, and Edward the Confessor, contemporary of Macbeth, intended to go.

Macbeth was succeeded, within a few months of his death in 1057, by Malcolm III (Canmore), whose first wife was a connection of Earl Thorfinn and whose second wife was the English Margaret, a member of the old English royal family which had been excluded from the throne by the Danish kings, and during their exclusion her father had taken refuge in Hungary. It has been suggested that Margaret's zeal owed something to her experience of a land where Christianity was an exciting novelty and where, after the death of St Stephen (1038), the Christian party had had to contend with a pagan reaction. However, as it had been only about 995 that the Earl of Orkney had been coerced into baptism, Malcolm's first wife may also have imbibed the zeal of recent converts and he may have been the victim – if that is the word – of two demonstratively zealous wives. Margaret's great-uncle, in her own English family, was Edward the Confessor, who has been characterised as not an English king but a French monk, under whom a Norman conquest of England began by peaceful penetration before William the Conqueror crossed the Channel in 1066.

Margaret's piety showed not only in 'rather ostentatious acts' like washing the feet of the poor but in discussions with the Scottish clergy. One of the points concerned reluctance to receive Communion. The natives quoted St Paul, 'He that eats and drinks unworthily eats and drinks judgment upon himself' and went on, 'Therefore because we recognise that we are sinners, we dread to approach that mystery, lest we eat and drink judgment upon ourselves'. The Queen replied: 'Why then, shall all who are sinners not taste the sacred mystery? In that case, none ought to take it, because none is without stain of sin. . . . If none ought to partake of it, why does the gospel proclaim, in the Lord's words, "Unless you eat the flesh of the Son of Man, and drink His blood, you shall not have life within you?"' Margaret was making the valuable point that Christianity is designed not for saints but for sinners. St Paul, she added, was condemning those who presumed to communicate without confession and repentance, whereas 'we, who many days before have made confession of sins, and are scourged with penitence and made lean with fasting, . . . take the flesh and blood of the Spotless Lamb, Jesus Christ, not for judgment but for remission of sins'. Clearly both Margaret and her opponents had thought about this central point; but Margaret was in line with majority Christian opinion. Her words were to be echoed several centuries later by St Catharine of Siena and may well have been used again in more recent times to persuade West Highlanders to shake off the conviction some of them still have about their unworthiness. It emerges, incidentally, that in Margaret's day Communion was normally only at Easter, as it continued to be throughout the Middle Ages. Some points Margaret debated arose simply because the Scottish Church had not kept in touch with developments in the Western Church generally. One of her innovations was the strict observance of Sunday as a day of abstinence from labour: while the transference to Sunday (*dies Dominica*, the Lord's Day) of the reverence attached by the Jews to Saturday (*dies Sabbati*, the Sabbath) had been progressing on the continent since the early centuries of Christianity, successive acts of church councils had not yet succeeded in completing the process.

Edward the Confessor, that 'French monk', had no taste for matrimony, and his marriage was only a formal one. A preference for celibacy persisted among Margaret's kin. Her sister became a nun and her brother Edgar the Atheling never married. Among her six sons, four apparently did not marry, while Alexander I married but had no children by his wife (though he may have had an illegitimate son), and the youngest of the brothers, David, was the only one who, after marrying (but not until he was over thirty), had children by his wife. David's son Henry had several children, but of his three sons Malcolm was called 'The Maiden' because he was celibate and the second, William 'The Lion', did not marry until he was over forty. Distaste for matrimony in an individual does not necessarily imply a belief in the principle of celibacy, but a kind of monkish preference is somewhat remarkable in a royal family, where the continuance of the dynasty was important. However, Margaret herself was no celibate. She had at least six sons and two daughters, and her career as wife, mother, queen and saint suggests the phrase 'All this and heaven too'.

One Scottish historian, Hume Brown, described her as 'an able and ambitious woman, bent on the aggrandisement of her own family and the predominance of the English interest', and Eric Linklater, with typical forthrightness, characterised her as 'one of those strong, interfering, pious and persistent women of whom England has bred a considerable number'. Did she give the names of English kings to four of her sons – Edward, Edmund, Ethelred and Edgar – in the hope that one of them might displace the intruding Normans? Her piety did nothing to deter her husband from marauding raids into England.

Margaret's youngest son, David, was cast in his mother's mould, for he is said to have heard all the canonical hours or services each day and his munificence in founding abbeys is proverbial. He had to be dissuaded from going on crusade, and his grandson and successor, Malcolm IV, made a vow to go on pilgrimage to the shrine of St James at Compostella.

In investing in the Church, David, his grandsons Malcolm and William and other royal and baronial benefactors were not seeking only spiritual dividends: the ecclesiastical structure contributed to the consolidation of the kingdom, and monasteries did much for the development of its economy by sheep-farming, coal-working, salt manufacture, the wool trade and so on. That is a familiar story. But there were more subtle features. The monks' standards of devotion and conduct were a constant inspiration to men both within and without their walls; and their ordered life must have made them oases of stability in troubled times. So far as the emphasis was on the salvation of souls, the munificence to the Church in the twelfth century looks like the biggest investment in non-material activity that western Europe has seen. But whether religious functions required such massive and costly 'plant' is another matter. There were surely elements – sometimes competitive elements – of grandiosity and display among those who followed the current fashion of founding abbeys, and also among their favoured orders of monks. Could thoughts of the glory of God wholly exclude from the mind of the builder of an abbey all thought of the glory of his own family, in comparison perhaps with the glory of the Joneses in the next valley? Nor can one ignore delight in the achievements of architects, sculptors and artists who produced beautiful things which gave pleasure to the donor and through which he gave pleasure to others.

The religious, as distinct from the material, psychological or aesthetic, significance of the abbeys takes us back to some of the problems of the post-conversion period. As long as Christians had been a minority, sometimes a persecuted minority, only the deeply committed would have considered it worth while to face the associated inconvenience and perhaps risk. Even then, however, there seem to have been those who felt that they should shake off the world and withdraw to surroundings where its cares and temptations did not lie heavily upon them. There had been hermits and small communities in the east from the end of the third century, and the general breakdown of order during the dissolution of the Roman Empire probably encouraged such a trend. Then, when Christianity became a matter of social conformity, the more committed were inclined to draw apart as hermits or monks.

Those who gave of their substance for the endowment of monasteries may have had various religious motives. The earliest documents indicating reasons for the foundation of religious houses – with a phraseology perhaps less self-conscious than some of the more stylised language we find later – suggest that one thing the founder wanted was prayers – prayers for the wellbeing of himself and his kin in this life, for the wellbeing of their souls after death and for the souls of some already deceased. Prayers are mentioned in general terms in some of the earliest evidence, in the middle of the eleventh century – *pro suffragiis orationum* or *pietatis intuitu et orationum suffragiis*. About 1100 provision was made specifically for prayers for the souls of the granter's father and mother, for the safety of the granter's body, for the souls of the granter, his brother and sister and all his ancestors and successors, and for the safety of 'my lord the king and of his father, mother, brothers and sisters'. David I's charters nearly always allude to the souls of himself, his kin, predecessors and successors, but his grandsons tend to be less specific. The earliest known Scottish grants to religious houses had been made *in liberam elemosinam*, translated 'in free alms', which meant that there was no material *reddendo* or 'return' in secular service, goods or money, with the implication that the return was to be non-material, that is, prayers. Prayers continued to be thought of as a main reason for founding religious houses, right down to the reformation and beyond it: the phrase 'suffrages of devote orisoun and prayer' was used about 1570 to recall the reason for a foundation.[4] In hospitals and almshouses the residents who received charity were expected to pray and were in consequence known as 'bedesmen' (ultimately derived from the old English *gebed*, a prayer – same root as 'bid').

As time passed, the phraseology became less precise as to what the prayers were for, suggesting a concept of the monastic houses as power-houses of prayer, where prayers were offered generally for blessings upon the world and its needs, and it may well be that the general term 'prayers' was used to cover not only intercessions but any communication with God, embracing praise and thanksgiving – in fact the whole content of the monastic services, the divine office or *Opus Dei*. The answer to anyone who says, 'I don't approve of monasteries' is the question 'Do you believe in prayer?' To anyone who believes in prayer the case for monasteries seems unanswerable.

Another concept in the minds of founders may have been that their benefactions could in themselves benefit their souls, irrespective of prayers that might be said. Such benefactions were among the good works whereby, theologians as well as ordinary folk believed, the soul could be purged of sin. Munificence to a religious house *pro salute animarum* did not necessarily postulate the saying of prayers specifically for the founder's soul. The inmates of the institutions, as well as the founders, considered that acts of charity performed by the houses would benefit their own souls. Whether through prayers or through acts of charity, souls were to be saved, but it is not certain that altruistic thoughts of the well-being of others were the primary consideration.

Given the reasons for the endowment of religious houses, why was there an outburst of generosity in the twelfth century? It is true that Scotland was following a fashion widespread in western Europe and that, while some previous fashions had passed Scotland by, it was now, thanks to the Normans, integrated into European culture as never before. The papacy had been reformed and was offering renewed leadership, some novelties had been introduced into monasticism and the crusades stirred a general militancy. There is no reason to believe that there was a sudden increase of material resources or that the economy was much more productive in the twelfth century than in the eleventh. The possibility that the Normans injected into the Scottish Church wealth from their properties elsewhere can probably be dismissed. They had not come to Scotland as philanthropists. There was indeed one new channel whereby resources could conveniently be found for the maintenance of religious houses. The development of the parochial system involved the allocation of tithes or teinds to parish churches, the appointment of whose parsons commonly lay with a local landlord as patron. It was open to a patron to confer the office of parson on a religious house, which meant that the bulk of the teinds (paid by the parishioners) were appropriated to that house. But this merely enabled the landlord to provide funds without digging into his own pocket.

The motives of the inmates of the monasteries were as complex as those of the founders. There was the element of believing fervently in the power of prayer and consequently in the monk's life of prayer, for himself as well as others. There was the belief that by mortifying the flesh, to the extent that by becoming a member of a religious order he gave up a lot of what the world offered, he was doing something meritorious which could profit his own soul. To take monastic vows meant commitment to a standard higher than could be attained, so at least it would be thought, by all men; and the bringing together, in a community, of people who had taken this further step, which was a kind of 'conversion' – a change of mind and the turning over to a new way of life – created a community of 'first-class Christians'. The truly religious life could not be a half-measure. The very terms 'religion' and 'religious' were appropriated to monasticism: a monk's conventional designation was *religiosus vir* – 'a religious man' – and in taking his vows he had 'entered religion'. Few 'gathered congregations' have so unashamedly advertised themselves as 'holier than thou'. Some perhaps believed that the Church in general was not holy enough, others that the temptations of the world were too great for them to bear, and in effect they obeyed the injunction 'Come out from among them and be ye separate' (2 Cor. vi, 17). It was easier to attain holiness in a monastic community, sheltered from temptation, than in the world outside. (I recall a member of a boys' club once observing, with remarkable perspicacity, 'It's easy to be good when you're in the club'.) Admitting the value of the high standards, admitting the value of prayers for the rest of the world, was it really good for the community that the holiest people should be withdrawn into cloistered seclusion instead of mingling freely with everyday life and spreading their influence throughout it? To some extent monasticism represented a retreat from the ideal that Christians should aim at transforming the whole of society instead of forming a godly élite.

The principles and practices of monasticism had good support in the New Testament. The vow of chastity was strongly commended by St Paul, in whose eyes even marriage was no more than a second-best. Paul's emphasis, in Romans xiii and elsewhere, on subjection to authority, told equally strongly in favour of the vow of obedience. The third vow, of poverty, found support in the divine recommendation, 'Go and sell that thou hast, and give to the poor' (Matt. xix, 21) and in the examples of the Christians of apostolic times, when 'all that believed were together, and had all things in common; and sold their possessions and goods, and parted them to all men, as every man had need' (Acts ii, 44–5). However, a monk, on entering an order, surrendered his possessions not to the poor at the gate but to the abbey, so that poverty was of a somewhat formal kind: while technically owning nothing, he enjoyed the amenities of a comfortable residential club, perhaps a geriatric refuge, he withdrew from the obligations of society and gained the privileges of his community. Such 'poverty', especially in an age when there was so much insecurity, was a lesser sacrifice than a change in a man's nature, the total giving of his life to Christ.

The strength of the communal bond varied from order to order. The ideal of the eremitical way as nearest to perfection was strong, and the Carthusians were almost hermits, living each in his own cell and knowing no path save that between his cell and the church. Significantly enough, they were the order whose boast was *nunquam reformanda quia nunquam deformata* (never requiring to be reformed because never deformed) and their standards never declined, but – again significantly – they had only one house in Scotland, the Charterhouse at Perth, and it was founded so late as 1429.

The spiritual commitment of monks made them speak the language of evangelicals, unchanged throughout the ages. St Bernard of Clairvaux laid great emphasis on the appeal of the Passion: 'The nail calls, the wound calls that truly God has reconciled the world to himself in Christ'. Bernard's sermons on the Song of Songs took over the imagery of Christ as the Bridegroom not only in relation to the Church but even in relation to the individual soul, and St Mechthild of Magdeburg, a German nun (c. 1210–80), described her mystical experiences in a kind of elevated eroticism – being taken into Christ's arms and being kissed by Him. (I recall an ardent and much admired evangelical of my own acquaintance once remarking that 'finding Jesus is like finding your ideal girl'.) The thought of

Adam of Dryburgh (d. 1212), who was a Premonstratensian canon in Scotland before joining the more austere Carthusians in England, was based on fervent personal conviction and consciousness of 'the great mercy of God, who spared not His own Son, but delivered Him up for us all', because 'the Son loved us and washed us in His own blood to set the prisoners free'.[5] 'Salvation' in his vocabulary meant not merely the negative escape from the danger of hell (of which he had a good deal to say) but also the more positive consideration that the canon must love Jesus in all things and above all things.

Yet already in Adam's day, when monasticism still had all the vigour of youth, it did not achieve uniformly high standards. Some canons did not shed all thought of the world and would chatter and gossip all day or even engage in slander; others were preoccupied with the finance and business of the house; in the election of an abbot, jealousy and expectation, fear and favour, could all have their influence. One of the most difficult rules to enforce was the prohibition of private property, for which human acquisitiveness was too powerful.

The business of the monk was to flee the world and wait upon God, not to serve the altar or call people to God. The Carthusian order declared firmly that its members retired from the world to care not for the poor but for their own souls, and Adam of Dryburgh had nothing to say of the care of souls and little to say about charity to those outwith the house. There were, however, abbeys where the nave served as a church for the surrounding parish, and a monk could be detailed to serve the parishioners, while canons regular – Augustinians and Premonstratensians – acted as vicars in parish churches whose revenues were appropriated to their houses – an association with the world in which Adam of Dryburgh saw some risk.

Yet in general the care of the souls of laymen was in the hands of parish priests who were secular clergy and not members of a religious order. From this point of view the important development of the twelfth century was not monasticism but the emergence of the parochial system. We are apt to take it for granted – not surprisingly, for the parish is our oldest existing local institution – but its introduction represented an astonishing achievement. In 1100 there were indeed some local churches, but they were not yet parish churches; by 1200 nearly all of Scotland's 1100 or so medieval parishes were in existence. (Denmark claims the foundation of 2000 parishes in a century.) Every scrap of land in Scotland was within a definite territorial parish, every individual had his parish church and his parish priest, with obligations and privileges attached thereto. That was or should have been the framework for the expansion and fostering of Christian belief.

It fell to the parish priests not only to administer the sacraments and to instruct and exhort the people but also to operate the penitential system which should have directed and controlled their way of life. The public correction of offenders known in early centuries had already introduced distinctions between mortal and venial sins and other gradations, with corresponding degrees of penance. Such distinctions were carried over when the public correction of offenders was replaced by private confession, with penance following rather than preceding absolution. How severe penance could be in the eleventh century is indicated in Queen Margaret's remarks, already quoted, about the strenuous nature of her preparation for Communion, but even then such severity may have been exceptional and before many generations had passed there was considerable relaxation. Private confession was finally made the rule (along with the obligation of making an annual Communion at Easter) in 1215, and thereafter penance (imposed by the confessor) seems to have become increasingly nominal. Public penance in effect vanished until it was revived by some of the reformers in the sixteenth century.

The work of monks and priests alike, in all the aspects of ministry, was supplemented by the orders of friars, who originated in the early thirteenth century. Although they took the same three vows as monks, their establishments were generally not (as so many monasteries were) in rural surroundings, but in towns, where they were active as preachers and confessors, and they had undergone training which made them superior, at any rate as preachers, to the average parish priest. If monasticism had represented a retreat from the ideal that Christians should consider it their mission to transform the whole of society and not be content with achievement within a small group, the friars constituted a reaction against monasticism, for they represented the intention to lead all professing Christians, lay as well as clerical, into genuine discipleship, and this was in some ways more in the main stream of Christianity than was the work of the monks. It may well be that the task of the initial conversions was completed, in so far as it was ever completed, by the friars. One can almost see a progression – or should it be regression? – from hermits, through monks and friars, to parish priests; at each stage there was progressively more involvement with the people at large.

The connection of the early British churches with Rome had been disrupted when the pagan Anglo-Saxons arrived; later, Scandinavian settlements not only in the north and west but also in southern Scotland and northern England renewed a measure of isolation. While there has been speculation about doctrinal differences between the Celtic lands and Rome, and while there may well have been distinctive theological emphases, the only differences we know of were in practices and usages. However, Augustine had found, almost as soon as he landed in England, that the Celtic bishops would not accept Roman jurisdiction, and a century later, when a Northumbrian king had declared himself in favour of Rome, Scots declined to accept a Roman ruling even in such a minor matter as the date of Easter. By the eleventh century, however, when Macbeth went to Rome and Margaret was in communication with Canterbury, the links were becoming closer. The first papal bull addressed to Scotland and still extant dates from about 1112[6] and the first occasion when a papal legate held a council in Scotland was in 1138. In the medieval centuries the constant traffic between Scotland and Rome and the affiliation of so many religious houses in Scotland to the continental headquarters of their orders intensified the European dimension in the minds of the Scots. One never ceases to marvel at the courage with which our ancestors faced journeyings to and from Rome or other continental centres: in peril and discomfort in cockleshells of vessels by sea and on rough tracks by land and risking the violence of nature and man.

Integration with the western Church meant that many aspects of Scottish life and relationships were determined by canon law. But there were other, less direct, ways in which Christianity helped to shape law and men's attitudes to it. The mere facts that Christianity had grown up within the Roman Empire and that the Church's organisation had developed in association with the imperial structure made the Church a link with Roman law. Missionaries who were not professionally trained in law might nevertheless carry with them a working knowledge of some legal practice. The whole idea of something like a written code of law seems to have derived from Rome. Bede says that Ethelbert, king of Kent, put his laws into writing 'after the example of the Romans' (*juxta exempla Romanorum*), which may mean models brought by Augustine, though Kent had links with Romanized Gaul (and therefore the Empire) before Augustine came on the scene. No doubt one reason for written law was to ensure the protection of the Church's property and to add sanctions to its moral teaching. Early criminal law had been based on the idea of offences not against society or the government which ruled a community, but against individuals, so that the main penalty for crime was the requirement to make amends to individuals who had been wronged. The notion that families and kin-groups should take up quarrels and exact vengeance was not readily extinguished and it lingered on in the wergild and assythment which compensated the kin of victims.

Christianity introduced new concepts: the Ten Commandments (pre-Christian in origin and largely concerned with rules of conduct on the basis of prohibitions), which were instilled by the Church, used in the instruction of catechumens and integrated into the penitential system, were directed at offences against God as well as men. Besides, the whole idea of penalties following from sin facilitated the introduction of punishments for crime, the Old Testament and the New alike were stocked with allusions to punishments and there was scriptural approval of the powers of punishment exercised by the civil magistrate: 'Thou couldest have no power at all against me except it were given thee from above'. In this rather indirect way Christianity influenced men's actions. Trial by ordeal and by combat met with approval, for they could be seen as an appeal to a supernatural decision when men could not decide. However, after centuries during which the Church had given to trial by ordeal the sanction of clerical supervision, the Lateran Council of 1215 forbade clergy to take part, and this method of detection was soon abandoned. Trial by combat was also frowned on by the Church, but this, at least in the form of the duel, lingered for centuries. Christianity made its influence felt in civil as well as in criminal law. The making of wills no doubt spread as a result of acquaintance with Roman practice, but the Church, as a great beneficiary of bequests, had an interest in discouraging intestacy, and priests (who often drew up wills) could use persuasion. These were all matters of institutional Christianity rather than of personal faith.

Christian belief affected also the social and political structure. Some saw God as a King who sent his Son as a princely warrior to battle on earth for the souls of men; others strongly emphasised the kingship of Christ, whose place as Judge sometimes obscured His place as Redeemer. These thoughts had an effect on the attitude of men to their earthly kings, and few had any thought of a polity which had no place for a monarch. The Old Testament was full of information about kings, the New had much to say about the Kingdom of Heaven. Kings ruled under God – *deo rectore*, as some early charters or seals have it – and the fifteenth-century *Three Priests of Peblis* presented the Christian ideal of a 'noble king' who welcomed the clergy as his 'helmet, spear and shield' and as the 'rule and rod' of his kingdom. The Church was involved in royal inaugurations (despite the survival of pagan superstitions about a sacred stone), although Scottish kings were not anointed until the fourteenth century.

The Pauline injunction to obey 'the powers that be' could no doubt be cited to support the authority of local magnates as well as that of kings and to cement a society in which 'every man must have a lord'. People of rank and wealth had their private chaplains, and a medieval castle frequently had a chapel either within it or nearby, but often the parish church had originated as a private chapel of a landowner, and as he sometimes continued to have the patronage of the church, the parish system was to some extent integrated with feudal society.[7] Anglo-Saxon laws had been explicit and in Alfred's reign unique sanctions were claimed for the crime of treason against a lord: compensation might be accepted for every other misdeed, but for that offence 'they dared not assign any mercy because Almighty God adjudged none of them who despised Him, nor did Christ adjudge any to them that sold Him to death, and He commanded that a lord should be loved as oneself'.[8]

But was the king acting under God when he led his men to battle? Pacifism has never prevailed among Christians and it is only too easy to note that Our Lord did not, for example, go around advising Roman officers to resign their commissions. A distinction might have been drawn in favour of wars fought for the defence of Christianity against pagans, or even in favour of wars fought with the intention of spreading Christianity. Scotland had no experience of the latter activity, and so far as defence against pagans was concerned its only experience had been with the Norse.

It is wars against Christians that alone concern us in assessing Scottish Christianity. All the evidence suggests that a war by one Christian kingdom against another was expected to have supernatural blessing. There was the legend that St Andrew had intervened on behalf of an early king of the Picts in his wars against southerners, there was the belief that Scots had later been victorious with the aid of Columba.[9] These shadowy operations, against foes in the south, may well have been defensive, but battles about which we know more were very often not defensive. The pious Margaret's son, Edgar, had recourse to military operations to establish himself on the Scottish throne, and her brother, Edgar the Atheling, waged war on her son-in-law, Henry I, on behalf of Henry's brother Robert. Kinship among rulers was no more potent in checking warfare then than it was in 1914 – and no more potent than Christianity. David conducted campaigns deep into England, Malcolm the Maiden accompanied Henry II on a military expedition, and William the Lion raided England. When David invaded England in 1138 he no doubt argued that he was maintaining the just right to the English throne of his niece, Matilda, against her successful rival Stephen; but the English whom he encountered believed that they had divine support and came to the field of 'The Standard' under the banner of their own saints.

If what they said about the Scottish invaders was even partially true, they might have been amply justified in expecting heavenly protection. The 'atrocities' attributed to enemies have changed so little over the centuries that they have an air of the stereotype. What was said by Henry of Huntingdon, writing contemporaneously of 1138, comes close to what was said in the twentieth century about Turks in Armenia and Germans in Belgium: 'They cleft open pregnant women and took out the unborn babe; they tossed children upon the spearpoints, and beheaded priests upon the altars. . . . Wherever the Scots arrived, all was full of horror and full of savagery. There was the screaming of women, the wailing of old men; groans of the dying, despair of the living'.[10] The men of Galloway seem to have had a peculiar reputation for ferocity, and a little later (c. 1180 onwards) it was said that among them 'neither faith nor hope nor charity can long exist. There chastity suffers shipwreck as often as lust wills'.[11] This was about eight centuries after Ninian's mission and at a time when abbeys were being founded in Galloway.

Curiously enough, the Battle of the Standard took place a year after the foundation of a cathedral in honour of the only pacifist of that era – St Magnus of Orkney. On an expedition by King Magnus Barelegs in the Irish Sea, when the warriors took up their arms Magnus sat down on the foredeck and said that as he had nothing against anyone there he would not fight. The king told him to go below and get out of the way, but Magnus took a psalter and sang during the battle, instead of sheltering himself. Pacifism remained a deviation, and on the whole the idea of a Christian in arms for a just cause proved more than merely acceptable in the middle ages, while after the reformation each side in so-called 'wars of religion' fought for what was thought self-evidently a 'good cause'.

Scots shared in the crusades, but we know little of this, and some of the material which may throw light on the thoughts of Scots who took part came from individuals who were at least as much Irish as Scottish and were outwith the main stream of Scottish life. They indicate something like nervous apprehension about the dangers of Mediterranean voyaging and a considerable degree of sentimental homesickness.[12] The *Melrose Chronicle* gives some insight into crusading mentality when it remarks on the loss of Damietta in 1219: 'It is not known whether this came about by the demerits of the Christians or by the judgment of God, especially since at that time divine service was being carried out in that city with splendid magnificence'. This parallels a remark of Robert Baillie, the covenanting writer in the seventeenth century, who, observing the successes of the Marquis of Montrose against the Covenanters, was frankly incredulous: 'We are amazed that it should be the pleasure of our God to make us fall thus the fifth time before a company of the worst men in the earth'.[13]

Beyond the classical crusades, operations went on for the extension of Christianity in the Baltic lands and the reconquest of Spain from Islam, while, after the Holy Land was lost, the islands of Cyprus, Rhodes and finally Malta were held as Christian outposts by the Knights of St John. Scots were involved in such activities, but it is difficult to deny that Christian motives merged with those of mercenaries.

Meantime there was no cessation of war between the states of western Europe, and not least, after 1296, between Scotland and England. Although any Christian ideal in international relations was giving way to a narrow nationalism, nations professing Christianity hardly differentiated themselves from Mohammedans who believed that death in battle in the cause of Islam is a passport to paradise; the Christian assumption that death in battle for the sake of one's country is a similar passport is not even now extinct. Divine support was sought by means of relics.

The Brecbannoch, that relic of Columba, was produced at Bannockburn to aid the Scottish army to victory, and David II took with him to his defeat at Neville's Cross the Black Rood of St Margaret, supposed to contain a piece of the true cross. It is hard to distinguish that kind of thing from the Fairy Flag of Dunvegan which was supposed to bring victory to the MacLeods or even the Raven Banner of Sigurd the Stout of Orkney, which brought death to the bearer but victory to him before whom it was borne.

3

THE LATER
MIDDLE AGES

'The High Middle Ages', the thirteenth and fourteenth centuries, are apt to be thought of as 'The Ages of Faith', when there was unquestioning acceptance of certain beliefs and practices (often wrongly identified with those known later in the Roman Communion). One reason for this idea may be the splendour of the churches surviving from that period.

There was at any rate no doubt about the prominence of ecclesiastical structures. There were far fewer (and mostly smaller) churches then than there were in the intense ecclesiastical competition of the nineteenth century, but their settings made them more conspicuous. A rural parish church dominated the scene in contrast to the humble dwellings of the parishioners, scattered here and there in small groups, always of a single storey and often of a single apartment. It was the only public building and, despite periodical legislation to protect its sanctity, it served the purposes of theatre, newspaper, local government offices, council chamber, law courts and social centre. Sunday mass was the great occasion for public announcements; and the place for public notices was the church door. The bell summoning the parishioners to services proclaimed the time; and every church, east-west orientated, served as a sundial.

In an urban parish, where most of the dwellinghouses were still of modest height, and no industrial premises, office blocks or factory chimneys marked the skyline, the massive burgh church was the dominating feature. In its tower was a clock which gave the time to all who heard the quarter hours strike. In country and town alike many people lived within earshot of a religious house, whose bell, marking the times of the 'offices' in the church, not only punctuated the working day of the outside world but reminded those who heard it of the sacred functions of the house. The church was audible as well as visible.

It was hardly possible to hear or see the building without thinking of the clergy, who in any event, simply because of their numbers, were conspicuous in the daily scene. Endowed as they were with spiritual authority which, if taken seriously, was nothing short of terrifying, they enjoyed important privileges in law and could also gain their ends by withholding their ministrations. A clerical 'strike', whether or not in the shape of an interdict imposed by the pope, could be a formidable weapon for political purposes. The Church was more than a mere pressure group.

The solidity, symmetry and sophistication of the buildings of the medieval church matched its theology as it developed in the thirteenth century. All was explained, all was rational, there was an inexorable logic in the teaching about man's sin and its consequences and equally about the consequences of divine intervention in the shape of the life and death of the Second Person of the Trinity. The response which could come from man also fell within the divine scheme. In a system so logical there was little room for eccentricity and there was strong pressure to conform.

As the medieval centuries proceeded, new institutions and new methods helped to spread the faith. The three universities established in the fifteenth century combined religious and secular aims: King's College, Aberdeen, was founded 'for the praise of the Divine Name, the exaltation of the Catholic faith, the salvation of souls and the good order, profit and advancement of the region and the nation'. It was no longer necessary to go abroad for higher education, though many continued to do so. Some sixty schools are mentioned in extant records, and there were certainly many more. Only about half of the sixty-odd were based on a cathedral, collegiate church or abbey and some which had in earlier times been under ecclesiastical management passed to the administration of town councils before the reformation; but teachers would be clerics and the teaching at least formally Christian. Friars continued to attract fresh endowments, if only on a modest scale, and their reputation as preachers was maintained. A few additional friaries were established, including a batch of reformed ('Observant') Franciscan houses which were noted for their high level of devotion. The invention which brought printed books into the country before the end of the fifteenth century and which led to a very small output of printed books within Scotland in the sixteenth did something to facilitate teaching and learning – not always along the lines of orthodoxy. The means were there for the wider dissemination of Christian belief.

The older monasteries, meantime, which had never played a very positive part in ministering to the people, now came to have a rather negative significance, in the sense that their falling away from their ideals brought them into something like contempt and may have encouraged criticism of the beliefs on which they were founded. The attraction of the 'religious' life was blunted by familiarity, the number of vocations fell off and only one major monastery was founded after 1273. David Knowles, in the final chapter of the final volume of his great work on *The Religious Orders in England*, divided the English houses into the good, the bad and the indifferent. The same three categories can be detected in Scotland. Among the good may be placed the more recent foundations – the Charterhouse at Perth, the nunnery of Sciennes and the Observant friaries. Secondly there were the bad, of which Knowles said that their 'continued existence served no good purpose whatsoever'; among them can be placed all the nunneries except Sciennes and probably most of the smaller and more remote men's houses, like Strathfillan, Ardchattan, Canonbie, Monymusk and perhaps Iona. The great bulk of the houses fall into the third category – the indifferent, or perhaps respectable but dull. The rule of individual poverty was discarded and each monk came to have his own chamber and yard and his own 'portion', a sum of money and victual secured to him like a salary. Knowles said that the number of religious in England who were seriously striving after perfection was small, that 'the monasteries of England, taken as a whole, were far from fervent' but that 'many were harmless, and respectable enough to pass muster'. These words, 'pass muster' were used by another scholar, G. G. Coulton, who, though approaching the subject with different presuppositions from Knowles, judged that most of the sixteenth-century English monasteries were merely marking time and good enough to pass muster. If Knowles and Coulton are in agreement the debate is closed. It is true that in Scotland as in England there were occasional bouts of zeal, but the real enthusiasts were apt to find the older orders wanting and took refuge in more austere institutions. Monasteries were no longer the places to look for the most committed Christians. Religious orders may have enjoyed rather less respect in Scotland than they did in England, but even there attachment centred largely on houses which had high standards – Carthusians and Observant friars – or which served as parish churches.[1]

The main pastoral responsibility continued to lie with parish priests. If we knew more about their origin and training in early times we might be on surer ground in assessing their efficacy. It has been suggested – though not with reference specifically to Scotland – that a lord sometimes simply seized on one of his serfs (perhaps one not of much use for other work) and compelled him to be ordained. A priest's training would then be no more than a kind of apprenticeship. He is unlikely to have had much influence, though his sacramental ministrations, being totally objective – *opus operatum* – and not dependent on the disposition of either priest or recipient, were valid. There probably was an improvement in later medieval times, as higher education became more available and there were arrangements if not for training at least for examination. However, contemporary authorities, even at the end of the middle ages, were much concerned about the poor education of the parish clergy, and it was revealing that the subprior of St Andrews, when preaching against a man accused of heresy, admitted that 'the cause of heresy is the ignorance of them which have the cure of men's souls'.[2] There were faults at higher levels, in that there were some long vacancies in episcopal sees, especially in the Highlands, and some bishops were themselves sadly in need of discipline; besides, papal dispensations for irregularities of all kinds could frustrate the most conscientious oversight.

Priests who did have the ability and the will would catechise children in at least the Lord's Prayer, the Creed and the Commandments, and sometimes they would supplement those elements with exposition of the Epistle or Gospel, the deadly sins, the sacraments, the works of mercy and the Hail Mary.[3] How far priests possessed written or, later, printed, guidance is not quite certain and at the best such guidance would seem to have been scarce. Among the books which Bishop Elphinstone presented to King's College in 1505 was a *Manuale parochialium sacerdotum*, a brief practical guide to ministry produced in the thirteenth century of which there were many editions after the invention of printing. The same collection included a *Modus confitendi* or Guide to Confession. The *Manipulus Curatorum*, a compendium of 'Necessary information for the use of those to whom the cure of souls was committed' was popular in England and may have circulated in Scotland also.[4]

The spoken word, which should have been the main channel of communication from priest to people in a largely illiterate society, had to be supplemented. There were books for those who could read, and printing made them cheaper and more plentiful. We have a certain amount of information about the printed books which were possessed by individuals (mainly clerics) and by a few libraries of ecclesiastical institutions.[5] While the books which bear a man's name on the flyleaf or stand on his shelves provide inconclusive evidence about his tastes and interests, especially in a period from which relatively few books have survived at all, some deductions can be made. General intellectual interests as well as the preoccupation of some clergy with their duties or their ambitions are reflected in Greek and Latin classics, the writings of the Christian Fathers, medieval and reformed theology and controversy, sermons, canon and civil law and some history. Devotional works are distinctly scarce, but *The Golden Legend* (a thirteenth-century Italian devotional manual focussed on lives of saints and the Christian year, translated for Caxton in 1483 and printed at least seven times before the reformation) enjoyed popularity suggestive of somewhat credulous piety. Three copies of *The Imitation of Christ* are noted, though one of them, published at Lyons in 1560, hardly ranks as medieval. As the books which were most popular and most read may have been thumbed to death, fewer copies survived of them than of volumes which were merely consulted. That could explain the scarcity of *The Imitation of Christ*. First printed in 1472, and in Germany alone reprinted more than a score of times before the century was out, it had been known in English in MS and was printed in England early in the sixteenth century. This classic of Christian literature did good service in Scotland both before and after the reformation.

Bibles had long existed in expensive MS form and in Latin. The medieval church sometimes gets less credit than it deserves for its work in not only transmitting the Bible down the centuries but also in devoting intensive study to it. Possibly post-reformation attitudes of Protestants, who have been apt to preen themselves on their own foundation in the Bible and to despise Roman Catholics for supposedly depreciating it, have cast their shadow back to shape attitudes to the medieval church. Few might readily consider that church to have been 'a Bible Church', but that is what it was. Not only did Breviary and Missal in the hands of priests and Books of Hours in the hands of the literate laity bring scriptural passages to the level of everyday familiarity, but the amount of scholarship devoted to Bible study was impressive by any standards. The labours of the learned, not infrequently acquainted with Greek and Hebrew (and sometimes profiting by the collaboration of Jews) produced commentaries, 'glosses' and guides of various kinds, including concordances and dictionaries. Those who studied the Bible worried over every detail of every Old Testament story, every New Testament parable, and they tried to extract both the literal and the spiritual sense. Much of the work was related to the potential use of scripture in preaching at popular level, and in general it was true that a priest who had been trained at all had access to equipment enabling him to instruct his people.[6] The findings of biblical scholarship were spread far beyond academics (though not to the illiterate, still less to 'the poor') in the pages of the *Biblia Pauperum*, a work produced in woodcuts to bring out an elaborate inter-relation of incidents and themes from the Old Testament and the New.[7] Another best-seller based largely on scripture, *The Mirour of Mans Saluacioune*, existing in nearly 400 manuscripts, was an aid to devotional meditation. As these works were so popular in other countries and left their mark in so many ways it is hard to believe that they did not circulate in

Scotland also, and the illustrations in the *Biblia Pauperum*, at any rate, could have been used to instruct the illiterate.

However, not even a printed New Testament in English was available until the 1520s, and English translations in print were harbingers of the reformation rather than instruments of instruction in traditional belief. Besides the texts of the Bible which existed in MS there were evidently a number of metrical paraphrases. Perhaps they were mainly of the Passion narratives, like this:

> In the tolbuth Pilot enterit in,
> Callit on Crist, and sperit gif [asked if] he wes king.
> Crist ansuerit, inquirand first at him
> Gif of himself, or uthiris rehersing,
> He sa inquirit gif he as prince suld ring [reign].
> Pilot ansuerit: 'I am na Jew to knaw.
> Thy awne pepill hes brocht ye to my law'.

But there were paraphrases of parts of the Old Testament as well, though a portion of a verse paraphrase extending from the Fall (Gen. iii, 1–6) to the birth of Joseph (Gen. xxxiv) probably belongs to the 1550s[8] and perhaps should not be credited to the medieval church.

Primers were readily available from England. The earliest Primers had been in Latin and contained a Kalendar, the Hours of the Virgin, some Psalms and the Litany, but already in the fifteenth century Primers in English had appeared, to serve those who did not know Latin. By the 1530s there were printed Primers with a wider range of devotional material. Well over 100 editions of Primers are known to have been printed before 1558 and between 1534 and 1547 there were 28 wholly in English. These later Primers were, like the English Bible, products of the reforming movement and some of them contained material condemned as heretical.

When we glance at illustrated Books of Hours we are apt to think that this is how medieval people got their Christianity, but Books of Hours must have been extremely costly and only the affluent could afford them. It may be that pious individuals would show their servants or dependents the illustrations in the books, but the extent of the impression so made can have been only limited. Printed texts, equally, did nothing for the illiterate, though the woodcuts in some printed books would be meaningful to a wider public. It was in general through other visual aids that knowledge of the contents of the Old and New Testaments was acquired.

Of painting in medieval churches very little has survived. Outstanding are paintings on oak panels at Fowlis Easter in Angus, dating from the fifteenth and sixteenth centuries. A crucifixion scene with more than twenty figures measures over 13' by 5', and there are panels with other figures. The church possesses so many features that a visit to it might teach more about late medieval religion than many words can do.[9] There are dimly visible traces of painting at Dunkeld and Dunfermline and a well-preserved piece of work at Inchcolm. It would be surprising if Scottish churches were not adorned, as were the Danish churches which so many Scots knew well, with paintings which sometimes covered almost the entire wall surface and might depict the whole scheme of salvation from the

Fall to the Last Judgment, but there is no evidence that this was so. We know even less about what appeared on stained glass. Tapestries hung in castles or houses sometimes depicted scriptural subjects, and the same is true of some of the abundant mural painting in private homes, but little has survived of pre-reformation date. One extensive mural decoration based on scripture, and well preserved, is not in a church but in Kinneil House, near Bo'ness, where vivid and realistically portrayed scenes are dated to the 1550s and may reflect the approach of the reformation. When assessing medieval paintings – and the same applies to sculpture and drama – we have to remember that the characters were usually shown in contemporary dress and that as many biblical scenes, depicting the activities of labourers and craftsmen, were set in the countryside or a small town – surroundings familiar to people in their everyday life – their relevance was at once evident.

The art-form of which most survives is sculpture. This was nothing new in the later middle ages, for some of the great stone crosses of early times were decorated with scenes and figures from the Old Testament and the New. However, the work of *The Medieval Stone Carver in Scotland* was surveyed by the late Dr J. S. Richardson. The carvings contain Christian and moral teaching, for they depict the deadly sins and the Christian virtues, works of charity, parables relating to the struggle between good and evil, scriptural scenes and even the Last Judgment, but there is also a high proportion of purely secular subjects, including animals real and imaginary and a proliferation of grotesque masks of human and animal heads. The mingling of the sacred and the profane is similar to what occurs in medieval drama. And, as in the drama, there is a strong element of humour. Life may have been hard, but men refused to be unduly depressed by it.

What the church did through the medium of drama must, like much else, be seen in the context of the problems of communicating in a largely illiterate society. Shops or similar premises carried symbols, some of which have survived in the mortar and pestle outside a chemist's, the striped pole outside a barber's, the three balls outside a pawnbroker's, and indeed the pictorial signs at public houses. It has become easier in the later twentieth century than it used to be to appreciate the medieval dependence on such devices, for now, after more than a hundred years of compulsory schooling, we have reverted to symbols and signs to meet the needs of our post-literate society: colours on taps, figures outside public conveniences, the ingenious and sometimes cryptic signs which puzzle and distract motorists on the road. But in the middle ages symbolism extended beyond static artefacts. Conveyances of property and appointments to offices were completed by giving delivery of earth and stone, or of the fastenings of a door, or of a penny, a bell-rope or a missal; ownership of a house could be conveyed by introducing the new owner into the building and closing the door behind him. Such symbolism lingers today when a newly appointed dignitary is formally ushered into his stall or even when a graduate is 'capped'. There was, and is, an element of acting about it.

Similar acting could develop out of the reading of a lesson in church: first a straightforward narrative by one person, then different persons reading the words of different characters, and finally some action. It was especially appropriate for such a development to centre on the most dramatic episode in the gospels, namely the events of Easter morning, of which the Bible gives a circumstantial narrative relating not only speech but lively action. The narrative compulsively moves the hearer, and it is impossible now to divorce it from the King James version: 'Woman, why weepest thou? Whom seekest thou?', and that most perfectly rhythmical sentence, 'They have taken away my Lord and I know not where they have laid Him'.

The narrative tied in with certain actions. On Maundy Thursday or Good Friday the altar-cross and reserved sacrament had been deposited in an 'Easter sepulchre' or recess in the wall, whence on Easter morning they had to be returned to their usual places. The way was open for drama and those who took part were free to move about as actors. Three clergy would take the parts of the Maries, two would take those of Peter and John, others might be angels, and there would be a performance: 'Let one... approach the sepulchre... and sit there.... Let the remaining three follow... and, stepping delicately as those who seek something, approach the sepulchre.... When he who sits there beholds the three approach... let him begin... to sing *Quem quaeritis*.... The three reply in unison *Jhesum Nazarenum*. So he, *Non est hic*.... Those three turn to the choir and say *Alleluia! Resurrexit Dominus*.... Let the one, still sitting there and as if recalling them, say the anthem *Venite et videte locum*. And saying this let him rise and lift up the veil and show the place bare of the cross, but only the cloths laid there in which the cross was wrapped.... Let them sing the anthem *Surrexit Dominus de sepulchro* and lay the cloth upon the altar'.

There were twelfth-century playlets on other Gospel incidents. Initially all would be in Latin, but translations – perhaps at first for use in nunneries, where Latin was less well understood than it was by priests and monks – meant popularisation, and the next stage was taking the performances outside the church. The authorities sometimes tried to check this, but forbidding the clergy to act outside the church drove drama into the hands of laymen and made it more secular.

Cycles of plays came to be associated with Corpus Christi Day, fixed in 1264 on the Thursday after Trinity Sunday, a date near Midsummer, with long days and warm weather, and, whereas a commemoration of the institution of the Eucharist on Maundy Thursday would have had a specific focus on the Last Supper, a festival on the Thursday after Trinity could range widely. Of the 48 plays in the York Cycle 11 are drawn from the Old Testament; with play No. 25 we come to the entry of Jesus into Jerusalem and with 27 to the Last Supper, so that half of the cycle deals with events before those of Holy Week, but nearly half with the Passion and its sequels.

Each play was presented on a four-wheeled platform of two decks: the lower, enclosed, was the dressing-room, the upper, the stage, is described as 'all open', but some pictures show it like a modern stage, open only to the front, giving the whole structure something of the appearance of a Punch-and-Judy show. As the 'pageants' moved on from point to point, sometimes the action spilled over into the street, presenting simultaneously two scenes like the Last Supper and the convocation of the Jewish priests. Plays drew on apocryphal gospels and legends as well as canonical scripture, supplemented by humorous improvisation, as in the relations between Noah and his wife. The picturesque, rather than theology, sometimes dominated, and there was no squeamishness in presenting the Passion.

Some of the milder realism is indicated by references to 'two vices' coats', 'three flaps for devils', 'a coat with hose and tail for the serpent', payments 'for cock-crowing' and 'two worms of conscience', as well as by the allocation of scenes to appropriate craftsmen: shipwrights constructed the ark, goldsmiths undertook the adoration of the Magi, vintners the marriage of Cana and bakers the Last Supper. The evidence goes a long way to substantiate the account given by Charles Reade in *The Cloister and the Heart* of what passed before Gerard's eyes when 'he went and saw the Mystery':

> In this presentation divine personages, too sacred for me to name here, came clumsily down from heaven to talk sophistry with the cardinal Virtues, the nine Muses and the seven deadly Sins, all present in human shape, and not unlike one another. To enliven which weary stuff, in rattled the Prince of the power of the air, and an imp that kept molesting him and buffeting him with a bladder, at each thwack of which the crowd were in ecstasies. When the Vices had uttered good store of obscenity and the Virtues twaddle, the celestials, including the nine Muses, went gingerly back to heaven one by one; for there was but one cloud; and two artisans worked it up with its supernatural freight, and worked it down with a winch in full sight of the audience. These disposed of, the bottomless pit opened and flamed in the centre of the stage; the carpenters and Virtues shoved the Vices in and the Virtues and Beelzebub and his tormentor danced merrily round the place of eternal torture to the fife and tabor.

One cannot help feeling that there must have been something of the atmosphere of Pyramus and Thisbe as performed by the craftsmen of Athens. Earnest men, such as Wycliffite preachers, had doubts about the merits of religious drama, but its defenders argued that 'nowadays men are not converted by the earnest doing of God or men, so it is time to essay to convert them by play and games; some recreation men must have, and it is better and less evil to have it by playing of miracles than by other pastimes; just as it is lawful to have the miracles of God painted, why should not they be played, when men may read them even better'.[10]

Religious drama in Scotland shared much the same development as in England.[11] The Scots term 'clerks' plays' suggests that they began in churches, with clerical actors. It appears that the authorities tried to suppress them: there was certainly a thirteenth-century statute against priests looking on 'at actors performing'; and a ban on *ludi* ('games' or 'plays') in sacred places may refer to dramatic performances.[12] The term *ludi* was certainly used to denote dramatic performances in the royal court at Christmas, in Lent and at Easter in the reigns of James III and James IV.[13] The performances in burghs, associated with Corpus Christi Day, became secularised in the hands of guilds or crafts, among whom scenes were allotted. In Aberdeen there was a *ludum de le Halyblude*, a Passion play, on Corpus Christi day in 1440, and in Perth there was a 'Corpus Christi Day Play' (*ludum Corporis Christi*) in 1485. There is some evidence of Corpus Christi Day cycles at Lanark, Haddington, Dundee and Edinburgh.

Reformers seized upon dramatic performances as instruments of propaganda. In 1535 or 1536, when Friar Kyllour 'set forth the history of Christ's Passion in form of a play' produced before the king at Stirling on Good Friday, the chief priests and pharisees were dressed to resemble bishops and regular clergy.[14] About 1540 James Wedderburn (who was partly responsible for the 'Gude and Godly Ballads' of which we shall hear more) composed plays 'wherein he nipped the abuses and superstitions of the time', including one on 'the beheading of John the Baptist, which was acted at the West Port of Dundee, wherein he carped at the abuses and corruptions of the papists'.[15] Dramatic art was not extinguished by the reformation and received a measure of encouragement from the reformed church down to about 1600.[16]

What was presented through the media of painting, carving or acting, was, one imagines, very much what was, and perhaps still is, taught in junior classes in Sunday Schools and some day schools. Men and women of all classes were certainly made familiar not only with Bible stories but with what may be called The Bible Story of salvation. Certainly biblical allusions were readily understood and scriptural phraseology was in common currency. Formal documents alluded to 'hardening the heart in the manner of Pharaoh' and a comprehensive excommunication included a catalogue of punishments which befell biblical characters – Dathan and Abiram, whom the earth swallowed up, Korah who was consumed by fire, Absalom hanged by his hair from a tree, Holofernes beheaded by Judith and so on. One of the favourite proverbs on everyone's lips was 'Put the mote out of your awin eye and then cast out the beam of your neighbour's' – but not all who used it so inverted scripture.[17] Such familiarity did not give men a faith by which to live, but visual aids provided a basis on which faith could be built by an intelligent learner or a trained teacher. That is where parish priests should have made their contribution, but all too often the hungry sheep – if they were hungry – looked up and were not fed.

We know a good deal about church attendance and about behaviour in church, both of which limited the influence which even the best of priests could exert. Attendance was hindered by the distance of many homes from a place of worship, especially as churches were not always centrally placed and some parishes were very large.[18] However, the geographical and weather hazards on which proposals for additional parishes were based were not the only reasons why people stayed away from church, and the Scottish complaint in 1552 that 'very few indeed' were in church was no novelty: in 1291 the Archbishop of Canterbury had urged his archdeacon to persuade more people to go to church and in 1303 it was observed that when the church bell rang many people preferred 'to lie and sweat and take the merry morning sleep' in bed.[19] When people did go to church, attention was apt to be distracted by thoughts of the secular activities carried on in the building, ranging from reputable legal proceedings, like the handing over of money to redeem lands, to the highly disreputable. Despite the notion that a church's sacred character provided sanctuary, even the presence in it of 'the most holy sacrament' did not ensure safety for either persons or property. The reconciling of churches which had been polluted by the effusion of blood was just a routine operation, constantly referred to as a regular episcopal function and one for which, in fourteenth-century England, there was a standard charge of 40s.[20] Only milder irreverence was indicated when worshippers were told to refrain from talking and laughing and 'sit still with devout heart and mind' or were denounced for preventing the service from being 'heard and seen by the devout people'.[21]

Most rural churches were modest in size and equipment and there is ample evidence that the condition of many ecclesiastical buildings was often such as hardly to encourage reverence, let alone devotion.[22] Some find the facts so shocking as to be incredible, but those who have studied the more ample evidence for England even in the thirteenth century have become, in words which David Knowles used in a different context, 'in some measure immune to moral shock'.[23] If standards were low throughout the country generally, they were worse in the Highlands.[24] It was said in the sixteenth century that people in the remote islands were not receiving baptism or other sacrament, not to speak of Christian teaching.[25]

In a rural parish church, whether lowland or highland, there was as a rule neither music nor choir; at best the proceedings were shared between the priest and a clerk, who made the responses. John Major, who was a prime example of the Scottish inferiority complex and thought that England was in every way miles better, considered it a scandal that in Scotland men who had no skill in music were advanced to the priesthood. It has been remarked that when congregational singing of metrical psalms came in with the reformation it did not replace plainsong, it replaced silence. Only in a cathedral, abbey, great burgh church or collegiate church, where at high mass there were several ministers of the altar, with incense and ceremonial, would there be an organ and choir (though even cathedral services were not conducted with the long files of choristers, the splendour or even the decorum customary today). But whether it was a high mass or a low mass the congregation were mere spectators. The priest was indeed instructed to read the service clearly and distinctly – the 'blessed mutter of the mass' was not encouraged – but when priests could not be trusted to read Scots without rehearsal it is hard to believe that they would be very proficient in Latin – and if the people did not understand the language, did audibility matter? At the best, 'they heard with their ears only, and their hearts, spirit and mind have not been edified'.[26] Sermons by parish priests were clearly rare, and the only vernacular many people would hear in church would be the periodical denunciation of offenders in a highly seasoned excommunication or 'cursing'. The appeal in the 'cursing' was to the fear of hell, and as long as people took it seriously it may have served as a moral sanction, while there must have been more than mere respect for the priest's claim to have power to commit a soul to hell and even to rob it of the merits earned by its good deeds.[27] But by the sixteenth century cursing had come to be derided. If sermons were rare, so also was Communion. Easter was the Communion season, when those who did not make their Communion had to pay a fine while those who did had to make an offering – a delightful application of the principle, 'Heads I win, tails you lose'.

In general, therefore, there was little or nothing for the people to say or sing, to hear with understanding, even to see. The devout occupied themselves with their private devotions (guided by manuals if they were literate). There was a divorce between what the priest was doing and what the worshippers were doing, and little to hold their attention except at one point which brought them and the priest together. The climax of the Mass was the moment when the priest, taking the wafer in his hands, pronounced the words 'Hoc est Corpus Meum' and then held it above his head so that the people behind him could join in adoration of the God who, they believed, was now present on the altar. Wherever the consecrated wafer was, there Christ could be adored – locked in an aumbry or sacrament house in the wall of the church, carried in procession, visible in a monstrance or glass case. And, because of the association of the Mass mainly with the death of Christ, the Real Presence in the consecrated elements was thought of as the presence of the dead, the sacrificed, body of Christ and not the presence of His living self. The medieval concentration on the Passion stood in the way of a full understanding of the Real Presence.

When the channels of instruction and communication were restricted, the faith which was implanted, or which grew in response, can hardly have been complex. The preoccupation, almost the obsession, was with the fate of the soul after death and the means by which it could escape torment. Each individual could do his best to avoid falling into sin, but that represented a counsel of perfection – perfection of which man always fell short – and the usual practice was or should have been the way of self-examination followed by confession, absolution and penance. In 1215 this procedure was formally made obligatory once a year and it was associated especially with Fastern's Eve or Shrove Tuesday, but it was recommended after the committing of any sin. However, the individual could rely on acts performed by his fellow Christians as well as by himself. Prayers for the departed had been regular practice long before Christianity prevailed in Scotland. St Augustine of Hippo (354–430) argued that prayers, the eucharistic sacrifice and alms were all efficacious for the 'relief' of the souls of the deceased. Gregory the Great (d. 604) emphasised the importance of prayer and the Eucharist for the same objective, Gregory III declared in 732 that each person might make offerings for his own dead, and his contemporary, Bede, asserted that persons not immediately received into paradise might be delivered by the prayers, alms, fasting, tears and masses of their faithful friends.[28] That emphasis on prayers for the dead was intensifying is suggested by the regularisation, from the end of the tenth century, of the commemoration of All Souls on 2 November (the day after All Saints' Day). The *Decretum*, which codified canon law in the middle of the twelfth century, quoted Gregory III and laid down that the souls of the departed are delivered in four ways – masses, the prayers of the saints, the alms of friends and the fasting of kinsfolk.

Notices of deaths in the Chronicle of Melrose indicate the thoughts of Cistercian monks. In earlier generations almost a stereotyped phrase, used especially of bishops, is 'migravit ad Dominum' or similar words. Does such language reflect confidence that the soul, at the moment of death, passes immediately into the Divine Presence, or merely the convention sometimes followed by a minister conducting a funeral service for someone of whose faith he has no knowledge? Even in the thirteenth century King William 'felici exitu migravit ad Dominum', and the same words were used of an abbot of Newbattle who died in 1275. Yet on the whole this tone of confidence faded. Queen Margaret had indeed 'rendered her holy soul to heaven', but of her sons Alexander I merely 'went the way of all flesh' while even the pious David 'died, commending his soul to God'. (Those three entries are all in the same thirteenth-century hand.) Explicit petitions for the departed begin to appear in the late twelfth century (1177 and 1184), when the deaths of two lay benefactors of Melrose are noted (separately) with the words 'may his blessed soul live in glory', and in 1218 the Chronicle, noting the deaths of the Count of Burgundy and the Count of Montfort, adds, 'may their souls rest in peace'. This echoes the phraseology, already surely long-established, of the Requiem – 'Eternal rest grant unto him, O Lord, and let light perpetual shine upon him'. Even the note of the death in 1216 of Pope Honorius III, 'father and defender of the Cistercian order' though he was, is accompanied by the petition 'may his soul live in glory'. Sometimes, too, confidence about the destination of the soul was qualified by 'ut credimus' – 'as we believe': Bishop Adam of Caithness, who was burned to death in 1222, 'by his sufferings deserved, as we believe, to reach the company of the citizens of heaven', and Alexander II's 'happy soul was snatched from this light and gathered into heaven with all the saints, as we believe'. A somewhat cursory examination of other thirteenth-century material suggests that there was still some reticence about the fate of the departed and that the naming of a person deceased was likely to be accompanied by the non-committal 'bone memorie'. What became and long remained the almost invariable phrase used when referring to the deceased – 'quham God assoilyie' (whom God absolve) – may have been in regular use for generations before it is found on paper, for it occurs almost as soon as written vernacular appears at all, namely in 1389. So far as this scanty evidence goes it suggests that men felt a growing need to pray for the dead.

They also craved a clear explanation of the whereabouts of the faithful departed before they reached heaven. Some thought of their being in some place of torment on or under the earth, others of their being in a place not in this world. The latter view prevailed, though emphasis on physical torment continued to encourage a somewhat materialistic view of 'purgatory'. Formal definition came in a letter of Pope Innocent IV in 1254 and not long after with the Council of Lyons (1274) and the writings of St Thomas Aquinas (d. 1274), who worked out in detail the theology of intercessions for the dead. Souls in purgatory were by definition souls destined for heaven, but few were in such a state of grace at the time of death as to escape purgatory. Contrition might be complete, a worthy confession made, absolution granted and guilt (culpa) erased by such means or by extreme unction, yet punishment (pena) might still have to be completed. Purgatory was seen as a place of punishment rather than of cleansing as its name suggests.

The obligation of annual confession after 1215 had the effect of tightening up the penitential system. At the same time, the growing clarification of the relationship between that system and purgatory gave the Church a kind of jurisdiction over the latter. Purgatorial pains could now be quantified in terms of an equivalent amount of 'enjoined penance' in this world. When punishment of sufferers in purgatory became to this extent measurable it was logical to focus on any means of abridging the term of that punishment.

Indulgences, remitting amounts of purgatorial pains measured in terms of the equivalent duration of earthly penance, had become common when crusaders earned plenary indulgence, and they were built into the general theory of a 'treasury of merits' accumulated from Our Lord and the Saints and doled out by ecclesiastical authorities. It was something of a landmark that in the jubilee year of 1300 Pope Boniface VIII granted full pardon from sins to pilgrims to Rome, for this implied papal power to release souls from purgatory. In 1343 Clement VI defined the treasury of merits as the source of indulgences and referred to Boniface's example of granting plenissimam veniam peccatorum – full pardon to sinners – as something which he proposed to imitate, though still with the prerequisites of personal penitence and confession. It was not until 1476 that Sixtus IV offered indulgences which could be purchased by friends or kinsfolk of the deceased. In 1510, under Julius II, indulgences were granted without preconditions, simply on payment of money, and this continued under Leo X, who professed to grant reconciliation with God and to be able to 'close the gates of hell and open the gates of pardon'. There had been a change from the remission of a penalty (*pena*) to the remission of guilt (*culpa*).

There is no evidence that Scotland saw the gross abuse of indulgences which occasioned Luther's revolt in 1517, and indeed Scotland had not been among the countries in which Leo X authorised the collections for the building of St Peter's with which the abuses were associated.[29] At one stage an indulgence for building Glasgow Cathedral had been couched in quite vague terms, with no period of penance specified, but in the early sixteenth century relatively innocuous indulgences issued by Scottish bishops granted remissions of specified periods of 'enjoined penance' to contributors to the repair of bridges or churches,[30] e.g.

> So that Christians may more readily hold out helping hands to the repair of the said bridge... we, trusting in the mercy of Almighty God and the authority of the blessed Peter and Paul, His apostles, release all Christians, being truly penitent and having confessed, who hold out helping hands to the repair of the said bridge, from a hundred days of enjoined penance.

The system does not seem to have figured prominently among the abuses which Scottish reformers condemned, though there had been attempts to curb the possible excesses of 'pardoners' who brought papal letters granting various remissions,[31] and Sir David Lindsay, in *The Three Estates*, introduced a pardoner who offered a remission of no less than a thousand years. Perhaps it is fair to add that it did not seem irrational in a religious house to arrange that prayers should be said for the souls of specified benefactors of the house 'everilk Sunday till the day of dome'.[32]

Intercession in the sense of prayer offered in any circumstances and on any occasion was increasingly absorbed in the saying of masses. And views of the Mass itself had changed. In earlier medieval times it had been held that the Mass could be called a sacrifice because it was a memorial, a re-presentation, of the Passion of Christ, through which men partook of the benefits of that Passion. However, in later medieval times that view was effaced, at least in the popular mind, by the less subtle belief that the Mass was in itself a real sacrifice, in which Christ, bodily present under the forms of the consecrated elements, was offered afresh on the altar. If the Mass was a real sacrifice, it could reconcile man with God, take away the guilt and penalty of sin, free souls from torments after death. Moreover, since each Mass was a sacrifice the idea grew that the more masses that were said the greater benefits would be produced. There was something perilously like 'accounting', almost of simple arithmetic: so many sins, so many masses; and the soul remained in purgatory until the masses offered on its behalf balanced the sins with which it had been stained before death. A Mass could still be offered for any purpose or 'intention', but most masses were for the release of souls from purgatory. The Mass had come to be, above all else, a Mass for the dead.

The idea of the Mass as a corporate action, in which a congregation could take part, had been largely lost sight of. There was no need for anyone to be present except the priest, and when masses were being offered literally by the dozen any other arrangement would have been impracticable. The action must have been seen as very much that of the priest, and consequently it could be reckoned among the 'works' of man, although theologically speaking it was not the work of man but the work of Christ on Calvary. How far did the man in the street or field really think in terms of presenting Christ's eternal sacrifice? The Mass was seen rather as just one way of gaining benefits either material or spiritual.

Altars and chaplainries proliferated so that masses could be multiplied. It is in this context that we must view the collegiate churches, forty or fifty of which were founded, mainly between about 1440 and 1550, each of them served by several priests. Some were parish churches, and one reason for their existence was to provide the staff to conduct worship with ceremonial and music not possible in an ordinary parish church, but another was to provide masses for the souls of the founder and his family. When people looked at those churches, the main idea in their minds must have been the multiplication of masses for the souls of the dead.

Information about individual faith comes from testamentary dispositions, of which thousands are engrossed in the Records of Testaments. There was some stereotyped phraseology, possibly imposed on the testator by a priest framing his instructions. It ran (much more frequently in Latin than in the vernacular), 'I commit (or commend) my soul to God Almighty, the Blessed Virgin Mary and all the Saints'. This occurs in the testaments of Sir James Douglas of Dalkeith (1390), Alexander Sutherland of Dunbeath (1456) and Sir David Sinclair of Sumburgh (1506), and it is all but invariable in the earliest extant volumes of the Record of Testaments -- St Andrews 1549-51, Dunblane 1539-47 and Glasgow 1547-55. Occasional variants, especially the omission of reference to the Blessed Virgin and the Saints, are probably not significant, especially as 'God' is sometimes followed by a convenient 'etc.' Executors were frequently empowered by the testator to dispose of goods for the benefit of his soul, and bequests were often made to chaplains, curates or friars to pray for the soul of the deceased or to say masses for him.

The well-to-do could make lavish provision. Sutherland of Dunbeath left £10 yearly for a priest to sing perpetually in Rosslyn Chapel (a collegiate church where Sir Alexander was to be buried), £100 towards the building and repair of that church, and funds for a priest to sing perpetually in Fortrose Cathedral, for masses there and in Fortrose, Fearn, Tain, Dornoch, Kinloss and Orkney. Sinclair of Sumburgh, in 1506, was less generous, especially with hard cash. He left his red velvet coat to Kirkwall Cathedral, one third of a black velvet coat to the church of the archdeacons of Shetland at Tingwall and another third of it to the Cross Kirk of Dunrossness (a collegiate church in Shetland). He bequeathed two nobles (probably about £3) and *The Book of Good Manners* (printed by Caxton in 1487) to Magnus Harwood, archdeacon of Shetland, and, mindful of his interests across the North Sea, he left a gold chain to St George's altar in Roskilde Cathedral, the burial place of Danish kings.[33] That the instructions of the wealthy thus varied makes one hesitant about judging the motives of the less well-to-do, but when a man provided for intercession for his soul for only one year it is hard to know whether he was poor, parsimonious, or merely confident that his stay in purgatory would not be a long one. Yet it does not seem to have occurred to the medieval mind that the whole system of paying for masses made it easier for a rich man to enter the kingdom of Heaven than Our Lord's own words had suggested – certainly easier for a rich man than for a poor man.

Statements quoted earlier about the means of shortening the sufferings of purgatory emphasised the part of friends and kinsfolk, who were expected to form a kind of rescue service for their kinsmen in the other world. Beyond the family there was a similar cohesion in groups formed by landlords and vassals or tenants. This fitted into Scottish society, and one wonders how far collegiate churches, often endowed by heads of great families and sometimes bearing the names of those families, were regarded as contributing to the well-being after death of dependents, followers and bearers of the name of those families. Beyond links arising from blood and tenure there were the more artificially created bonds of confraternities or guilds in the burghs, which were friendly societies but also Christian fellowships, perhaps under the patronage of a saint and committed to prayer for any member after death.

Another possible source of information about belief is tombs and memorials. Most surviving medieval tombs had recumbent effigies, usually in mural recesses, and such effigies may have been thought of as an invitation to pray for the soul of the departed.[34] In a class by themselves are a number of West Highland grave-slabs.[35] Not many of them display specifically Christian symbolism, though a few show crosses bearing the figure of the crucified Lord, an Iona slab depicts a priest saying Mass and a mere handful (out of a total of 109) have inscriptions indicating concern for the welfare of departed souls. However, four at Iona, of varying dates from c. 1400 to 1543, contain express formulae craving God's mercy on the soul of the defunct. The unique monument at Rodil in Harris, dated 1528, contains a kind of litany of intercession to many named saints, presumably on behalf of the deceased. A stone at Kilchoman in Islay (fourteenth or fifteenth century) has phraseology which might have been copied from a charter granting land to a church in the twelfth century: 'pro animabus patris et matris et uxoris sue ac omnium fidelium defunctorum' (for the souls of his father, mother and wife and all the faithful departed). And at Inchmahome, which was really in the Lowlands and where there were Augustinian canons who knew some theology, a stone displays the petition 'ut deus solvat animas eorum a pena et a culpa' (that God may release their souls from penalty and from guilt). What does impress is the genealogical flavour of the inscriptions, which suggests a certain parallel with the collegiate churches, of which there was no example in the Highlands except at Kilmun, which is as nearly out of the Highlands as it is possible to be.

Among Scots of the later medieval period who committed their thoughts to paper was Robert Richardson, who was an Augustinian canon, first at St Andrews and then at Cambuskenneth, and later entered the ministry of the Church of England. He wrote a *Commentary on the Augustinian Rule*, published at Paris in 1530,[36] in which he deplored the decay of discipline among canons, sometimes at the level of such *trivia* that his concern seems to be with the Law rather than the Gospel. But he added an 'Alphabet of the religious', consisting of passages from *The Imitation of Christ*, whose author, Thomas à Kempis, had himself been an

Augustinian canon whose references to 'conversion' meant the change which took place when a man decided to live according to a monastic rule, and whose 'community' was a monastic establishment. The *Imitation*, while providing, almost line by line, ample food for meditation and challenging thoughts, has plenty to say about men's sins and shortcomings and may well have been used mainly as a guide to self-examination before confession. Richardson's selection has only one paragraph which rises above the level of a guide to conduct, running 'Let Christ be your life, your lesson, your meditation, your speech, your desire, all your hope and reward'. Richardson's compilation ends with seven thanksgivings and prayers, one for each day of the week, with reference to the Lord's Prayer and the Words from the Cross, focussed on the seven deadly sins. One can see profound devotion in Richardson, and there is a little in *The Imitation* about contemplation of the Passion, but in neither is there assurance of salvation through the Passion.

Another Scottish writer of the time was, like Kempis and Richardson, an Augustinian. This was Adam Abell (or Bell), a grand-nephew of Robert Bellenden, abbot of Holyrood. He was a canon of Inchaffray, but, for reasons he makes clear in his 'Roit or Quheill of Tyme',[37] he moved over to the stricter discipline of the Observant Friars at Jedburgh. He tells us that his uncle, Abbot Robert, encountered such opposition among his canons to his strict discipline[38] and was so unpopular with the courtiers who came to Holyrood with the king that he ultimately, like Adam, moved to a stricter order, in his case the Carthusians at Perth. Abell, who condemned sins, crimes and abuses like pluralism, non-residence and the holding of the headship of a religious house by an unqualified person, praised a prior of St Andrews who, despairing of restoring obedience to the Rule, gave up his dignity to become a novice at Coupar-Angus, a Cistercian house which had no involvement with the service of parishes and no association with the royal court. It has been claimed that Abell was the first Scot known to have been interested in foreign missions, for his attention had been captured by the work of Franciscan friars in Mexico and Africa.[39]

Richardson and Abell were writing when the reformation was already touching Scotland, but they were not explicitly on the defensive against it. Other works, very little later in time, were upholding medieval thought against the challenge of the reformers. The study of Archbishop Hamilton's Catechism (1552) has frequently emphasised its novelties and its concessions to growing protestant thought: for example, it has something to say of the Church Invisible but nothing about pope or hierarchy; its language on justification stresses faith, it denies that the Mass is in itself a sacrifice, and indulgences are not mentioned.[40] But the great bulk of the Catechism was what must have been taught for generations – transubstantiation, purgatory, prayers for the dead, the perpetual virginity of Mary and the decisive importance of 'our works' on the Day of Judgment. All was presented in a simple and unaffected manner, quoting many passages of scripture in a dignified vernacular and assuming that allusions to incidents and parables in the Gospels would be understood.

Sermons by John Watson, canon of Aberdeen, belonging to the 1540s and 1550s, attempted to reach a middle ground between traditional theology and that of the reformers. His answer to the doctrine of Justification by Faith was that works are the fruit of faith, in which faith becomes practical. On the claim that only 'the elect' are saved, he replied that 'God desires the salvation of all, and offers grace to all; He also gave us free will. The elect are those who serve God for love'.[41] Quentin Kennedy, commendator of Crossraguel, had in 1558 roundly denounced the corruptions in the old system, upheld the authority of general councils and ignored the Pope, much as Hamilton's Catechism had done, but in 1561 he dealt explicitly with the contentions of the Protestants. He argued for the Real Presence in the sacrament, but he showed a disposition to compromise by saying that instead of maintaining that Christ is contained in a small quantity of bread and wine it would be sounder to state that He is present 'under the forms of bread and wine', since He does not occupy space and has the qualities of a spirit – which would seem to exclude transubstantiation but might admit something like the Lutheran theory of consubstantiation. He stops short of declaring the Mass a repetition of Our Lord's sacrifice as in itself propitiatory, and, like Archbishop Hamilton, sees it as a sacrifice of commemoration by which we are made partakers of the fruits of the Passion.[42]

Behind such works by scholars, there is material which may bring us closer to the mind of the common man. One can only speculate how far medieval hymns, some going back many centuries, were familiar to the people. True, they were in Latin, but usually extremely simple Latin and, while they often fall short of being great poetry, their rhymes jingle easily, some having refrains, they are eminently singable and they contain, in succinct form, a lot of basic truths about the Incarnation, the Passion and the Eucharist. Some of them may have been translated into the vernacular, and there were some hymns written at least partly in the vernacular. William Dunbar (c. 1461– c. 1520), best known for his earthy, sometimes scurrilous, satire (castigating the clergy among others), his vigorous 'flyting' and his whining appeals for royal patronage, should be numbered among Scotland's very few hymn-writers. His verses 'Of the Nativitie of Christ', with the refrain 'Nobis puer natus est', can stand comparison with any of the innumerable carols which express the joy of Christmas:[43]

> Syng hevin imperiall, most of hicht,
> Regions of air mak harmony;
> All fishe in flud and foull of flicht
> Be myrthfull and mak melody;
> All *Gloria in excelsis* cry,
> Hevin, erd, se, man, bird and best,
> He that is crownit abone the sky
> *Pro nobis Puer natus est.*

Equally, Dunbar's verses 'On the resurrection of Christ', with the refrain 'Surrexit Dominus de sepulchro', have the thought and words of familiar Easter hymns. 'Ane ballat of Our Lady' piles extravagant language around the repeated greeting, 'Ave Maria, gracia plena', but winds up

> Thy birth hes with His blude
> Fra fall mortall, originall,
> Us ransoumed on the rude.

(Thine offspring has with His blood
From fall mortal, original,
Us ransomed on the cross.)

Another 'Ballat of Our Lady', not by Dunbar, similarly uses as its refrain 'O mater Jhesu salve Maria'.[44] Dunbar wrote a long meditation (144 lines) and an even longer (168 lines) 'Tabill of Confession' to stimulate and guide self-examination. The latter is addressed 'To Thee, O merciful Saviour mine, Jesus, my King, my Lord and my Redeemer sweet' and it has the refrain, 'I cry thee mercy, and leisure to repent'. Dunbar's 'The Maner of passing to Confession' is a more general guide to penitence.

Dunbar was not the only poet of the time whose lines echo Christian sentiment: in Robert Henryson's *Testament of Cresseid* 'there is no direct Christian reference whatsoever', yet one of his *Fabillis*, that of 'The Frog and the Mouse', concludes:

> Now Chryst for us that deit on the rud
> Of saule and luf as thou art Salviour,
> Grant us to pass in till a blissit hour.[45]

Many items of simpler type than the polished (or sometimes laboured) work of poets find places in a collection titled *Devotional Pieces in Verse and Prose*.[46] The 'pieces' were not all original Scottish contributions to devotional literature, but they all circulated in Scotland. The longest, 'The Contemplacioun of Synnaris', by William Touris, a Scottish Franciscan, had been printed in England in 1499. Another of Scottish authorship was 'The Passioun of Christ', by Walter Kennedy, a vigorous and often moving metrical paraphrase of the Gospel narrative. Verses called 'Ane devoit exercicioun' form a meditation on the Passion, addressed 'Sweet Lord, I desire richt hertlie to loif and thank you with all my hert for all the panis that ye thollit in your blist tender heid', somewhat parallel to the hymn 'O sacred head, sore wounded'. The theme of dependence on Christ's Passion and on it alone runs strongly through the whole collection: for example, 'O Lord God, makar of hevin and erd, that hes designed to mak me like thyne awin ymage and with thy precious blude hes bocht me'. In the reiteration of the everlasting cry of the sinner for the mediation of Christ, and trust in redemption through His sacrifice, the timelessness of Christian devotion strikes one forcefully. The eternal essence of Christian truths was being presented to the people in their everyday idiom, with all its homeliness and directness.

Such concentration on the Passion is not surprising in view of the emphasis on the re-enactment of the death of Christ in the Mass, but there are signs that devotion to the Passion might displace the purchase of prayers and masses. Feasts introduced in the later middle ages included those of the Five Wounds (in Scotland by 1491) and the Crown of Thorns (in Scotland by c. 1520),[47] and there was something of a cult of the instruments of the Passion, which attracted the art of the stone carver, for instance at the collegiate church of Seton. 'Andrew Lundy's Primer', belonging to the early sixteenth century, contains acts of devotion focussed on the Passion and Psalms related to it;[48] the Book of Hours of Mary of Guise contains a 'Devotion to the Passion' and an illustration of the Five Wounds.[49] In Aberdeen by the end of the fifteenth century there were altars to the

Holy Blood and the Five Wounds, and at Haddington it seems that an altar previously known as St Salvator's received an additional dedication to the Holy Blood in the early sixteenth century. In Edinburgh and Aberdeen there were confraternities of the Holy Blood. The Fetterneir Banner, which has been credibly associated with a confraternity of the Holy Blood, probably in Edinburgh, shows a figure of Our Lord covered with wounds from which drops of blood exude and depictions of the instruments of the Passion – scourge, nails, ladder, spear, reed, sponge and column of scourging. The same emphasis appears in the crucifixion scene at Fowlis Easter. There was plenty to 'concentrate men's thoughts on the Passion of Christ'[50] and 'the increasing emphasis on Christ's suffering humanity in many ways reflected... an awareness of, if not genuine sorrow for, sin'.[51]

There was, as always, plenty of sin to be sorry for. Although we have ample knowledge of wicked deeds, thanks to records of criminal proceedings, we know little or nothing of wicked thoughts which fell short (if that is the proper phrase) of crime. Perhaps the teaching of the Church encouraged emphasis on deeds rather than thoughts. The basis of moral teaching was the Commandments, under which almost the whole range of human thought and action can be subsumed. But the obvious emphasis of most of the Commandments is on prohibition. Equally, the Seven Deadly Sins were indeed expressed in terms of abstractions – gluttony, lust and so forth – but they were manifestly much concerned with deeds. And the general excommunication, which people were supposed to hear read in church four times a year, denounced wrongdoers in deed – sorcerers, fire-raisers, forgers, notorious usurers, perjurers, robbers and their accomplices, those who meddled with churches and church property.[52] One hears far less about Our Lord's positive commands to love God and your neighbour as yourself. An awareness of sin neither led men to refrain from it nor, after committing it, to reach a state of contrition.

The three and a half centuries of the later middle ages leap from an atrocity in 1222, when Bishop Adam of Caithness was roasted to death by his people, to another atrocity in 1570, when the commendator of Crossraguel was roasted (not indeed to his death but to his permanent injury) by the Earl of Cassillis; in each case the cause was human greed. The twelfth-century description (quoted earlier) of south-western Scotland as 'full of beastly men and altogether barbarous' can almost be paralleled by the description of north-eastern Scotland in the late fifteenth century as 'rude, ignorant of letters and almost barbarous'.[53]

To serve as a report on Scottish morals on the eve of the reformation there is a group of acts of parliament passed in 1552 – the year of Hamilton's Catechism – which might suggest that all the efforts of medieval centuries, whatever effect they had on faith, had done little enough to raise the standard of conduct and that the achievement of the medieval church, measured by its end-product, is far from impressive. The first of them contains an explicit confession of failure: 'notwithstanding the oft and frequent preachings in detestation of grievous and abominable oaths, swearing, execrations and blasphemy of the name of God, swearing in vain by His precious blood, body, passion and wounds,... yet the same is come in such an ungodly use among the people of this realm... that daily and hourly may be heard among them open blasphemy'. Two other acts imply equal failure by disclosing that people 'under process of cursing' (i.e.

excommunication) refused to leave divine service when charged to do so and that such persons compelled priests to say Mass in their presence. Bigamy and adultery, fraud by notaries, overcharging by tradesmen and tavern-keepers and the commercial offences known as 'paking and peling, regrating and foirstalling' were the targets of subsequent acts in the series.[54]

The sovereignty of God in human activity was often proclaimed. The words 'In the name of the Holy and Undivided Trinity' were perhaps peculiarly appropriate to preface acts of Robert I regulating the succession to the throne, where kings reigned 'by the grace of God' and where the will of God, operating through birth and death, was necessarily involved; but quite routine statutes, such as those of James IV in 1490, began with the same formula. Acts passed by a legislature including lords spiritual must be seen as at least a formal expression of the intentions of men who professed Christianity; and, reading through the statutes, with their frequent solicitude for the welfare of all classes, not least 'the poor people that labour the ground', one would never conclude that a clique of landed magnates, or an ambitious king, controlled affairs for their own ends. How far the apparent concern for social justice reflects the presence either of prelates among the legislators or of ordained men among the 'clerks' of the civil service might be debated; the pious opening of acts of parliament can hardly in itself mean more than the opening with the words 'In Dei nomine Amen' of all notarial instruments, dealing with the most mundane matters and having no motive beyond human acquisitiveness.

Of course something was done to sanctify human conduct by the place assigned to 'good works' in the scheme of salvation. True, there might be ostentation. Our Lord's example was at one time followed when, on Maundy Thursday, abbots washed the feet of their monks, bishops those of their clergy and sovereigns those of their subjects. The symbolic acts of successive Scottish sovereigns (like sovereigns elsewhere)[55] survived the reformation, though, because of the reformers' disapproval of the Christian Kalendar, the date was transferred from Maundy Thursday to the sovereign's birthday. In 1583 James VI, on his seventeenth birthday, distributed a blue gown and a purse containing seventeen shillings to each of seventeen poor men.[56] Such 'bedemen' were, like other recipients of alms, to reciprocate with their prayers, in this case for the king, and it has been observed that as they had an interest in the increase of the king's years – and his shillings – their intercessions must have been sincere.

There is any amount of evidence of less showy ways in which 'practical Christianity' operated and indeed left its mark on the map. Relief of the poor was certainly regarded as one of the functions of monastic houses, and the tradition, at least, survived to the reformation. When the prioress of Haddington made up what might be called her income tax return in 1561 she optimistically claimed among her expenses payments to 'six auld servitouris and gentilmen, . . . auld failyeit men and wedowis . . . and puir pilgrimes and indigent persounes cumand daylie to the place . . . and to the pure solles almous daylie'. Abell in his Chronicle considered it worthy of remark that his uncle the abbot of Holyrood (c. 1500) distributed four bolls of wheat, baked into bread, amongst the poor, and money if that did not suffice for the throng.[57]

Then there were the 'hospitals'. A list recently compiled runs to upwards of a hundred and seventy names, even although, as the scholarly compiler states firmly, 'nothing like finality' can be claimed for it[58] – establishments for lepers, for the poor, for the sick, for travellers and pilgrims, and almshouses where bedesmen resided. Some were appendages of religious houses, occasionally of a collegiate church, but most seem to have been independent foundations, established usually by some individual, whether layman or cleric, and occasionally by a burghal guild. By the sixteenth century there were cases where the original intention had been lost sight of, the hospital suppressed and funds diverted, but new foundations were still appearing and many medieval hospitals provided continuity into post-reformation times. Some of the hospitals were designed to assist travellers on routes leading to ferries and bridges; the erection of bridges (which could save lives) was itself a recognised work of piety, which could be encouraged by indulgences, and a number of them originated with a cleric or an ecclesiastical institution.

Charitable works were enjoined by Christianity: not only did St Paul exhort 'Let us not be weary in well-doing' and 'Let us do good unto all men' (Galatians vi, 9–10), but there was the Lord's own implied recommendation: 'I was an hungered, and ye gave me meat, . . . I was sick, and ye visited me'. It must be said, however, at the risk of seeming cynical, that charity was not necessarily disinterested. The words just quoted were set in the context of the Last Judgment: those who acted thus charitably looked for welcome to 'the kingdom prepared for you from the foundation of the world' and hoped to avoid the 'everlasting fire, prepared for the devil and his angels'. This should be kept in mind when one looks at the Doom which was kept before the eyes of medieval man in sculpture, in drama and mural paintings. Medieval acts of charity were not a kind of unselfish 'social gospel', but a way to salvation for those who performed them.

Besides the obvious acts of charity, there were other 'works' which might be reckoned among the means of salvation. There were still 'hermits', but how many of them were enthusiasts for secluded devotion must remain uncertain.[59] Pilgrimage must likewise be viewed with reserve. Scots took the well-trodden paths to the Holy Land, the shrine of St James at Compostella in Spain, the Holy Blood at Hailes Abbey in Gloucestershire, and remote Scottish shrines.[60] There was an element of sight-seeing, almost of tourism, and much of the traffic seems to have been fairly well organised, though even so the perils were so considerable that some at least of the pilgrims deserved to have their excursions reckoned among their merits.

Setting 'good works' against sins is a venture in accounting almost as profitless as setting off masses against sins, but looking at one alongside the other – without attempting to balance them – brings us to the crucial point of relating principle to practice. The medieval mind seems never to have been unduly perturbed by the divorce of principle and practice – perhaps one of those 'childlike inconsistencies of the medieval mind which no mere history can make clear to the modern reader'.[61] This is conspicuous in secular affairs, for many well-intentioned statutes regularly passed by the Scottish parliament were at best only imperfectly put into effect and no one seems to have been greatly concerned by the divergence between the statute book and current practice. (To be fair, how many people, walking in our streets today, would guess from what they see that there are laws against dogs fouling the pavements or against the dropping of litter? Perhaps in this as in pandering to the illiterate there has been a reversion to medieval practice.) It was the same in the Church. Its day-to-day working was, one might almost say, based on the principle that the law should not be observed. Canon law was there, but seems to have been thought of as representing the kind of unattainable perfection of which sinful men always fell short. At any rate, canon law was constantly set aside by papal dispensations. When the reformers came along to castigate the corruptions in the Church they took a malicious delight in observing that if only the clergy would obey 'their own laws' all would be well.

Possibly the divorce was not between principle and practice but between faith and works. Works were separated from faith, and, in theological language, medieval man was antinomian to a degree not surpassed by the most extreme predestinarian of the eighteenth century: if he kept to his faith, works might be disregarded. However, this inconsistency in outlook compounds the difficulty of assessing the impact made by medieval Christianity. The suggestion that the great mass of the people were not instructed Christians at all has been seriously advanced, for instance by the late Dom Gregory Dix, who will hardly be thought a friend to the reformation:

> All through the dark and middle ages there is an immense drab mass of nominal Christianity in the background, looming behind the radiant figures of the saints and the outstanding actions of the great men and women who make up the colourful foreground of the history – a mass of ignorance, squalor and poverty.... Down to the end of the middle ages this great lay mass, the product of the mass-conversions, was never fully absorbed by the church.

Keith Thomas, in *Religion and the Decline of Magic*, concludes that 'it is problematical as to whether certain sections of the population [of England] had any religion at all' and quotes contemporaries to the effect that the people were as 'heathenish' as the natives of Africa and America.[62] It would be hard to prove that things in Scotland were any better.

If this was so, then pagan beliefs and superstitions lingered on, sometimes perhaps not consciously distinguished from Christian beliefs. Whether or not the invocation of saints was defensible, the association of particular saints with particular powers – like Triduana with defective eyesight or Anthony with erysipelas – looked more like magic. There was the obsession with relics, which was mentioned in the previous chapter in relation to attitudes to war and which, by attributing supernatural power to artefacts, went a long way to efface the difference between the spiritual and the material. Some trusted in the arm of St Andrew, some women in labour trusted in the 'shirt' of St Margaret. When any man-made object – houses, tools, ships – as well as animals and crops, could be 'blessed' (perhaps accompanied by another material object, holy water) the frontier with magical spells was a thin one. An amulet like an Agnus Dei looked like a lucky charm. Magic spells were wrought by human power, while prayer required the co-operation of God, but the distinction was blurred in practice. Prayers could look much like spells, and the belief that sacraments were effective irrespective of the disposition of priest and recipient made even them look like magic.

The idea that heathenism persisted in the shape of a witch-cult, though attractive, seems now to be generally discounted,[63] but witchcraft was believed to exist all through the middle ages. The earliest extant ecclesiastical statutes, in the thirteenth century, included witches, male and female, among the offenders to be excommunicated four times a year.[64] It is possible that there was increasing concern about witchcraft as time went on, but perhaps all that happened was that evidence increased as prosecutions became more common or were better recorded. In 1484 Pope Innocent VIII encouraged inquisitors to act against witches as well as heretics and three or four years later the *Malleus Maleficarum* described their alleged practices along lines which were long to be familiar. There were some prosecutions for witchcraft (associated with heresy) in the 1540s,[65] and Hamilton's Catechism declared witches damned but did not say that they should be executed. It is an all too common piece of nonsense to believe that either then or later witchcraft trials were conspicuously more frequent in Scotland than they were in many other countries.[66]

It is safe to say that, despite difficulties, setbacks and human failings, the middle ages had seen an increasing penetration of at least a modicum of knowledge of essentials. The monasteries may have represented mainly the interests of the aristocracy, who were almost alone at that stage in having access to or regular communication with intellectual leadership. However, the friars, as was mentioned in chapter 2, represented an extension of Christian teaching down the social scale, especially in the burghs, where there was increasing wealth to endow both friaries and other ecclesiastical institutions. Besides, it was people in the burghs who derived most benefit from schools, the religious activities of guilds, the plays and the pageants. We know that in some countries, though not specifically in Scotland, there were various movements among relatively humbler people, movements which were on the fringe or beyond the fringe of strict orthodoxy. The likelihood is, though, that even in the burghs the very poor were those who benefited least.

Gregory Dix, who had doubts about the extent to which Christianity prevailed, was nevertheless prepared to concede that 'a noble and faithful pastoral work must indeed have been done by the nameless and rustic clergy of the dark ages and by the early medieval parish priests'.[67] One might say that such work was still being done right down to the eve of the reformation. Ill-educated as parish priests often were, falling short of the standards of conduct which their own code laid down, ill-supplied with equipment, they may still have been passing something on to the people, in simplicity but in sincerity. If the verses quoted earlier were current and their thought was in men's minds as well as their words on men's lips, then the situation could have been healthier than might appear from other evidence – admittedly harder evidence. Academic competence is not and never has been an essential qualification for effective pastoral work, and it was perhaps less essential in the sixteenth century, when the congregations on their side had less education and lower intellectual equipment, than today.

The next chapter will show that the teaching of some of the earlier reformers, even though it had an immediate Lutheran origin, was hard to distinguish from what was officially countenanced by the Church. Archbishop Hamilton would have found nothing wrong with some of the material which will be quoted in the next chapter from *The Good and Godly Ballads*. It is not too fanciful to visualise a humble priest, with a true vocation, who had been brought up on material reflecting late medieval devotion to the Passion, using the Catechism or some similar production, encouraging his people in the use of verses like those in the Ballads, and carrying on a successful ministry, in spite of all the material difficulties surrounding him. But of course if this was going on, the contrast between the eternal essence of Christianity and a great deal of the existing ecclesiastical system would be all the more marked. There was something of a paradox: the better a parish priest was doing his job within the ecclesiastical system – doing his job even on that lowly, non-intellectual level – then the more likely was the reformation to take root among his people. So the very merits of the individual, within a defective system, contributed to the downfall of that system.

If to maintain the law in theory but disregard it in practice is inadequate, insincere or hypocritical, then the middle ages stand condemned. But if it is meritorious to uphold certain standards, irrespective of enforcing them, then they deserve some credit. The medieval church, with all its failings, had not the kind of depravity which is all too familiar in the twentieth century, when the differences between right and wrong are blurred or effaced and when churchmen prefer to find excuses for sinners and reach an accommodation with sin, rather than demand either penitence or amendment.

4

THE REFORMATION

In the era of reformation the proliferation of personal writings enlarges our knowledge of what was in men's minds, yet the externals of church life rather than the substance of the faith continue to command attention, because it was in organisation that the reformation made the most obvious changes. The religious life of monasteries and friaries came to an end, the diocesan boundaries were to be rationalised, the machinery for appointing bishops or other overseers was altered, the long-familiar courts held by bishops' officials ceased to function and their jurisdiction was largely transferred to secular courts, the traditional privileges of the clergy ceased and some ecclesiastical authority passed into lay hands, whether through nobles, burgesses and shire commissioners in parliament and general assembly or through annually elected elders at congregational level. Such an extensive structural overhaul may be likened to the changes of the twelfth century, when the dioceses and parishes were organised and the new religious orders introduced, but the reformation, which made innovations in doctrine as well, was a revolution of such magnitude that the parallel should perhaps be rather with the initial 'conversions'. (The reformers, who took an exaggerated view of their achievement in rescuing people from 'ignorance', would have appreciated that comparison.)

The reformation was the product of attacks on the church system on national, economic and rational as well as theological grounds, but it is mainly the last that concern us here. The previous chapter showed that late medieval men were much concerned about sin, some of them no doubt merely by habit and convention, but others in sincere penitence, and, in the belief that a remedy could be found in the Passion, their thoughts turned much to Our Lord's sufferings:

Throu thy marcy and this memour	*Through thy mercy and this memory*
Off thy panis and the dollour,	*Of thy pains and the sorrow*
Grant at the mynd of Thi Passioun	*Grant that the memory of Thy Passion*
Be to me full remissioun.	*Be to me full remission.*

or

Gif thou thi life in syn hes led	*If thou thy life in sin hast led*
To ask me marcy be thou nocht dred;	*To ask me mercy do not dread;*
For the lest drop I for the sched	*For the least drop I for thee shed*
May clenge thee sone	*May cleanse thee soon*

| And all the syn this warld within | *And all the sin this world within* |
| That thou hes done. | *That thou hast done.* |

As the benefits of the Passion could be mediated through the Mass, thought of this kind could find expression and practice within official teaching, but, while some therefore still invested in masses for the souls of the departed, clerical eyebrows must have been raised by lines like these:

> Continuall and devoit meditation of the passioun is better na to fast a yer [on] bred and watter and daly scurge him self quhill the blude ryn . . . our [over], or daily reid a psalter.
>
> Suppois all haly kirk pray for a man, he may get mair grace himself for remembring of the passion.
>
> Devoit remembrance of the passion is better than our Lady and all the sanctis prayit for him.[1]

Such emphasis on individual, personal faith was in line with teaching outside rather than inside the Church. And such teaching there was. Hardly anything is known of the enduring influence of the earlier movements for reform which had reached Scotland with Lollards from England and Hussites from Bohemia in the early fifteenth century, but certain radical views did here and there survive as late as the 1490s: 'After the consecration in the mass there remains bread. . . . The mass profiteth not the souls that are in purgatory. . . . We should not pray to the glorious Virgin Mary, but to God only'.

As Scotland had strong commercial links with Germany, the Low Countries and ports on both sides of the entrance to the Baltic (where Scots settled in significant numbers), news of Luther's defiant challenge in 1517 did not take long to reach the eastern coastal burghs. Soon impetus was coming not only from the other side of the North Sea but also from the other side of the Border, for in 1526 Tyndale's translation of the New Testament into English became available in print and in a matter of months it reached Scotland. An act of parliament against Lutheran books, passed in 1525, was ratified in 1535 with an addition to the effect that anyone who had such books must hand them over to the bishop within 40 days, and in 1541 parliament issued nine acts which would have been unnecessary if earlier legislation had not been worse than fruitless: the sacraments were to be respected; the Blessed Virgin was to be the object of worship, honour and intercession; papal authority was not to be impugned; 'kirks and kirkmen' were to be reformed (the former in their fabric, the latter in their 'habit and manners'); 'congregations or conventicles to commune or dispute of the holy scripture' were prohibited; heretics, even if they abjured, were to hold no public offices; assistance was not to be given to fugitive heretics; informers were to be rewarded; and statues of saints were not to be 'cast doun' or otherwise treated irreverently.

These statutes indicate in a general way what had been going on, and there was a whole series of specific incidents – iconoclastic outbreaks, violence against clergy, disturbances in churches, prosecutions for heresy and a few executions – as well as expressions of contempt for the irregular lives of priests and for superstitious devotion to relics. As the evidence relates to only the proportion (presumably small) of illegal activities which came to light and as it derives not from any archives of ecclesiastical courts (which are not extant) but from stray pieces of information which happen to have survived elsewhere, it must reflect only a minute fraction of the disaffection which existed. The overwhelming majority of the incidents which are mentioned took place on or near the east coast, from Lothian to Aberdeenshire, where burgesses and lairds were exposed to protestant winds from Denmark and Germany; only about a tenth of them were in Glasgow and the south-west.[2] But the influences were Anglican as well as Lutheran: Sir John Borthwick, a Lothian laird, was indicted in 1540 not only for reading the works of Lutheran divines but for approving 'the English heresies' and urging them on his fellow-countrymen.[3] In the later 1540s and the 1550s Swiss and French contacts reinforced these other influences.

There is plenty of evidence of growing dissatisfaction with the medieval system and of agonising doubts focussed on the persistent question, 'What must I do to be saved?' The answer came. 'Patrick's Places', a digest of evangelical theology attributed to Patrick Hamilton, who was executed for 'heresy' in 1528 after associating with Lutherans in Germany, put strong emphasis on the Passion as the remedy for sin, with the reiterated proclamation: 'Christ bought us with His blood, Christ washed us with His blood, Christ came into the world to save sinners, Christ was the price that was given for us and our sin.' The stress was on the futility of works and the necessity of faith, by which alone sinners can be justified: 'Whosoever thinketh to be saved by his works, denieth Christ is our Saviour, that Christ died for him. . . . To what end should He have died for thee, if any works of thine might have saved thee?' Such an exciting manifesto offered, with complete assurance, the message that men had been craving.

Such teaching found ample support in scripture: 'a man is justified by faith without the deeds of the law' (Rom. iii, 28); 'being justified by faith, we have peace with God' (Rom. v, 1); 'if thou shalt confess with thy lips that Jesus is Lord and shalt believe in thine heart that God hath raised him from the dead, thou shalt be saved' (Rom. x, 9); 'justified by his grace' (Titus iii, 7). No mere moral perfection could ensure salvation. 'All our righteousnesses are as filthy rags' (Isaiah, lxiv, 6); or, in New Testament language, 'all have sinned and come short of the glory of God. There is none righteous, no not one' (Rom. iii, 10, 23). Works were devalued, though they were not to be dismissed in relation to faith: 'faith, if it hath not works, is dead' (James ii, 17, 20, 26). The two had to be brought together: 'Works done before . . . the inspiration of [Christ] are not pleasant to God . . . they are not done as God hath willed and commanded them to be done and even have the nature of sin'.[4]

There were variants within the theme of justification by faith. The name of John Calvin is associated with 'predestination', the belief that 'the Elect' are foreordained to salvation, others to damnation. This, in its most rigid form, was to have considerable influence in Scotland from the seventeenth century to the nineteenth, and it became an article of faith that there was only a 'limited' atonement, as Christ died not for all men but only for the Elect. This idea, however, is not to be found, at least unambiguously, in the Confession of Faith prepared by the Scottish reformers in 1560. It does say that the regeneration of men is wrought by the Holy Spirit, which works 'in the hearts of the elect of God an assured faith in the promises of God', that God had 'of mere mercy elected us in

Christ Jesus His son, before the foundation of the world was laid' and that the Church contains 'the Elect of all ages', who are known only to God. But the document also states that Jesus gave power to *so many as believe in Him* to be sons of God, that He offered himself generally 'for us . . . for our transgressions' and that, whereas those who suffered for righteousness' sake would inherit immortality, sinners would be cast into outer darkness: this seems to come close to declaring that works are after all decisive and that men may be faithful of their own free will. However, good works are brought forth not by free will but by the spirit of the Lord in men's hearts: all 'workers of iniquity' have neither true faith nor sanctification *so long as they continue in their wickedness,* but when 'the spirit of the Lord Jesus . . . takes possession of the heart of any man, so soon does He regenerate and renew the same man' so that he hates sin. There is a reference to such works 'as please God and as He has promised to reward', but

> we utterly abhor the blasphemy of those that affirm that men which live according to equity and justice shall be saved, what religion soever they have professed. For as without Christ Jesus there is neither life nor salvation, so shall there none be participant thereof but such as the Father has given unto his Son Christ Jesus, and those [that] in time come to Him, avow his doctrine and believe into Him (we comprehend the children with the faithful parents).

Yet, despite this devaluation of good deeds, the Last Judgment is depicted as committing to 'the fire inextinguishable' such as 'delight in vanity, cruelty, filthiness, superstition and idolatry', while 'such as continue in well doing to the end' shall be received into heaven. The Confession is rambling and repetitive and looks like the work of a committee whose members were not all of one mind, but it could be interpreted to mean that an individual could choose faith and virtue or unbelief and sin and in doing so could determine his fate. There is nothing here of the unrelenting predestinarianism so emphatically and succinctly set down in Archbishop Whitgift's Lambeth Articles of 1595:

> God from eternity has foreordained some to life and has condemned some to death. The moving or effective cause of predestination and life is not the acceptance of faith or perseverance or good works or anything in the persons predestined, but the will of God alone. The number of the predestined is already defined and certain and can neither be increased or diminished.

These articles read almost like a refutation of some of the clauses of the Scots Confession. Their purpose, of course, was presumably to furnish a more rigid interpretation of predestination than the Thirty-nine Articles had done – though Article XVII, with its explicit rejection of any merits in works done without the inspiration of the Holy Spirit and its reference to a divine decree 'before the foundations of the world were laid', is as emphatic on election as is the Scots Confession. The documents show what nonsense it is to speak of the Church of Scotland as theologically more 'Calvinist' than the Church of England.

The reformers forcefully rejected the Mass. In their eyes it was idolatrous, because it involved the worship of a wafer; it was blasphemous, because it detracted from the uniqueness of Christ's Passion as the only true sacrifice; it was undermining in its moral effects, because by purchasing masses men could hope to make satisfaction for sins; and it detracted from the majesty of God and the position of Christ by giving the priest a place as a mediator between man and God. The reformers were nowhere more forthright than in their insistence that the only sacrifice which availed with God was Christ's own sacrifice. The words in which the Thirty-nine Articles of the Church of England denounced the Mass are often quoted: 'The sacrifices of masses, in which the priests are said to offer Christ for the quick and the dead, are blasphemous fables and dangerous deceits'; but the Scots Confession of 1560 used very similar language: 'The priests, . . . as mediators between Christ and His Kirk, do offer unto God the Father a sacrifice propitiatory for the sins of the quick and the dead. Which doctrine, as blasphemous to Christ Jesus, and making a derogation to the sufficiency of His only sacrifice, once offered, we utterly abhor, detest and renounce'. In the emphasis they laid on the sacrifice of Calvary and in their determination to eliminate the notion that men could be worthy to offer any other sacrifice, the reformers rejected the concept of the eucharistic oblation. While their Communion was emphatically a commemoration of the death of Christ, showing forth that death and recalling it to the minds of men, the idea that the worshippers were making an act of remembrance before God, that they were presenting before the Father the passion of Christ and thereby associating themselves with the work of Christ as the Great High Priest, ever pleading His sacrifice – all that was lost sight of.

Yet in the Communion of the Scottish reformers a Real Presence was unambiguously proclaimed: 'In the Supper, rightly used, Christ Jesus is so joined with us that He becomes the very nourishment and food of our souls. . . . The faithful, in the right use of the Lord's Table, so do eat the body and drink the blood of the Lord Jesus that He remaineth in them and they in Him'. No doubt the compilers of the Confession were eager to insure against the accusation of being Zwinglians, who held that the elements and the service were no more than symbolic, but the unmistakeable warmth in this part of the Confession suggests deep feeling.

The reformers had no desire to depose the Eucharist from its centrality in public worship or even from its weekly celebration. But as they would not celebrate with few or no communicants in the medieval manner and as the people were accustomed to communicate only once a year, celebrations became infrequent. The reformers proclaimed that their clergy were ministers of Word and Sacraments: no one was to administer the sacraments unless he could also preach and indeed the sacraments were not to be celebrated without an accompanying sermon. But, while they would no doubt have liked to give equal emphasis to Word and Sacrament, in practice the emphasis changed from the sacramental to the prophetic and the sermon became predominant. Scotland was now on the road which in time led the typical Scot to speak not of 'going to church' but of 'going to hear Mr So-and-So'. Churches were reconstructed to focus not on the altar at the east end but on a pulpit placed against one of the long walls, not infrequently with an extension opposite the pulpit to make the church T-shaped. Initially the arrangements provided also for a long Holy Table in a prominent position, or sometimes, in a large church, a special 'Communion Aisle'. Later, churches were built undisguisedly as preaching-halls.

The attack on the Mass, which involved an attack on the priesthood, led logically to an anticlericalism which would in any event have stemmed from the new emphasis on the individual's responsibility. Anticlericalism has often done much to shape opinion, because healthy-minded laymen are usually anti-clerical: 'those who are attached to the clergy seldom realise how very few laymen are not in their hearts opposed to clerical influence' wrote David Mathew, who as a Roman Catholic archbishop ought to have known. The reformers intended – they did not succeed – that the new ministers should not have the dominating position which priests had had. It is easy to see how anticlericalism worked out in worship. The use of the vernacular in place of Latin, metrical versions of the psalms which could easily be sung, service books – of Common Prayer or Common Order – in the hands of the people and no separate books for the clergy: worship became something in which everyone would join, indeed something in which everyone was expected to join. The people were now invited, expected, to communicate at every celebration, the cup was restored to them. Minister and people were to assemble round a table, set lengthwise in the chancel or the nave.

Much of the reformers' thought sprang from their acceptance of the concept of the priesthood of all believers. They did not take that to mean that every man was his own priest and that there was no need for a professional ministry; what they did believe was that the essential priesthood or ministry was a kind of corporate ministry residing in the congregation, from whom authority came up to the minister instead of descending on him from a bishop. This had been put into practice in congregations which met without any formal authorisation before 1560. After the reformed church was formally organised it was proposed not only that the people should elect their minister but that the people should have power to depose him. This particular piece of anticlericalism was never, so far as we know, put into practice, for ministers were disciplined by superintendents, but the proposal indicated the belief that the minister derived his authority from the people.

Just as the eucharist became a corporate act, performed by minister and people together, so the priestly powers of excommunication and absolution were to pass to the congregation; instead of confession in private to the individual priest and imposition of penance by him, the congregation or its representatives were to examine members and decide whether they should be admitted to Communion and whether they should be subjected to penance – penance in face of the congregation. Somewhat similarly, baptism ceased to be a rite performed in private by the priest, and instead was performed in face of the congregation, which thus, as a kind of corporate priest, admitted the newly baptized into its fellowship.

The changes in worship could hardly have been more revolutionary. Yet in popular belief – which theologians might not have approved – there was a good deal of continuity, shown plainly in *The Good and Godly Ballads*. About 1542 John Wedderburn, in Dundee, a town which had a great reputation for 'godliness', 'translated many of Luther's dytements into Scottish metre' and 'turned many bawdy songs and rhymes into godly rhymes'.[5] This compilation, originating in the earlier phase of the Scottish reformation, reflected something of the warm passion of Luther and hardly fitted with the coolly intellectual emphasis of Calvin, but it was several times reprinted, down to 1621, no doubt with official approval.

Wedderburn obviously believed, like General Booth, that, far from letting the devil have all the best tunes, there was something to be said for setting sacred words to melodies which had been used for secular or even improper verse.[6] In 1549 a church council ordered enquiries about 'books of rhymes or popular songs containing calumnies or slanders defamatory of churchmen and church institutions, or infamous libels or any kind of heresy'; and three years later parliament legislated against 'bukis concerning the faith, ballatis, sangis, blasphematiounis [and] rymes als weill of kirkmen as temporal and uthers'.[7] The *Ballads* have achieved notoriety because they contained some scurrilous verses about the pope, and they may have been the very material condemned in 1549 and 1552, but they contain other matter which shows how truths were rendered easily memorable, in vigorous but tender and sometimes moving language. There is, for example, a metrical version of the Creed, combining impeccable orthodoxy with vital faith:

> We trow in God allanerlie,   [believe
> Full of all micht and majestie,
> Maker of hevin and eird sa braid,
> Quhilk hes himself our Father maid:
> And we his sonnis ar in deid,
> He will us keip in all our neid,
> Baith saull and body to defend
> That na mischance sall us offend:
> He takis cure baith day and nicht
> To save us throw his godly micht
> Fra Sathanis subteltie and slicht.
>
> We trow in Jesus Christ his Sone,
> God, lyke in gloir, our Lord alone;
> Quhilk, for his mercy and his grace,
> Wald man be borne to mak our peace,
> Of Mary mother, Virgin chaist,
> Consavit be the Haly Gaist,
> And for our saik on croce did die
> Fra sin and hell to mak us fre,
> And rais from deith, throw his Godheid,
> Our Mediatour and our remeid
> Sall cum to judge baith quick and deid.
>
> We trow in God the Haly Spreit,
> In all distres our comfort sweit,
> We trow the Kirk Catholick be
> And faithfull Christin companie
> Throw all the warld with ane accord,
> Remissioun of our sin we trow;
> And this same flesche that levis now
> Sall stand up at the latter day
> And bruik eternal lyfe for ay.   [enjoy

This creed begins 'We...', a usage advocated nowadays to make the creed acceptable to those who recite it without believing it. Archbishop Hamilton had by anticipation rebuked such dishonesty: 'Quhi sais thow in the beginning of the Crede *I beleve*, spekand in the singular nowmer? To signifie and declare that ilk ane of us suld haif in our awin hart ane special faith in God... sa that thow may saie with sanct Paule, *In fide vivo filii dei, qui dilexit me et tradidit semetipsum pro me* – I leive in the faith of the sonne of God, quhilk hais luffit me and gaif himself for me. And than may our Salviour say to the: *Fides tua te salvum fecit* – Thi faith hais maid the saif'. It might have been argued that the concept of justification by faith demanded an affirmation of personal belief. Another of the 'ballads' clearly rejects works as the way to salvation:

> Quhair I culd not the law fulfill,
>   My warkis maid me na supplie;
> Sa blind and waik was my fre will,
>   That haitit the veritie;
> My conscience kest me ever in cair,
> The Devill he draif me to dispair,
>   And hell was ever befoir myne eye.

Remarkable stanzas combine warm evangelical fervour, focussed in the late medieval manner on the Passion, with devotion to the Blessed Virgin:

> For us the blissit Bairne was borne,
> For us he was baith rent and torne;
> For us he crownit was with thorne;
>   Christ hes my hart aye.

> For us He sched his precious blude;
> For us he was naillit on the rude;   [cross
> For us he in mony battell stude;
>   Christ hes my hart ay.

> Nixt Him, to lufe his Mother fair,
>   With stedfast hart, for ever mair;
> Scho bure the birth, fred us from cair:
>   Christ hes my hart ay.

Other verses link the Passion with the Eucharist in impeccably orthodox terms:

> Our Saviour Christ, king of grace,
> With God the Father maid our peace;
> And with his bludie woundis fell
> Hes us redemit from the Hell.

> And He, that we suld not foryet,
> Gave us His body for to eit
> In forme of breid, and gave us syne
> His blude to drink in forme of wyne.

> Quha will ressave this Sacrament
> Suld have trew faith, and sin repent;
> Quha uses it unworthelie
> Ressavis deid eternallie.
>
> Thou suld not dout, but fast belief
> That Christis body sall releve
> All them that ar in hevines
> Repentand sair thair sinfulness.

The first of those four stanzas take us back to an item in *Devotional Pieces*:

> Jesu Christ hang on the rude:
> With lufly speche and myld mude
> He schew till man
> How he fra hell with panis fell
> Oure saulis wan.

And the second echoes other phraseology in that collection ('ordained His precious body to us as sacrament in form of bread') as well as in a suggestion of Quentin Kennedy quoted earlier.

Is it in those verses, with their evangelical fervour, rather than in Catechisms and Confessions, that the essentials of the Scottish reformation are revealed? They are as far as possible removed from bickerings about ecclesiastical polity. And, laying the *Devotional Pieces* alongside the *Ballads*, can one really believe, as some silly people said in 1960, that in 1560 one religion, the Catholic, was swept away and another religion, the Protestant, introduced in its place? Catholic and Evangelical approximate far more than is often believed and share attitudes which cut them off from the detachment of those who take what they think a middle way. The Mass is so closely tied in with the Atonement and with Redemption that belief in the Mass (as itself the work of Christ) comes very close to the belief of evangelical Christians. The whole concept of salvation by the Blood of Christ, through vicarious suffering, is common to both and this gave a strong element of continuity.

We know well enough where the reformers stood, what they believed, but it is not so easy to be clear about how widely and how rapidly they spread their message. There was, to begin with, a core of singularly committed people, some of whom were martyrs, some of whom risked but escaped martyrdom. The whole question of commitment at the reformation has been raised: 'So much doubt is cast on the political, economic and religious motives of the participants in the reformation that the ordinary reader might be forgiven for wondering how sufficient motivation remained to accomplish anything of historical consequence'.[8] But however strong self-interest, nationalism or politics, they would not make a man face the stake. In the heat of battle he might kill or be killed without any very clearly understood motive save self-preservation, but in the cold-blooded choice between recantation and an agonising death it is hard to see that anything other than religion could have been of account. It was indeed self-preservation, but preservation of the soul, not the body: only a desperate belief that a man's eternal welfare was at risk can explain it. G. M. Trevelyan, reflecting on Thomas Cranmer's 'magnificent gesture' of thrusting into the flames the right hand which had, in a moment of weakness, signed a recantation, wrote: 'Had the men of those days a less highly strung nervous system than ours, or can the power of a scholar's mind be so triumphant over physical pain?' In the humane atmosphere of Scotland few were put to the ultimate test. In 1893 the Marquis of Bute, himself a Roman Catholic, remarked that the number of persons 'put to death in connection with the Reformation [in Scotland] is stated to have been nineteen on one side and five or six on the other. Admit the twenty-five. Henry [VIII] or Mary [Tudor] would have consumed them in a month.'[9] As one of the 200-odd papists who were put to death by Elizabeth Tudor happened to have been born in Scotland, Roman Catholics now speak of them as 'British martyrs', just as English football hooligans are styled 'British' with the same intention of shifting blame to Scotland, but also to mitigate Roman mortification at the scarcity of real Scottish martyrs.

It has been remarked that we know about the 'diers' – the martyrs – and the 'flyers' – those who left Scotland for realms where protestants could live in safety – but that we can do little more than guess at the number of 'liars' who had turned to protestantism in their hearts but continued to conform outwardly. However, when the parliament of 1560 suppressed the Latin rite, abrogated papal authority and adopted a reformed Confession of Faith, its legislation was following, not leading, the examples of several local authorities, in places like Dundee, St Andrews and Ayr, where already the old worship had been suppressed and reformed congregations organised.

Testamentary dispositions illustrate how protestant beliefs were adopted, for the soul was now usually commended to God alone, without intercession. Conservative elements survive, but mainly in wills drawn up before 1560 for people who died after that year. A Glasgow Testament of 1564 (written in the vernacular in presence of the vicar of Bothwell, who had not yet entered the reformed ministry) commends the soul to God, the Blessed Virgin and 'all the halie fallowschip of hevin'; and a few others in the early 1560s mention the Virgin and the Saints or 'all the company of hevin'. One empowered executors to dispose of the deceased's goods 'for the helth of his saull', another appointed executors 'for almous of his saull' and one in 1564, which made the traditional committal to the Virgin and the Saints, authorised executors to act *pro salute anime mee* and bequeathed fourpence to the fabric of 'the church of Glasgow' (a gesture of contempt?). As traditionalists thus retained medieval formulae, committal 'to God omnipotent' can be taken to indicate rejection of prayer for the dead and of invocation of saints, though it might have appealed to some who did not feel able to use a more positive expression of the reformed faith. Of the latter there are plenty of examples. One testator in Glasgow, in 1561, declared, 'I commend my saull to Almyghty God, the Redeemer of mankynd', and another, in 1563, put it, 'I leif my saull to God Almichty, and beleifis to be savit be the schedding of Christis bluyd and be na uther menis [means]'. At St Andrews one testator leaves his soul to God and his body to be buried until the day of the General Resurrection; another gives 'declaratioun of his faith that his salvation consisted only in the death and passion of Jesus Christ' and commits his soul to the 'protectioun of God eternal'. An Edinburgh testament of 1594 gives what has been called 'a classic statement of the protestant faith': the testator committed 'hir saull in the handis of Almychtie God, certanelie hoiping that be the merreitis and passioun of Jesus Chryst the samyn salbe ressavit to the eternall bliss and joy of hevin' and that on 'the day of resurrectioun' her body 'sall ryse and be placit with the elect'.[10]

Changing beliefs about the souls of the dead affected treatment of their bodies. According to the Book of Common Order and the first Book of Discipline there were to be no burial services, though a sermon of thanksgiving for the faithful departed, such as preached by Knox for the Regent Moray, was permissible. The recumbent effigy of the deceased, the main feature of medieval tombs, survived here and there, but became much less fashionable. There were many well-executed monuments which incorporated recesses too shallow to have ever contained a three-dimensional representation of the deceased and which look curiously impersonal and frigid. The significant novelty to emerge was the sculpture representing the deceased not in death but in life, either kneeling or standing. Such a monument almost excluded any concept of prayer for the dead and certainly did not invite that practice.[11]

There long remained much to keep the old ways in mind. As parish priests were no longer saying masses for their deceased parishioners, the customary offerings and mortuary dues came to an end, but endowments (often explicitly provided 'for the salvation of souls') were in general safeguarded by law and practice. It was rare to find the plain speech heard in the English Short Parliament, to the effect that funds 'granted to pray for their souls' were obsolete because 'no more purgatory, so no need for prayer'. Yet craft guilds hastened – sometimes even before parliament had abolished the Mass – to eliminate references to their patron saints and their altars and to prayers for the souls of deceased brethren.[12] It is naive to think that because a guild still had a 'chaplain' the members were still hearing Mass.

As the reformers' teaching was to be grasped by the intellect, they thought that symbolism and ceremonial designed for the illiterate were as superfluous as the striped pole outside a barber's shop. Their services were designed to reach the intelligence through the ear and not to reach the senses through the eye and possibly the nose. This must have limited the appeal of the new programme. Many must have felt that with the suppression of the Latin rite and the erosion of belief in the sacrificial character of the Eucharist something which for centuries had nourished the devotion of the saints and of countless other Christians was being abruptly discarded. Looking over the whole of Scottish Christianity it is hard to avoid the conclusion that the biggest breach in continuity was, to put it in the simplest possible terms, what happened to the Eucharist at the reformation. The term 'Eucharist' is meaningful (Greek for 'thanksgiving'), and to call the central rite of the Christian religion by nothing better than the words of dismissal at the end of the service, 'Ite missa est' is silly. Yet the popular term 'Mass' acquired its significance because it gathered to itself a whole complex of ideas and associations. Dom Gregory Dix, recalling how it all started with the words, 'Do this in remembrance of me', went on:

Was ever another command so obeyed? For century after century, spreading slowly to every continent and country and among every race on earth, this action has been done, in every conceivable human circumstance, for every conceivable human need from infancy and before it to extreme old age and after it, from the pinnacles of earthly greatness to the refuge of fugitives in the caves and dens of the earth. Men have found no better thing than this to do for kings at their crowning and for criminals going to the scaffold; for armies in triumph or for a bride and bridegroom in a little country church; for the proclamation of a dogma or for a good crop of wheat; for the wisdom of the parliament of a mighty nation or for a sick old woman afraid to die; for a schoolboy sitting an examination or for Columbus setting out to discover America; for the famine of whole provinces or for the soul of a dead lover; for a village headman much tempted to return to fetich because the yams had failed; because the Turk was at the gates of Vienna; for the repentance of Margaret; for the settlement of a strike; for a son for a barren woman; for Captain So-and-So, wounded and prisoner of war; while the lions roared in the nearby amphitheatre; on the beach at Dunkirk; tremulously, by an old monk on the fiftieth anniversary of his vows; furtively, by an exiled bishop who had hewn timber all day in a prison camp near Murmansk; gorgeously, for the canonisation of St Joan of Arc – one could fill many pages with the reasons why men have done this, and not tell the hundredth part of them.[13]

Now of course this did not all come to an end at one stroke. Perhaps it had been undermined before 1560, for an emphasis on Communion rather than sacrifice appeared in a 'Godly Exhortation' issued early in 1559.[14] On the other hand, the reading of the history of Christ's Passion at the reformed Communion helped to maintain the concept, but celebrations were very infrequent. More persuasive is the evidence of continuity already cited from popular verse, which proves that the idea of the eucharistic sacrifice was not readily extirpated from men's minds. Nor did the concepts which had underlain medieval thought exist in later times only in the Roman Communion. Many Anglicans have believed that in their Communion – at first styled 'the Order for the Lord's Supper or Holy Communion commonly called The Mass' – they are doing very much what medieval men thought their Mass was doing. The idea is explicit in some Anglican liturgies, not least in the Scottish Liturgy in the form it had from 1764, if not earlier, until 1929. It is possible, too, to read much of the traditional view into services in the Church of Scotland's present Book of Common Order, but infrequency of use militates against their moulding popular belief in the way the medieval Eucharist did.

At the time, the more intellectual appeal of the sermon must have seemed a cold and comfortless novelty, and a God who no longer was brought down from heaven to be adored on the altar must have seemed a remote deity with whom it was harder to communicate. Surprise is sometimes expressed at the likelihood that no more than a minority of Scots accepted reformed teaching before or in 1560, but the really surprising thing is that so many did accept such a wrench with the past. One can well understand what lay behind the poignant cry of one parishioner of the Canongate, who agreed to use the reformed church for marriage and baptism but drew the line at its Communion: 'William Anis biand callit and accusit quhy he brak divers and sindre promissis to the kirk oblising himself to renunce idolatrie and jone himself to the companye of Godis pepill, ansueris: "I confes I wes marrit and gat my child baptiset, bot my hart gevis me to the mes, and thairfoir I can nocht come to the Comonion"'.[15] There must have been many whose hearts prompted them in that way. Others were more forthright than William Anis. William Balfour in Leith demanded, 'Is this your Communion? The Devil burst me when ever it come in my belly and the devil burst them in whose belly it comes'.[16]

However, as opposition was seldom militant or confident, sympathy for the old ways was largely latent. Three or four peers voted against the Confession of Faith in the 1560 parliament, numerous priests were prosecuted for violating the proclamation by which Queen Mary forbade the saying of mass on pain of death. But nothing was done to rally the multitude whose hearts still 'gave them to the Mass'. Archbishop Beaton of Glasgow, who should have led them, went off to France in 1560, never to return; the bishops who declined to approve the Confession were either conscientiously hesitant or timid; the definitions of the Council of Trent (1563) came too late to help Scottish conservatives by at last making it clear what doctrines they ought to defend. In any event, whatever the attachment to the Mass, there are few indications of any strong attachment to the papacy, the hierarchy or even the apostolic succession. Leaderless, and despondent about prospects at home, the more intransigent, including Ninian Winyet, who in 1562, in his *Certane Tractatis*, had posed questions which searched out the weaknesses and inconsistencies in the reformers' position, followed Beaton to the continent. With their retreat, the reduction by death of the number of priests in the country, and the lack as yet of measures to mount a counter-offensive from the continent, the prospect facing Scottish Romanism in the 1570s was one of extinction.

It is not surprising that the protestant challenge to long-established belief was not the only challenge. Traces of radical deviation from orthodoxy can be seen now and again in the middle ages: in 1277 a list of propositions taught by the masters of arts at Paris included statements that theology rests on myth, that religion is a bar to enlightened education and that there is no happiness except in this life.[17] Academics in other periods have indulged in similar speculations without attracting much attention. However, in the era of the reformation much had been happening to shake loose the foundations of long-held beliefs – geographical discoveries seemed to weaken the presuppositions of scripture, the growth of nation states weakened the notion of a united Christendom, and printing enormously facilitated the dissemination of novel ideas. The challenge to traditional theology was accompanied by the appearance of scepticism and even atheism. Sir Richard Maitland of Lethington (1496–1586) wrote:

> Religion now is reckoned as a fable,
> All hope of heaven is holden vanity
> And hell's pain is counted poetry.

'Fable', it should be said, was then a stock term to express scepticism.[18] Sir Richard's son, William, who as Secretary of State was prominent in the revolution which brought the protestants to power but whose motives were political, is alleged to have declared that the devil was only 'ane bogle [scarecrow] of the nursery' and very possibly did so, though the words have never been conclusively traced to him. In the 1590s an Edinburgh minister remarked that 'men doubt if there be a devil'. In contemporary England, while 'atheism' was used to cover any kind of immorality or nonconformity, Marlow denied Christ's divinity, Ralegh rejected heaven and hell and there seems to have been a good deal of scepticism at lower social levels.[19]

In 1560 and 1561, when one system had been effaced but another had not yet fully taken its place, there had been some cynicism and a tendency to cry 'a plague on both your houses'. A canon of the collegiate church of St Mary of the Rock declared that he was 'nether ane papist nor ane Calvynist, nor of Paul nor of Apollo, but Jesus Cristis man'.[20] William Balfour in Leith declared the reformed religion and worship contrary to the Word of God and argued that Holy Communion should be abolished, and when the reader of the parish of Canongate was asking a woman 'if she had any hope of salvation by her own good works', Balfour condemned the reader as a very knave and his doctrine as false.[16] There was some choice language in St Andrews: 'I sall by [buy] ane poynt of wyne and ane laif [loaf] and I sall haif als gude ane sacrament as the best of them all sall haif.... The Divell knok out John Knox harnes [brains].... The Divell ane kirk will I gang to. The Divell burn up the kirk or [before] I come into it'. The son of a Fife laird, who was also a parson of a parish, retorted to the superintendent's demand that he contribute to the repair of the church, 'The devill ane penny he wald spend upon the kyrk'.[21]

Such deviations, if they took much root at all, were likely to wither away, for as the reformed faith increasingly prevailed there would be if not less scepticism at any rate less recklessness in expressing it. While it might be possible to draw a parallel between the work of what was initially a mere handful of protestant preachers and the work of stray missionaries in the period of the 'conversions' a thousand years before, the difference was that this time there was systematic shepherding of the converts through an organisation which had government backing to establish a reformed ministry throughout the country. We can do little to quantify the support reformed teaching gained among the laity, but the likelihood that many were receptive and most were ready enough at least to acquiesce can perhaps be inferred from the example of the clergy. Many may have had no better principles than the Vicar of Bray, but, even so, instructive comparisons can be made: when in 1573 it at last became impossible to retain a benefice without professing the reformed faith, a mere handful of clergy were deprived, whereas in 1662, when a presbyterian system was superseded by an episcopalian system, about 270 ministers were deprived and when the episcopalian system in turn gave way to presbytery in 1690 about twice that number were deprived. The conclusion is inescapable that there was far less attachment to the pre-reformation system than there was to either of the two systems which competed later. There was also far less personal animosity after 1560 between those who conformed and those who did not than there was in the following century.

Standards of education among the ministers rapidly improved, and within half a century or so it was rare to see in a pulpit a man who was not a graduate. More than that, evidence that many ministers were earnest in their studies comes from what we know of their books – not only those they possessed (and perhaps did not read) but from those they lent and borrowed. East Lothian ministers in the late 1560s were exchanging Calvin on the Lesser Prophets, Bullinger against the Anabaptists, Musculus on Matthew and John, and Calvin on the Acts.[22] At various dates between 1583 and 1598 Thomas Swinton, minister at Kirkwall, borrowed books which included works of the Zurich theologian Gualter, Calvin's Institutes, works by Musculus (Berne), Melanchthon the Lutheran, Peter Martyr (Strassburg), Erasmus and many more, as well as *The Imitation of Christ*.[23] The books which Clement Litill, a leading Edinburgh lawyer, put at the disposal of the ministers of Edinburgh included an astonishing range – medieval doctors, Anglican, Lutheran, French and Swiss divines (as well, again, as *The Imitation of Christ*).[24] A vast amount of protestant literature was available in England and surely found its way to Scottish readers, as primers had done earlier – to an extent indeed that the output of Scottish printers was extremely meagre because of competition from material produced in bulk for the large English market.[25]

Congregations were taught from the pulpit and children were taught in schools, which by the middle of the seventeenth century existed in most parishes in the Lowlands. In church and school alike the main vehicle of instruction was a Catechism. As in the middle ages, the minimum belief was crystallised in the Commandments, the Creed and the Lord's Prayer, ability to recite which could be required of couples intending marriage and of paupers seeking relief, as well, of course, as of intending communicants.[26] But the direct access of the Christian to God, without a human mediator, postulated something more than learning by heart: the Christian should be able to turn to the Bible with understanding and not rely on tradition or on what he was taught by clerical mentors. Help came from a Catechism.

Catechisms, like other books, were easily obtained from England. Calvin's Catechism, first printed in Scotland (so far as we know) in 1564, had been printed in England in 1561, and subsequently there were more editions in England than in Scotland. The Prayer Book Catechism had been available since 1549 and was in 'the book set forth by godly King Edward' which was widely used in Scottish churches in 1560. Besides, a version modified for Scottish use was printed separately: two leaves which survive show Scotticisms of spelling and the insertion of the Summary of the Law after the Commandments – a feature which does not occur again until the Scottish Prayer Book of 1929.[27] A Catechism was contained in some editions of the Book of Common Order, including the Gaelic version of 1567. The Scots Confession of 1560, printed in 1561 and 1565, could have served in place of a Catechism, but the first known native Catechisms were in Latin (Adamson and Pont, both in 1573); John Craig's *Short Summe of the Whole Catechism* appeared in 1581 and went through five editions before 1600. Craig also produced *Ane Forme of Examination before the Communion* in 1592, and in the same year the Catechism of the English puritan Dudley Fenner was printed in Edinburgh. There seems to have been some assertion almost of individualism and reluctance to be tied to a standard version. Thus a Stirling Register contains, in March 1591/2, 'The Maner of the Examination befoir the Lord's Supper', which has been conjecturally attributed to Robert Pont. Its sacramental theology seems Zwinglian rather than Calvinist and it does not teach predestination. Another *Maner of Forme of Examination before the Admission to the Table of the Lord, used in Edinburgh*, printed in 1581, had little similarity to the Stirling version and reflected current opinion during a kind of 'Popish Scare'.[28] It would be reckless to think of the reformed church presenting a uniform scheme of instruction or of all Scottish protestants being indoctrinated with the same theology.

Some of the warmth which sermons and catechism lacked may have been supplied by the verses and hymns already mentioned, for the use of the sung word to familiarise people with the scriptures was popular. William Tyndale, who translated the New Testament into English, had written, 'If God spare my life, ere many years I will cause a boy that driveth the plough shall know more of the scriptures than thou doest', and a farther step was taken by William Samuel (d. 1569), who composed many paraphrases of the Bible in verse and wrote in his *Abridgments of Goddes Statutes* that his mind was to 'have my country people able . . . to sing the whole contents of the Bible' in place of ballads. The Preface or 'Prologue' to the *Good and Godly Ballads*, quoting St Paul's advice to teach and exhort 'with psalms and hymns and spiritual songs', contended that 'the Word of God increases plenteously in us by singing . . . and that especially among young persons and such as are not exercised in the scriptures, for they will sooner conceive the true word than when they hear it sung in Latin'. While the place of hymns – good, godly or other – in Scottish worship may not then have been significant, there was no doubt about the value of music as a vehicle of religious expression. Calvin wrote: 'Among other things which are suitable for the recreation of men and for giving them pleasure, music is the first or one of the chief, and we should esteem it a gift of God bestowed for that end. In truth we know by experience that song has great force and power in moving and inflaming the heart of men to invoke and praise God with more vehement and ardent zeal', though he seems to have thought that only psalms were appropriate in church.[29] The Prologue already quoted went on to say that when young people hear the word of God 'sung in the vulgar tongue or sing it themselves, with sweet melody, then shall they love their God with heart and mind and come to put away bawdry and unclean songs'.

It was altogether too optimistic to believe that any amount of godly balladry would at once eliminate ungodly bawdry. The parliament of 1563 (ignoring the adoption of the reformers' standards by a somewhat dubious parliament three years earlier) serenely re-enacted statutes which had been passed in 1552, in what Knox would have called the days of ignorance – ignorance, that is, of the gospel. Brothels, fornication, adultery and swearing were all now condemned afresh, and not for the last time.

We know far more about the sins of Scots after the reformation that before it, not because they sinned more but because their sins were systematically recorded in extant archives. What the reformers did was to restore something like the ancient penitential system for which purgatory had been in a sense the substitute. Guilt (*culpa*) for sin could indeed be remitted through faith in Jesus Christ as Saviour, but penalties or retribution (*pena*) had still be be exacted, not now by suffering after death but by discipline and punishment in public. Thus purgatory in some sense recovered its location on earth. The medieval penitential system has left no records, and in so far as penance was imposed privately by a confessor it was by definition unrecorded; but after the reformation penance was a public matter, and it figures largely in kirk session records, which survive in growing numbers from 1559. In dealing with sexual offences, profanity, assaults on parents and on wives, the kirk session imposed not only the formal penance of exposure of penitents to the public gaze on 'the stool' (which might be a bench for five or six persons) but also fines and the physical ordeals of the 'jougs' (equivalent of the stocks), ducking and banishment, and sentences passed by the session could be executed by the secular arm, at least in towns, where the bailies (often themselves elders) were at hand to exert physical force when it was needed. Elders themselves were not always models of rectitude, even if their delinquency went no farther than playing golf when they should have been at a session meeting,[30] but this did not check their censoriousness towards others. The whole topic is a very familiar one and can be assessed in various ways. It has been said that the proceedings provided free advertising for the immoral and that they enlivened public worship with entertainment now purveyed by the less reputable Sunday newspapers, but the sessions have also been given credit for acting as general watchdogs in the parish and thereby helping to create the growth in respect for the law which characterised seventeenth-century Scotland. The system did hold up certain standards and publicised clear distinctions between right and wrong, though few might go so far as the scholar who wrote: 'Those who did not learn to love righteousness were taught to dread the punishment of sin; and the shame of public appearance was designed to deter the innocent as well as to express the grief of the guilty. It was thus that a healthy public opinion was formed'.[31]

The reformers believed that one of the 'marks' or distinguishing features of the Church was 'discipline', which included the belief that laws were there to be obeyed, not to be disregarded or set aside by dispensations. One cannot overlook the sharp distinction between the medieval church, when delinquency among the clergy was generally accepted as the norm, and the later situation, in which scandals among clergy became so rare that when they occurred they reached the headlines. The reformers proclaimed that their intention was to redress the balance between faith and works in favour of faith, but from one point of view their achievement was to redress the balance in favour of works, by insisting that would should accord with faith. Behind all the changes lay the concept that the individual was responsible for his own salvation and did not rely on religious specialists in monasteries or elsewhere; he could no longer secure vicarious salvation by buying the prayers of others. God was to be found by each individual's experience through His Word. There was no more segregation of the holier people in monasteries, no formal distinction between first-class and second-class Christians. The same standards were expected of all. The Church as consisting of 'The Elect', known only to God, was invisible, but those who had been baptized and who were communicants formed a visible institutional Church. The reformers set their sights high in postulating the thoroughgoing commitment of all Christians. In any event, the offer of justification and salvation by faith, though made to sinners, did not prevent sin. No one who witnessed the unending stream of sinners passing through the hands of the kirk sessions could have failed to feel disappointment at what could only have seemed the failure of the hopes of the reformers. What happened, though not at this early stage, was the emergence of the 'gathered congregation' of the more committed.

'Works' in the sense of uprightness of life might not be without merit, but salvation was not to be attained by the 'works' which had been deemed salutary in the middle ages – going on pilgrimage, mortifying the flesh by fasting and other hardships, doing good to the poor and the sick. Nor was there merit in acts of charity in the ordinary sense. Yet there was no lessening of emphasis on the significance of what is usually called Christian charity or of social commitment.

Before the reformation there had been clear signs if not of social unrest at any rate of uneasiness about the sufferings of the poor. Sir David Lindsay, who wrote so vigorously on the topic in his *Three Estates*, is not to be numbered among the religious reformers, if only because he died in 1555, before the explosion came, but the persistent theme of his Satire is the need for 'reformation' – a word he used again and again – and in 1547, after the murderers of Cardinal Beaton had seized St Andrews Castle, he turned up there, perhaps expecting the explosion. Lindsay most likely thought primarily of a social reformation and certainly not of a social, still less a political or ecclesiastical, revolution. But the religious reformers took up his theme and seem to have deliberately appealed to the lower classes by adopting the cause of those whom they called 'the poor labourers of the ground'. The obvious contrast between the poverty of the apostles and the wealth of the prelates provided background for an economic element in the revolt against the old church system.

It was hardly accidental, and it may well be significant, that the chain of events which led directly to that revolt started with a document known as 'The Beggars' Summons' which ran in the name of 'the blind, crooked, bedridden, widows, orphans and all other poor' and called on the friars to terminate their possession of properties which had been intended for charity. Due notice to flit was given, and it was when the date named for removal came round, in May 1559, that there began the violence which continued until the triumph of the reformers in July 1560.

Once the reformers were in the saddle, laws were passed to give some protection to tenants; revenues of friaries and some other establishments were assigned to hospitals, schools and other 'godly uses'; and action was taken to ensure funds for poor relief. Apart from such direct involvement, the reformed church continued to exert some pressure by making its views known. The Second Book of Discipline (1581) urged 'relief' for the 'haill common people' and especially for 'the labourers of the ground' who had been 'rigorously handled' by extortioners.[32] In 1596 the general assembly drew attention to the 'cruel oppression of the poor tenants' and to the ancient malpractices of 'forestalling and regrating' in the tradition of medieval legislation against sharp practices in the market-place.[33] One must reflect that medieval parliaments had been dominated by magnates and the reformation was led by magnates, and that measures in favour of the poor were not passed by a self-seeking proletariat.

The Church never shirked the responsibility proposed for it by the first Book of Discipline of 1560–61, to the effect that 'every several kirk must provide for the poor within the self'. But the poor were apt to be mobile and it was not enough for parishes to act. In August 1562 the magistrates and council of Edinburgh, on the ground of the needs of the poor and the burden which fell on the capital, to which 'resortis mair pouir than to ony uthir of this realme', asked the queen for help in the creation of hospitals and schools.[34] The queen agreed to do something, but voluntary contributions were required as well, and they were forthcoming – an action which has been patronisingly and insensitively called 'the acceptable face of protestantism'.[35] Continuity there was and to spare: old endowments for the poor, not least through 'hospitals', were maintained or even recovered, sometimes under the supervision of kirk sessions, and the familiar 'beddellis' or gownsmen survived.[36] In Perth ('St Johns toun'), where a new hospital for the poor was planned by the kirk session in 1579 and where one of the three weekly meetings of the session was for 'helping the poor', the session still licensed beggars by giving them a badge of the 'Holy Lamb, the town's mark and token'.

Modest contributions towards the relief of the poor came from the fines which kirk sessions levied from delinquents and from 'mortifications' or bequests by individuals, a 'good work' which still had its appeal. But for nearly three hundred years the main source of the poor fund was the collections taken at public worship. As the upkeep of churches and manses and ministers' stipends was the responsibility of the heritors, money raised in church could be wholly devoted to the poor. For generations there was no question of 'taking up a collection' for general church purposes, which is very much what is done now and which, if not a selfish exercise, is at any rate largely an inward-looking exercise (though some of the money raised may go to mission work). Instead, the emphasis was on giving alms for the poor – a more personal, less institutionalised, act of charity, which the donor no doubt thought was good for his soul as well as for the bodies of the recipients. The Prayer Book imaginatively associated this collection of alms with the offering of the elements for the Communion; the service-books of the Scots did not generally go as far as that, but it was made clear that what was collected, whether at the church door or in wooden ladles during the service, or given on approaching the Holy Table, was the *alms for the poor*, and the level of giving was always conspicuously higher at Communion services. This, by contrast to the modern collection, was unselfish, because the giving was for the benefit of others. To the extent that, as often alleged, it was sometimes the smallest coin and not infrequently base money (sometimes of no value except as metal) which went into the box, practice may have fallen short of the principle which was nonetheless maintained.

The role of the Church in education is too well known to require elaboration. The reformers were committed to education, partly because of their emphasis that each individual's responsibility for his salvation lay, under God, on his own shoulders rather than on a priestly caste and partly because schools were the channels by which the faith could be instilled and protected; little time was lost in making it the law that schoolmasters must be vetted by the reformed church. The first demand for a school in every parish came in the first Book of Discipline (1560–61), and a good deal towards that end was achieved before legislation first came from the secular government in 1616. But, despite government intervention, education was no more nationalised or secularised than poor relief was: although the Church had no financial responsibility for schools – the heritors paid for them as they paid for churches and manses – the Church did a lot to stimulate the establishment of schools and directly supervised their work.

Poor relief and education were the most obvious fields of social concern, but Christian influences on society were working less obtrusively in the background. The reformed church took very seriously its duty to reconcile its members one with another, especially before they came to Communion. The Prayer Book's exhortation to attending communicants to be in love and charity with their neighbours laid the onus on the individual, but in Scottish parish churches minister and elders took a real part in quenching quarrels and ending disputes – something which they could well do in the small populations of rural parishes where all local differences would be well known.

'THE DISTRACTED TIMES'[1]

There have not been many reigns when a Secretary of State, much involved in court life and public affairs and personally ambitious, not only wrote a long work called 'Doom's Day or the Lord's Great Day of Judgment' but also collaborated with his sovereign in producing 'The Psalms of King David translated by King James'. The king was James VI, who wrote Paraphrases and Meditations based on scripture and who spoke with little hesitation as if he knew the mind of God. The Secretary of State was the poet Sir William Alexander, Earl of Stirling.

If the first sovereign in the seventeenth century was a scholar, the second, Charles I, was a man of taste and a patron of the arts, and the third, Charles II, had an intellectual curiosity which made him the patron of scientists as well as artists. Nobles and lairds engaged in literature, encouraged writers, commissioned portraits of their ancestors and the decoration of their walls and ceilings to illustrate the diverse interests (including religion) of the time. Among the kings' subjects were artists and builders, and growing prosperity made resources available for the erection of handsome structures which still delight the eye.

The material needs of the Church were not ignored. The stock of church buildings surviving from the middle ages was more than adequate for most needs, and efforts went mainly into conservation and renovation[2] but as it took a long time to remedy the results of pre-reformation neglect there were still complaints. Nor had the reformation brought a sudden access of decorum, for there could be 'great misorder' in 'rash and sudden coming to the Table, in spilling of the wine and in thrusting and shouting at their passage out at the kirk door after the ministration'.[3] Almost the first experiment in new building was the bold experiment at Burntisland (1592), which William Laud thought looked like 'a large square pigeon house', but the traditional rectangular plan was soon reinstated. In 1617 parliament required every parish church to have its own Communion plate, and there is evidence of the purchase of bells and candelabra. An English visitor in 1629 heaped up superlatives in praise of Scottish churches: Leith had 'two fairer churches for in-work than any I saw in London' and Galashiels had 'the finest seats I have seen anywhere, and the orderliest church'.[4]

Given the example set in high places, the general pattern of life, the cultural setting and the growth of law and order during 'King James's Peace', evidence that Christian profession was fashionable need not surprise. Among the friends of the poet-Secretary Alexander was a better-known poet, William Drummond of Hawthornden, for whom we have information about not only books he owned and books he gave away (to Edinburgh University Library) but of books he read.[5] The wide reading of this cultivated man included *The Holy Love of Heavenly Wisdom*, *The Sanctuarie of a Troubled Soul*, *An Exhortation to Repentance*, an *Oratio Eucharistica* by G. du Val, and Philippes de Mornay's *De la Vérité de la Religion Chrétienne*, besides going back nearly a century to the *Treatise on Justification* by Henry Balnaves, an associate of John Knox. He read some books of the Bible as literary exercises – the Psalms in French, the Epistles and the Acts in Italian – but he went systematically through the books of the Old Testament from Joshua to Ezekiel, presumably in English, and like many another in that century he felt the fascination of the book of Revelation, three works on which were among his reading. In Drummond's library,[6] a sixth of the books were theological (but at the time a third of all books printed were theological), ranging from the scriptures in Hebrew and Greek through many of the Fathers and medieval doctors on to Lutheran and Anglican divines, the decrees of the Council of Trent and post-reformation controversy.

Many of Drummond's earlier poems contained little that was religious and less that was specifically Christian. With the *Flowers of Zion* (1623) there enters a more distinctly Christian element, in hymns of the Passion, the Resurrection and the Ascension, recalling the work of Dunbar more than a century earlier. Despite the absence of official blessing, hymn-writing had not been extinguished, for in 1599 Alexander Hume, minister of Logie, had produced *Hymns or Sacred Songs*, of which Drummond had a copy. Drummond's verses on 'The Angels for the Nativity of Our Lord' anticipated by six years the 'Ode on the Morning of Christ's Nativity' of John Milton, whose classical obsessions did not obscure his Christianity any more than Drummond's obscured his.

It was true, as a contemporary (himself a sincere believer) remarked, that 'men are unwilling to quarrel with the religion of their country, and since all their neighbours are Christian, they are content to be so too'.[7] It was also true that certain standards of belief were officially upheld. The Confession of Faith approved by parliament in 1560 and 1567 had been supplemented by the 'Negative Confession', first adopted at the time of a 'Popish Scare' in 1581 and repeatedly signed as a test of protestantism. In 1616 the general assembly adopted a new Confession of Faith[8] which was more explicitly predestinarian than the Confession of 1560: 'God, before the foundation of the world was laid, according to the good pleasure of his will, for the praise and glory of his grace, did predestinate and elect in Christ some men and angels unto eternal felicity, and others he did appoint for eternal condemnation'. However, 'albeit we be not justified by good works, . . . yet they are the way to the kingdom of God and are of necessity to be done for obedience to God, for glorifying of his name, for confirming ourselves anent our election and for good example to others; and constantly we affirm that faith which bringeth not forth good works is dead and availeth nothing to justification or sanctification'. The 1616 assembly also adopted a new Catechism (printed in 1619)[9] which was more reserved on 'election' than the Confession was, for the answer to the question, 'Are all men saved by Him?' was 'No, but only those who have true faith'.

Meantime, on the continent a reaction against the strict determinism associated with Calvin had been headed by Arminius, but it was condemned by theologians of several nations at the Synod of Dort (Dordrecht) in 1619. Whether or not as a direct result of the continental movement, in both England and Scotland some theologians adopted more liberal views. Among the 'Aberdeen Doctors'[10] Robert Baron maintained that Christ died for all men, and both he and John Forbes agreed that God predestined the wicked to hell only in the sense that He foresaw their evil deeds, while John and William Forbes saw good works as the product of the operation of the Creator, who made a man righteous.

In the 1640s, after the success of the covenanters against Charles I, the general assembly adopted the Confession of Faith and Catechisms produced by the Westminster Assembly of Divines. This Confession was more emphatic than ever on predestination: 'By the decree of God... some men and angels are predestinated unto everlasting life and others foreordained to everlasting death.... Their number... cannot be increased or diminished. Those of mankind that are predestinated unto life, God, before the foundation of the world was laid, according to His eternal and immutable purpose and the secret counsel and good pleasure of His will, hath chosen'. And it went on to remarks which would appear to have opened the way to the possibility of an antinomian interpretation – that is, the belief that the elect did not require to turn aside from their sins: God had chosen them 'out of His mere free grace and love, without any foresight of faith or good works or perseverance in either of them'. Again, as in 1616, the Catechism was milder than the Confession: 'Justification is an act of God's grace, wherein He pardoneth all our sins and accepteth us as righteous in His sight.... Sanctification is the work of God's free grace, whereby we... are enabled more and more to die unto sin and live unto righteousness'. There seems to be little stress here on 'election', some encouragement to perseverance in an upright life and less of an opening for antinominianism. When in 1661 the covenanters' innovations were in the main swept away, nothing was said about doctrine, and the 1616 Confession seems to have been ignored; the Confession of 1560 was resurrected in the Test Act of 1681, to meet the objection that it was quite unfamiliar. The Westminster Confession and Catechism remained in use, though without any legal basis, and were more than once reprinted.[11]

Apart, therefore, from a few years in mid-century when the Westminster Confession may have been enforced, it would have been hard to find grounds for condemning any thought as 'unorthodox' in the sense of being contrary to officially upheld standards. When we turn to the papers to which representative figures, laymen as well as churchmen, committed their thoughts, we find little awareness of doctrinal standards to which they could look for guidance, still less from which they dared not deviate.

Collections of sermons survive from the late sixteenth and early seventeenth centuries, the most noted by Robert Bruce (1554–1631), Robert Rollock (1555–99), John Welch (1570–1622) and William Cowper (1568–1619). All have been praised, but relatively few seem to represent the actual pulpit eloquence of the time: some were originally in Latin, others were anglicised either in MS or for publication. Bruce, however, not only preached in the vernacular but, at a time when it was being superseded in the printed word, made his own translations, into vigorous Scots, of the scriptural passages which he had occasion to quote. His preaching was rooted in his experience when at the age of twenty-seven, struck by consciousness of his sins and appealing to God's mercy through the Passion of Christ, he gained an assurance of pardon and salvation. His abiding awareness that God was with him he found so deeply moving that in private prayer and public intercessions he gave way to tears and in his sermons he moved his hearers to tears. Several of his extant sermons deal with the Eucharist, in thought fairly close to that of the Scots Confession of 1560: 'Christ Jesus His true body and blood... are spiritually present, really present,... present inwardly to thy soul as the bread and wine are present inwardly to thy body'. In other sermons his constant stress is on 'a true and lively faith', a 'bruised and broken heart' and 'the cross of Christ'. Good works 'are given thee in this life to be a gage and sure pledge that the perfect justice of Jesus Christ pertains to thee.... If I... wrought not according to the Lord's command in my calling, my conscience could never be persuaded of a remission.... I am not justified by the works which proceed from me, but by the works which proceed from Jesus Christ my Savour'.[12]

Bruce, although for years under severe royal displeasure, seems to have had little taste for the ecclesiastical politics which distracted so many of his contemporaries, not least Samuel Rutherford (1600–1661), minister of Anwoth, whose hostility to the high church tendencies encouraged by Charles I led in 1636 to his deprivation. 'In the pulpit he had a strange utterance, a kind of skreigh, that I have never heard the like. Many a time I thought he would have flown out of the pulpit when he came to speak of Jesus Christ'.[13] (Knox, it will be recalled, was 'like to ding the pulpit in blads and fly out of it.') However, even before Rutherford lost the use of a pulpit he had begun to transmit his views by letters, selections from which, often reprinted, were formerly found in many Scottish homes. When he turned his attention to the spiritual counselling of an individual he was forthright in his belief in predestination, for God's 'book keeps your name and is not printed and reprinted and changed and corrected'; but he also wrote with tenderness and with encouragement to trust in God:

> Your afflictions are not eternal; time will end them, and so ye at length see the Lord's salvation. His love sleepeth not, but is still in working for you. His salvation will not tarry nor linger, and suffering for him is the noblest cross that is out of heaven.... And this is the fruit, the flower, the bloom growing out of your cross, that ye be a dead man to time, to clay, to gold, to country, to friends, wife, children and all pieces of created nothings, for in them there is not a seat nor bottom for your soul's love.... God gave so much for your soul... and blessed are ye if ye have a love for him and can call in your soul's love from all idols and can make a God of God, a God of Christ, and draw a line between your heart and him.... Let the Lord absolutely have the ordering of your evils and troubles and put them off you by recommending your cross to him.

That was one side to Rutherford, but much of his concern was less with individual salvation than with the Church, afflicted in the 1620s and 1630s by the policy of Charles I and in the 1640s by the disputes among the covenanters. His passionate concern was expressed in highly charged, sometimes erotic, language:

Our blessed Lord Jesus, who cannot get leave to sleep with His spouse in this land, is going to seek an inn where he will be better entertained. . . . Christ is putting on his clothes, and making him ready, like an ill-handled stranger, to go to other lands. Pray him sister, to lie down again with His beloved. . . . We have cause to weep for our harlot-mother: her Husband is sending her to Rome's brothel-house. . . . Oh, what joy . . . to see Christ put on the glory of His last-married bride and His last marriage-love on earth; when he shall enlarge his love-bed, and . . . take in the Elder Sister, the Jews, and the fulness of the Gentiles.[14]

The Scotsman in this century about whose religious thoughts we know most was Archibald Johnston of Wariston (1611–63), whose Diary extends (with gaps) from 1633 to 1658.[15] His outpourings match those of Rutherford in their exuberance, but his range of devotion, of meditation and of self-revelation was uncommonly wide. His father had evidently undergone a conversion after what was apparently his first Communion, and this had conferred a kind of assurance of 'remission and reconciliation'. Archibald traced his own Christian conviction to his sixteenth year, with his own first Communion, but he seems never to have experienced such assurance.[16] How could one be sufficiently assured that he was numbered among the elect if the decision lay with God's arbitrary will? To see one's works as a sign of election, as Bruce had done, came perilously close to assessing one's salvation in the light of one's moral record. The 'federal theology' of the time, suggesting a covenant between a man and God on condition of perfect obedience and faith, on the whole made more difficulties for anyone who could not see faith as a free gift. At any rate, Wariston and others had no confidence in predestined salvation and, still tortured by doubts, continued to ask, 'What must a man do to be saved?' He still felt separated from God by his sins and enslaved to 'the devil and his lusts'. His consciousness of sin was over-powering, and constant self-examination led him to extravagant declarations: he had been 'guilty a thousand fold' of breaking all the Ten Commandments. After much experience he still seemed suddenly to realise, almost as a novelty, the message of the Gospel. In March 1634 he wrote:

On Sunday again between sermons God was sensibly present with me in meditation. After sermon he was wonderfully present with me in meditation with floods of tears, and in prayer he fixed and glued my thoughts and desires to the blood of Christ, that I might find the power satisfactory and meritorious efficacy of it in reconciling, remitting, abating of sin, . . . and, calling here by I wit not what sweet attractive power of mercy from God for this blood, I found my conscience much pacified and my heart inseparably glued to the blood of Christ.

One would have thought this conclusive, but the self-abasement went on and he saw God's judgment on him as a sinner. All his tortured soul-searching did not evolve merely from his own consciousness, but was stimulated by wide reading of devotional works. Many were Anglican, but there were those of the Lutheran John Gerhard (1582–1637), who translated into German that most moving of

Passiontide hymns, 'O sacred heart, sore wounded'; and even from the
Meditations of a Dominican friar he 'got some tears' – always his sign of efficacy.
He derived spiritual profit also from sermons he heard in Scotland, often from
bishops, including that very 'high' churchman Sydserf of Galloway, and from
Dean Hannay, at whom, according to legend, 'Jenny Geddes' was to throw her
famous stool. Wariston found a special place in his devotional life for Communion,
and he contrived, by going from parish to parish, to communicate at least five
times between April and November 1637. His religious exercises extended to
fasting and almsgiving and to an undertaking to dedicate to pious uses a tenth of
his income if God would 'mercifully and indulgently deal with this unworthy
worm'. 'The Lord's hand' was in everything he did – his professional work, his
personal relations and the running of his estate. One wonders how Wariston found
time for professional and political activities, and until 1637 secular concerns are
rarely alluded to. The copious tears as he 'poured out his heart' and 'his heart
melted like water' must surely have marked him off as a man apart, 'walking on the
dizzy verge of madness'.[17] Leader of the extreme wing of the Covenanting party
though he became, Wariston had a religious life less like that of an evangelical
protestant than that of a devout medieval Catholic. It has been remarked that the
committing of self-examination to the pages of a diary was something of a
substitute for the confessional, and there are examples of other similar diaries in
Wariston's time.[18] Reading Wariston agonising over his sins one feels that he
should have been in the confessional, but he would have needed a singularly
patient confessor. His appreciation of Roman Catholic and Anglican writings and
his own setting in the context of covenanting – and also pre-covenanting –
Scotland is eloquent of the widespread dissemination of essential Christianity.

　　Wariston had contemporaries who were equally self-revealing and shared his
deep religious experience, but without his frenzy. John Forbes, one of the
'Aberdeen Doctors', committed his inmost thoughts to his 'Diary, or Spiritual
Exercises', extending from 1627 to 1647. The pages contain extensive meditations
on scripture, with numerous quotations, from which he drew comfort and
consolation; like Wariston he often confessed his sins with tears, he 'renewed his
covenant' with God at Communion and again and again 'comfortably
communicated'; 'the Lord quieted [his] soul and filled [his] heart with peace,
strength and joy'. In his unaffected piety he opens a field far removed from the
events of the period and has hardly anything to say of public affairs before 1638,
though his own sufferings at the hands of the Covenanters are inevitably
mentioned later. The late G. D. Henderson, in one of the few books which has
attempted to explore Scottish spirituality – his *Religious Life of Scotland in the
Seventeenth Century* – wrote of how Forbes 'conversed with God' and was 'as a
little child when he came before God'. The Diary of Andrew Hay of Craignethan
for 1659–60 came from a layman who, like Wariston, was an extreme covenanter
but who preserved a balance among his various interests in a full daily record of
public and personal affairs, business and religious observance. He made extensive
notes of sermons he heard, but his approach was far more one of the intellect than
of the heart and the reading he mentions was largely in history and anti-Roman
polemics. Another diarist, Alexander Brodie of Brodie (1617–80), confessed his
sins like Wariston and Forbes, but was far more occupied with current affairs and

the state of his fellow-countrymen's morals than Forbes was. Yet another, Alexander Jaffray (1614–73), left a 'record of religious experience' in which he claimed to have undergone conversion but not to have known the time and place of it, because, he explained, it is one thing to desire that Christ would come, another to know that He is there already – an assurance which he does not seem to have achieved in full until after the passage of many years. Like Wariston, he engaged much in self-reproach, but his thoughts kept coming back to the affairs of state in which he was involved as a member of parliament of first the Scottish kingdom and then the Commonwealth and as a negotiator with Charles II and with Cromwell.[19]

There were others for whom mundane affairs clearly had priority over religion but who yet were not without Christian thoughts. Sir Thomas Hope of Craighall, Lord Advocate, who left a diary for 1631 to 1645, displayed little depth of religion in relation to everyday affairs, but a belief in more than conventional Christianity is suggested by the fact that when he sent off two sons, one to England and one to France, in 1636, he gave each of them a copy of *The Imitation of Christ*, telling them to read a chapter of it every night and morning. (That ever popular work was one of the 28 books, many of them devotional, owned by the wife of Sir Walter Innes of Balvenie about 1630.[20]) Sir James Hope, son of Sir Thomas, who himself became a Lord of Session, left a diary for 1646–54[21] which is concerned almost entirely with business and the births, marriages and deaths of his family, with no light on his religion. The diary of William Drummond, son of the poet, extant for 1657–9,[22] shows that he went to church fairly frequently, but as often stayed away, and while he sometimes noted the name of the preacher he never noted the subject of the sermon. Whether he was a communicant is not clear: one Sunday he noted, 'the Communion given in Edinburgh; I went to Leith church', which may or may not mean that he wanted to avoid the Sacrament. One Sunday when he did not go to church he read a prose essay by his father which is a meditation on death (though with hardly a Christian content), but on another he read the 'Devotions' of John Donne. It was on a Saturday night that he read Ovid's *Ars Amandi*. He noted his many bouts of heavy drinking, but gave no indication that they weighed on his conscience.

The intense fervour characteristic of the period could issue in occasional corporate outbursts. In 1625 David Dickson preached so forcefully in Irvine that some of his hearers fell down insensible, and people spoke of 'the Stewarton sickness' (Stewarton being the parish adjacent to Irvine). At Shotts in 1630 John Livingstone preached to a vast gathering in the open air on the Monday after the Communion, when some had spent the night in devotion. When he moved to Ireland he was accused of stirring up people to 'ecstasies and enthusiasms'.[23] But neither religious epidemics nor widespread evangelism provided the main outlet for fervour.

The truth was that not long after the reformation evangelical commitment was overlaid by what can only be called ecclesiastical politics. Firstly, there was from the 1570s the issue of whether the church should be administered by individuals (superintendents or bishops) or by presbyteries. Secondly, the presbyterians denied lay people any voice in church affairs, which meant that annually elected elders were superseded by elders ordained for life and that parliament must not legislate for the Church – or rather, must not legislate against presbyterianism: it was, illogically, welcome to legislate for presbyterianism.

The covenanting movement, as a revolt against the administration of Charles I, had its origins, much as the reformation of the previous century had had, largely in secular – constitutional, financial, social and nationalist – as well as ecclesiastical, grievances. No one can say how many of the people who gathered to sign the National Covenant were fully aware of the meaning of a document which would take about half an hour to read to them. Attention was caught at the outset by the stirring language of the 'Negative Confession' of 1581, which was inserted to appeal to the anti-popery of the multitude and to give the impression that nothing new was involved. Fewer would grasp the long and tedious list of statutes which followed; the drift of this was that the law was above the king. The sting of the Covenant was in its tail, where the signatories pledged themselves to disregard the changes made by Charles until they had been tried in free assemblies and in parliaments and to defend their cause 'against all sorts of persons whomsoever', which might commit them to action against the king. But the Covenant appealed to convictions deeply rooted in the national consciousness. The notion that the Scots were a chosen race went back at least to the Declaration of Arbroath in 1320, and it had been strengthened after the reformation by a belief that, whereas other churches retained 'some footsteps of Antichrist and some dregs of papistry', the Scottish church had nothing within it 'that ever flowed from that Man of Sin' and would become 'an example and pattern of good and godly order to other nations'.[24] Samuel Rutherford, five years before the Covenant, had described how the Church of Scotland had been made the bride of Christ, who would 'embrace both us, the little young sister, and the elder sister, the Church of the Jews' – so imputing incestuous bigamy to the Almighty. Taking other metaphors, he said that Christ 'got a charter of Scotland from His Father' and, 'seeing the ends of the earth are given to Christ (Ps. i, 8) and Scotland is the end of the earth', Scotland must be entailed to Him.[25] Johnston of Wariston considered the day of the signing of the Covenant to be the 'marriage day of the kingdom with God' and saw the parallel between Scotland and Israel as 'the only two sworn nations to the Lord'.[26]

The covenanting concept was only a passing phase, discarded by all save a small minority after little more than a generation, but for a brief space it captivated the vitality of the nation. Without appreciating the Scottish people's concept of a perpetual contract with God giving them an unique place in the Divine Purpose it is impossible to understand how ministers expounding the Covenant could stir their hearers to frenzy:

Immediately at his lifting up of his hand and his desiring the congregation to stand up and lift up their hands and swear unto the eternal God, . . . there fell such an extraordinary influence of God's Spirit upon the whole congregation, melting their frozen hearts, watering their dry cheeks, changing their very countenances, as it was a wonder to see so visible, sensible a change upon all, that Mr John, being suffocated almost with his own tears and astonished at the motion of the whole people, sat down . . . but presently rose again . . . and he and they for a quarter of an hour prayed very sensibly with many sobs, tears, promises and vows.[27]

That there were those who saw religion not in the individual soul but in the corporate consciousness of the nation comes out in the Diary of Sir Thomas Hope, who was led by his involvement in the rebellion to a novel personal devotion, undertaking to remodel his private life in response to the Covenant, in the context of which all his piety and personal commitment developed: 'I humblit myself on my knees to my Lord, and in prayer vowit to adhere to my o[a]th. . . . Being in a deip meditation of God's favours to the publick good of His Kirk, . . . I vowit to restrayne my soddan passions and to compose my mind, by God's grace, to patience and equanimity and to remit all to the Lord'. Later he recalled his 'holy vowis and promises to my Lord' and poured forth his heart in prayer and tears, again in relation to public affairs.[28]

Besides the frenzy, which found an outlet in ecclesiastical politics, there was another very different streak in the fervour of the period. This was a kind of quiet, withdrawn, individual piety, with no obvious setting in either predestinarian theology or politics. It is so directly at variance with the latter that it might be seen as a reaction against it but for the fact that it was not unknown before the Covenant. It can perhaps be traced back to Robert Bruce: 'Hell stands in these two points chiefly: an everlasting presence of sin and an everlasting feeling of the wrath of God. . . . No man shall be condemned but he whom his own conscience first damneth, nor no man justified but he whom his conscience first justifieth'.[29] To suggest that hell is nothing more than a state of mind seems far removed from both covenanting politics and the self-torture of Wariston. Hugh Binning (1627–53) – like Wariston a member of the extreme covenanting party, the Protestors – was not so obsessed by ecclesiastical politics as to have no room for personal religion, about which he wrote with profound conviction. It is hardly surprising that he denounced undue attachment to a place of worship or its services, but even so it must have taken courage for any covenanter, whose cause was centred on the church and not on individual faith or worship, to write:

> You think yourselves good Christians if you be baptized and hear the Word and partake of the Lord's Table and such like, though in the mean time you be not given to secret prayer and reading and do not inwardly judge and examine yourselves. . . . The Lord never commanded these external ordinances for the sum of true religion. . . . Prayer in your family is a more substantial worship than to sit and hear prayer in public, and prayer in secret is a more substantial worship than that.[30]

Such thought, eccentric in predestinarian and covenanting Scotland, is to be viewed in relation to what happened when schism first appeared. The aim of the reformers had been to reform the Church, not to split it, and Scots continued to oppose 'separation' from the one Church. Knox dealt briskly with the first English separatists, and the early disputes in Scotland between presbytery and episcopacy did not produce division. In the storm caused by King James's changes in worship about 1620 there had been a tendency towards separatist congregations, but the prevailing practice had been for men to acquiesce in much of which they did not approve rather than abandon the Church. In the 1630s, Rutherford, hostile though he was to the establishment, could not bring himself to the point of rejecting it as no part of Christ's Church: 'As for separation from a worship for some errors of a church, the independency of single congregations, a church of visible saints, ... they are contrary to God's Word'. That was a firm rejection of the concept of a gathered congregation of 'first-class' Christians. Even later, in the episcopacy of the Restoration period, a sincere Presbyterian could still adhere to the Church of Scotland and declare, 'I will not separate from the Church of God'.

However, in the 1640s the alliance of the covenanters with the English puritans brought the Scots into contact with English separatists, and quarrels among the covenanters made them apt pupils in separatism. The wranglings which split the assembly between moderate Resolutioners and extreme Remonstrants or Protestors led to divisions between rival synods and presbyteries and, at local level, to the emergence of something like independency. When one party formed 'a refined congregation of their own adherents', the 'gathered congregation', the 'church of visible saints', which Rutherford had abhorred, became a reality, and schism had appeared.[31]

Another novelty resulting from the association with England was Quakerism, which had affinities with some of the quiet piety which had already made some appeal. George Fox proclaimed that true religion was not a matter of religious observance, church order or dogma, but a spiritual awareness within the human personality, a sense of the nearness of God through the indwelling spirit of Christ. 'The inward light of Christ' or 'the inner light', or the 'that of God in everyone' was what mattered – an inward authority of the spirit, not the external authority of Church, tradition or even Bible. William Penn wrote: 'It is not opinion, or speculation, or notions of what is true, or ... the subscription of articles or propositions ... that ... makes a man a true Christian; but it is a conformity of mind and practice to the will of God, according to the dictates of the divine principle of light and life in the soul, which denotes a person truly a child of God'. It has been remarked[32] that 'Religious people of all ages have spoken of this experience as an encounter with God' – when 'we have discovered a new level of existence in which our spirit is fused with spirit itself in a creative encounter.'

Clearly there was much in Quakerism that would not commend itself to Scots who were thirled to the importance of the organised church, or even to Scots who gave first place to the authority of the Bible, but the emphasis on individual heart-felt conviction, as opposed to formal subscription of creeds or confessions, came close to the thought of a fair number of Scots. Robert Barclay of Urie (1648–90) wrote one of the classical expositions of Quaker principles in *An Apology for the True Christian Divinity* (1678). He put the Bible firmly into a secondary place: a man should be liberated from strict adherence to the letter of the Bible by a confidence in God's Spirit, which was 'certain and infallible' (unlike men's varying interpretations of the Scriptures). He went on to denounce the actions of those 'that lean to tradition, scripture and reason'; and he held protestants and papists as alike guilty under this head. One can understand how disgust with the outcome of the Covenant, the loosening of ties to the Church of Scotland, which had got itself into such a mess, and the shock to the national life from the abolition of the monarchy and the Cromwellian conquest, caused a tendency to drift away into private faith which could come near to Quakerism. One can think of a gathered congregation, drawing apart from the hurly-burly of ecclesiastical politics and basing its distinctive spiritual life on religion alone. Much of the essence of Quakerism extended beyond those who became members of the Society of Friends.

It seems to an outsider that the Quaker 'inner light', 'that of God which is in man' comes close to what is usually understood by the conscience, and this is an area in which one can detect some continuity. Robert Bruce had focussed on conscience as the source of justification or damnation. Hugh Binning, too, in a sermon on the text, 'God is a Spirit', wrote of the futility of conventional church membership without secret prayer and inward judging and examination, which surely means self-examination in the light of conscience. In the pages of Alexander Jaffray, who ultimately joined the Quakers, we find uneasiness about 'too much activity in a formal way of performing duties, such as prayer and fasting at set times', followed by a recognition that 'Christ is in the heart, as He was in the world, but is little known or observed' and a reference to 'the light in the conscience' which approached Quakerism. We move on to Robert Leighton (1611–84). Leighton, who reluctantly became bishop of Dunblane after the Restoration, was as far as possible removed from the ecclesiastical politics of Protestors – or from any ecclesiastical politics. He had, indeed, a reputation for disdaining most of the things of this world – food, amusement, pomp – and for concentrating on the spiritual. His theme in a paper on 'The Rule of Conscience' was that 'conscience is the clearest beam of divine light and of the image of God in the soul of man', phraseology which links his thought with that of the presbyterian Binning and of the Quakers and with that of his fellow-episcopalian Henry Scougal (1650–78). The title of Scougal's little classic, *The Life of God in the Soul of Man*, echoes Leighton. Its central theme is that a human being has a divine spark capable of knowing and loving and *enjoying* God – recalling the Shorter Catechism, which pronounced that 'the chief end of man' is 'to glorify God and to *enjoy* Him for ever'.

Scougal saw 'true religion' as 'a union of the soul with God, a real participation of the divine nature', so that 'Christ is formed within us' to create 'a divine life'. 'Let me never cease my endeavours', he declared in a prayer, 'till that new and divine nature prevail in my soul;' and he explained that 'The Holy Ghost must come upon us, and the power of the Highest must overshadow us, before that holy thing can be begotten and Christ be formed in us.' The life of God in man's soul leads to love, purity and humility, good works which are the fruit of the Spirit. Yet Scougal was much concerned with apprehension about the Last Judgment and the sight of 'the Blessed Jesus... appearing in the majesty of his glory and descending... to take vengeance on those that have despised his mercy'. The fear of hell should make men abstain from sinful pleasures, but the Son of God came to live and die for us to bring us felicity; he overcame the sharpness of death and opened the kingdom of heaven to all believers; he receives our prayers and presents them to the Father.

Scougal had much to say also about what true religion does *not* consist of and criticised not only those who were content with formal church membership and observance, ecclesiastical conformity, temperance and charity but also those who were 'affected with... expressions wherewith they court their Saviour, till they persuade themselves that they are mightily in love with Him and assume a great confidence of their salvation', yet remained 'strangers to the holy temper and spirit of the blessed Jesus.' Scougal knew the zealots, but he leaves the reader feeling that he dismissed most of his fellow-countrymen as sanctimonious humbugs.

Another writer who castigated erroneous impressions of what religion consists of was Laurence Charteris (1625–1700), who briefly held a chair of divinity in Edinburgh. In *The Corruption of This Age* (published posthumously in 1704), he countered antinomianism and stressed the need for high standards of conduct. Like Scougal he was critical of those who 'seem to place almost the whole of Christianity in covenanting with God, in closing with Christ and relying on Him' and think that 'when that is done all is done which is required of us'. But he laid greater stress than Scougal had done on 'works': 'our mental transactions with God' must be attended with righteous, sober and godly living. 'Some pastors . . . do not too much represent . . . the necessity of . . . charity, mercy, purity, patience, meekness, peacableness, humility and such other graces and virtues which Jesus hath specially recommended'.

Binning, Leighton and Scougal, if not Charteris, emphasised a transforming experience in an individual rather than the national commitment of the Covenant, but there is little indication how far their ideas spread, although the period was one in which libraries began to facilitate access to both evangelical and polemical works (a development considered in the next chapter).

As the First Part of Bunyan's *Pilgrim's Progress*, which appeared in England in 1678, was published in Scotland in 1680, 1681 and 1683, it evidently had many Scottish readers. The story of Christian's journey is represented in terms of physical obstacles – Giant Grim and his lions, Hill Difficulty, the dungeon of Giant Despair, the Valley of the Shadow of Death, the Slough of Despond – and, in so far as it presents the trials which had to be overcome even although the ultimate destination was assured, bears some resemblance to the concept of purgatory. As so often, the traditional and the evangelical approximate, and one feels that this work might have consoled the tortured Wariston. One attempt to revive the 'godly ballad' tradition of the previous century was made by William Geddes in 1683, but his *The Saint's Recreation upon the Estate of Spiritual Songs* has been characterised as an 'exquisitely wrong-headed anthology of execrable religious verse'.[33]

The antithesis between faith and works on which Charteris fastened may go some way to explain why a period which produced some striking Christian faith produced also some strikingly unchristian works. The century is one for which we have copious information about deeds, mainly deeds of violence, for violence hit the headlines then as it did in the tenth century and as it still does today. It is impossible to say, on the evidence of criminal courts and kirk sessions, that the covenants raised the standards of either public or private morality. Such records apart, much publicity was given at the time and has been given ever since to the brutalities committed in civil wars and rebellions. Controversy has persisted as to whether in the 1640s it was the covenanters or their royalist opponents who shed more innocent blood. Facts are not to be dismissed. They relate to the royalist Montrose, who sacked Aberdeen (not, as it happened, a stronghold of his enemies) and 'extracted a terrible price' for the life of the drummer who had been sent with envoys to negotiate with the magistrates: 'for three days the army indulged in an orgy of pillage, rape and bloodletting'. They relate no less to the covenanting David Leslie: at Dunaverty, 'warned by his chaplain of the curses which befell Saul for sparing the Amalekites', his men butchered 300 royalist defenders, and at Philiphaugh royalists who surrendered on promise of quarter were shot, with 300 camp-followers. The comment on the slaughter by one minister – 'the wark gangs bonnily on' – and the question put by a general to another minister (or it may have been the same one) – 'Have you not once gotten your fill of blood?' – have passed into folklore.[34] Most recent writers have regarded the atrocities of both sides with equal horror, but the completeness with which some minds are closed was illustrated by a newspaper correspondent who wrote in 1957, 'It is news to me that the Covenanters massacred women and children; I refuse to believe it.' (But if the Scots have forgotten what the godly Covenanters did, the Irish, it should be added, have not forgotten what that other godly man, Oliver Cromwell, did at Drogheda.)

When the army of the Covenant was first mustered to face the king in 1639, it represented 'the general body of the Scottish people', arrayed in arms under the traditional leadership of the nobility, in what professed to be a godly cause.

> Every company had flying at the captain's tent door a brave new colour stamped with the Scottish arms and this ditton, 'For Christ's Crown and Covenant' in golden letters.... The sight of the nobles and their beloved pastors daily raised their hearts, the good sermons and prayers morning and evening under the roof of heaven, to which their drums did call them for [in place of] bells, the remonstrances very frequent of the goodness of their cause, of their conduct[ing] hitherto by a hand clearly divine.... True, there was swearing and cursing and brawling in some quarters, whereat we were grieved. But we hoped if our camp had been a little settled to have gotten some way for these misorders.[35]

These comments, reflecting disappointment that the army did not display godly behaviour to match its cause, can probably be taken as erring on the favourable side. It should be added that if the rankers restrained neither their tongues nor their fists, the aristocratic officers had no intention of mortifying the flesh: one of them sent home for 'two night caps and two pairs of slippers, one grass green, the other sky colour, with gold and silver lace upon them'.[36]

Incredulity about the Covenanters' behaviour in victory derives from the sympathy attracted by their sufferings in adversity, after the Restoration. There has been controversy here too, this time over whether the punishments inflicted on rebels were as numerous and as brutal as tradition will have it. Hagiography has much to answer for, but perhaps the main trouble is the lack of a context, for although neither of the most publicised instruments of torture – the thumbscrews and the 'boots' – was invented by the Restoration government[37] we hear little of their application until they were used on the later Covenanters, for whom thumbscrews were made more severe. And, while the victims no doubt contended that they were suffering for their religion, their prosecutors were equally convinced that they were punishing breaches of secular laws. Besides, some of the victims were in truth guilty of murder or attempted murder.

In the middle ages we moved from the roasting of a bishop in 1222 to the roasting of an abbot in 1570. So in the period of the reformation and the Covenant we move from the murder of an archbishop – Beaton – in 1546 to the murder of another archbishop – Sharp – in 1679. It is a mystery why such murders should have been applauded by members of a supposedly Christian party. Yet applauded they were. John Knox related how 'a man of nature most gentle and most modest' began the 'work and judgment of God' on Beaton by striking him twice or thrice through with a sword. Similarly, Covenanters related that 'several worthy gentlemen, with some other men of courage and zeal for the cause of God and the good of the country, executed righteous judgment' on Sharp.[38] Nor did the Covenanters conceive that their licence to murder extended only to archbishops: 'It is lawful to prevent the murder of ourselves or our brethren, when no other way is left, by killing the murderers before they accomplish their wicked design, if they be habitually prosecuting it and have many times accomplished it before.... It is lawful – to kill Tories or open murderers, as devouring beasts'.[39] There is some unpalatable truth in what F. W. Maitland wrote: 'Faith may be changed; works are much what they were.... The blood-feud is no less a blood-feud.... "The bond" is no less a bond because it is styled a "Covenant" and makes free with holy names'.[40]

Slaughter on the field of battle, even political assassinations, may be comprehended within the scope of public morality. But the Covenant seems to have done little to raise the standards of private morality either. Perhaps the most unreliable of all evidence about such standards are the reminiscences of near-contemporaries, who, especially in old age, were much given to believing that morality (like the weather) had deteriorated during their lifetimes. Thus in 1639 an aged minister, John Wemyss, remarked, 'I do remember when the Kirk of Scotland had a beautiful face. I remember when there was a great power and life accompanying the ordinances of God, and a wonderful work of operations upon the hearts of people'.[41] Presumably he meant to refer to a period some forty or fifty years before, in the last decade or two of the sixteenth century. But the general assemblies of that period tell a different story: 'a great abundance of iniquity' over 'universally the whole face of this commonwealth,... stirring up the justice and equity of God to take judgment and vengeance';[42] 'the universal corruption of this realm;[43] a 'great dissoluteness of life and manners ... in every nook and part of this land;... swearing, perjury and lies, profaning the Sabbath-day, gluttony, drunkenness, fighting, playing, dancing, etc., incest, fornication, adulteries and all kind of impiety and wrong; neither religion nor discipline with the poor, but the most part live in filthy adultery, incest, fornication, their bairns unbaptized'.[44]

Similarly, David Calderwood (d. 1651), the historian, a contemporary of John Wemyss, has it that in 1596 'the Kirk of Scotland was now come to her perfection, and the greatest purity that ever she attained unto, both in doctrine and discipline, so that her beauty was admirable to foreign kirks'.[45] However, the general assembly, which in the previous year had alluded to 'great abundance and increase of sin and transgression of all the commandments of God by all the estates', now in this year lamented 'ane universal caldness and decay of zeal in all estates, joined with ignorance and contempt of the Word, Ministry and Sacraments,... great blasphemy of the holy name of God in all estates, with horrible banning and cursing in all their speeches,... adulteries, fornications, incests, unlawful marriages and divorcements,... and children begotten in such marriages declared to be lawful; excessive drinking,... gluttony... and gorgeous and vain apparel, filthy and bloody speeches'.[46] The ministers themselves were blamed for being slothful in administering the sacraments, being irreverent profaners thereof, even selling the sacraments; they did not have kirk sessions to strike 'on all sins repugnant to the Word of God, as blasphemy, swearing, cursing, profaning the Sabbath, disobedience to parents, drunkards, slanderers, brawlers' and so on. The members of the assembly responded by making public confession, during which tears were shed abundantly.[47] There is similar evidence in presbytery records: in the parish of Kilconquhar in 1596 there was 'great cauldnes in not regarding the Word and at variance amangis thameselffis', and in 1600 there was a lament about 'all kind of vice overflowing the land'.[48]

The contrast between the rose-coloured recollections of John Wemyss and David Calderwood on one hand and record evidence on the other can be paralleled half a century later. James Kirkton, looking back from about 1690 to the ascendancy of the Covenanters forty years earlier, reflected:

> Religion advanced the greatest step it had made for many years.... Hardly the fifth part of the lords of Scotland were admitted to sit in parliament, but these who did sit were esteemed truly godly men. So were all the rest of the commissioners in parliament.... Also, godly men were employed in all offices,... purging out the scandalous and insufficient and planting in their place a sort of godly young men, whose ministry the Lord sealed with an eminent blessing of success.... No error was so much as named; the people were not only sound in the faith, but innocently ignorant of unsound doctrine. No scandalous person could live, no scandal could be concealed,... in all Scotland.... Then was Scotland a heap of wheat set about with lilies.... This seems to me to have been Scotland's high noon.[49]

However, an English observer saw 'Scotland's high noon' differently: 'It is usual with them to talk religiously... and the very next moment to lie, curse and swear without any manner of bounds or limits.... How legally religious soever they pretend to be there is little or no conscience made of the breach of any one of The Commandments'. He then proceeded to expound, *seriatim*, how the Scots broke all ten. Instead of having no other God but one, they idolised their ministers, and 'the presbyterial government' was the graven image which they had set up, for 'all must fall down before this golden calf and submit to this government.... Taking the holy and dreadful name of God in vain, it is common in their ordinary discourse.... Although they pretend to be zealous observers [of the Lord's Day], yet to my observation I have not known any of them to spend that day in religious exercises, only in a bare cessation from labour and work'. Then 'respect in their children towards their parents' is 'like their parents' love to them, which is like Jockey's advice to Jany, "Throw away the bairn and save the baggage, God may send more bairns but ne'er more baggage"'. Adultery was amply vouched for in the kirk session records, and 'whoredom and fornication is the common darling sin of the nation'. Theft was common and covetousness is 'so predominate that many of them come to the [penitents'] stool for it'.[50] The Englishman's assessment finds some support from Alexander Brodie, who deplored in 1653 and 1656 that his country 'hath rested in a bare profession of religion..., dishonouring our profession by... profanity, ungodliness, pride, violence... profaneness, lying, cursing, whoredom, looseness in words and conversation'.[51] Such indictments find support in the records of the general assembly, which specifically make the point that lust was not mortified nor other changes wrought in men's lives by their taking the Covenant: swearing, profanation of the Lord's Day, fornication, drunkenness, lying and oppression still abounded, and a long series of remedies was proposed for swearing, drinking, mocking of piety 'and particularly for the better restraining of the sin of whoredom'.[52]

It was not because the restoration of the monarchy in 1660 led to a falling away from the Covenanters' standards that the so-called 'drunken parliament' had to pass a series of statutes, not unlike those passed in 1552, relating to the observance of the Sabbath, swearing, excessive drinking and profaneness. The privy council appointed each minister and certain gentlemen of his parish to enforce acts against fornication, drunkenness, swearing, Sabbath-breaking and other offences.[53] Bishop Leighton was meantime inveighing against 'cursing, swearing and rotten filthy speaking, as usual among the common sort'.[54] Had a century of kirk session discipline (maintained under episcopacy as under presbytery) been effective? Partly because of the rift between Resolutioners and Protesters, who excommunicated each other, celebrations of Communion had become very infrequent. At a time when so few could claim to be 'in love and charity with their neighbours' this should perhaps be counted on the credit side. Nor was it unknown for a minister to decline to hold a Communion on the ground that his people were not sufficiently instructed or prepared. Here and there the Sacrament was held in contempt. In Kildrummy in 1665 a man was in trouble for saying of the Communion that 'he cared not two pennies whether he got it or not', and in 1675 in Strathdon another said he could have 'bought as much bread and wine in Aberdeen for a bawbee'.[55]

Did Calderwood and Kirkton, whose impressions were erroneous, look no farther than the facade of ecclesiastical institutions and simply conclude that if the presbyterian system was officially approved then all was well? Was such an attitude another aspect of the tendency towards something like antinomianism – a belief at any rate that a man could be formally committed and yet not be converted to a life according to the precepts of Christ? The Covenant and the concept of the Scots as a Chosen People might encourage seriousness in life (as it did for Sir Thomas Hope); on the other hand, the Old Testament concept which identified the Scots as a Chosen People may have caused a disposition to see parallels in the actions of ancient leaders and captains whose behaviour, on any moral standards, was sometimes deplorable but who nonetheless were seen as the agents of their God. It almost seems that the Scots felt themselves to be so very special that they did not need Christianity, and one wonders how far the 'Chosen People' notion was buttressed by the Calvinist doctrine of 'Election' and perhaps even by the trend to antinomianism. Could a nation, as well as an individual, be numbered among The Elect? Was a member of the Chosen People individually one of The Elect? If the Scots did not feel that they needed Christianity, they certainly seem, in their distraction with politics, not to have wanted Christianity if it cramped

1 St Serf's Hermitage, Dysart

2 Pre-Christian and Christian symbolism
on Pictish stone

3 Tomb of Wolf of Badenoch, Dunkeld Cathedral

4 Typical medieval tomb, Seton Collegiate Church

6 The Agony in the Garden and the Betrayal

5 Administration of Last Rites

7 The Fall, the Doom,
  Heaven and Hell

8 The Priest and the Levite

9 Continuity, Fowlis Easter

10 Discontinuity, Oronsay Priory (note grave-slabs)

11 Symbols of the Passion or Arma Christi

12 Death and Resurrection

13 Monument of 1st Earl of Dunbar

14 Monument of Robert Wilkie,
who left 4200 merks to the poor

15 Menzies Monument, Weem, *c.* 1626 (re-using medieval stones)

16 Reid Memorial Church, Edinburgh, 1933

their political obsessions. There is the well-known story told of Robert Leighton when he was minister of Newbattle at the height of the quarrel between moderate and more extreme Covenanters – a political quarrel – and was rebuked for not 'preaching up the times': when he was told that 'all the brethren' did so, he replied that 'if all of you preach up the times, you may surely allow one poor brother to preach up Christ and eternity'.[56] Somewhat similarly, it was said that when presbyterian ministers were 'indulged' to preach under the episcopalian establishment 'at first the people of the country ran to them with a transport of joy, ... in hopes that they would have begun their ministry with a public testimony against all that was done in opposition to what they called the work of God; but when they found that they ... preached *only the doctrines of Christianity* they soon changed their sentiments'.[57]

If ecclesiastical politics did nothing for morals, it did not increase the social commitment of churchmen either. However, the concepts of the first reformers maintained their momentum, for through all the vicissitudes of the presbyterian-episcopalian controversy there was never any doubt about the Church's responsibilities. Education Acts were passed under episcopalian auspices in 1633 and under presbyterian auspices in 1646; under the episcopalian regime of the Restoration period a Poor Law was enacted which endured until nearly the middle of the nineteenth century. The most startling indication that social justice was not lost sight of was given when, in all the stress of the 1640s, the assembly mentioned 'oppressing and defrauding the poorer sort and the needy'.[58]

The violence and brutality bred by the covenanting revolt did not pass without challenge. Drummond of Hawthornden fastened on the unreasonableness of the policy of using force to impose presbyterianism on England. Did Our Lord and His apostles, he asked, 'propagate their religion by pikes and muskets?'.[59] He turned the tables on those who thought that they were justified in using force to resist the tyranny of a king, by accusing the insurgents of 'a vast arbitrary power of taxing the poor people, spoiling the country, turning all upside down by new magistracies and novations' and he directed against those insurgents the classic denunciation of unjust rulers: 'In the absence of justice what else are kingdoms than great brigandages (*Sublata justitia quid aliud sunt regna quam magna latrocinia*)?'[60] Drummond had written with sarcasm and scorn of 'presumptuous, ignorant and hypocritical churchmen, who not keeping themselves within their own vocation and limits do assume the power of kings and emperors to govern states, use an arbitrary power, first over the consciences, then upon the persons, goods and fortunes of men'.[61]

Leighton, attached though he was to the importance of the conscience, warned fanatics of the danger of setting their consciences above the law of the land and 'the express laws of Jesus Christ' and thinking they could engage in rebellion with impunity because 'we did it according to our conscience'. Almost like Elizabeth Tudor, who would not 'make windows into men's souls', Leighton observed that 'a man is not properly punished for his conscience, but for the evil, external acts of a wicked conscience'. Like others, he saw the absurdity of presenting the struggle as one of 'King Jesus' against 'King Charles', which implied disobedience to the laws of the land.[62] Some made a more far-reaching protest that although the Church 'had the keys of authority given her' she had not 'the keys of knowledge' and so could 'in many ways err, especially when she meddleth with matters which are not within her horizon'.[63]

That learned, thoughtful and versatile man, Sir George Mackenzie of Rosehaugh (1636–91), who, as Lord Advocate, prosecuted ecclesiastical dissidents, condemned, as Leighton did, those who thought that their consciences dictated disobedience to St Paul's injunction to be subject to the higher powers, and he emphasised, as Drummond did, that Our Lord never countenanced recourse to violence. He judged that immortal souls might be more imperilled by taking up arms and dying violently, suddenly and unprepared in the heat of battle than by unwillingly attending parish churches.[64] He also appealed to the Scottish dislike of schism, using Rutherford's metaphor of Christ and His Spouse, the Church, to plead with the dissidents who rejected any church which did not measure precisely to their own rules: 'It were absurd to think that He will divorce her upon every error, especially seeing His blessed mouth hath told us that it is not lawful to divorce upon all occasions'. Mackenzie also attempted to mount a recall from the diversion into politics with a reminder that 'True religion and undefiled is to visit the widow and the fatherless'.[65]

Another eminent lawyer, the first Viscount Stair, opened his *Institutions of the Law of Scotland* (1681) with a discussion of the 'Common principles of law' in which, besides a section on 'The Laws of God' in which he refers to 'Christ and His propitiatory sacrifice of Himself', he relates reason, the law of nature, the law written in man's heart, the human conscience, all alike to the guidance and direction of God. This echoes Scougal, Leighton and other divines. The fact that there were men in high places in the state – Sir Thomas Hope, Wariston, Mackenzie and Stair (all lawyers) who spoke freely of religion without being therefore regarded as in any way eccentric, must have had an enormous influence on the general standards and outlook and no doubt would encourage those who were less profoundly convinced about Christianity to adopt at least the jargon of the more committed.

There are indications of the faith of other lay people. Sir Robert Moray (1607/8–1673) had a military career in Britain and on the continent, but was drawn to philosophy and increasingly to science. In 1660, when he settled in London, he was one of the founders of the Royal Society. Sickened by ecclesiastical politics, he 'retreated entirely from religious conflict into a non-sectarian personal Christianity, strongly influenced by stoicism, in which public worship had little part but private prayer was of central importance'.[66] Patrick Lyon (1642–95), first Earl of Strathmore, commissioned the construction of a chapel in Glamis Castle, work on which was completed in 1688. There was an organ, and the walls and roof were decorated with paintings (apparently based on woodcuts in a Prayer Book) by Jacob de Wet, best known for the portraits in the Long Gallery at Holyroodhouse. In the year before he died the earl made provision for the care of the family burial place and loft in his local parish church and for the saying of prayers at his burial place – a direction which suggests that the reformers' prejudice against the offering at a tomb of prayers for the repose of the deceased's soul may now have been passing away.[67] Strathmore's contemporary, Lord Forbes of Pitsligo (1648–1717), was an admirer of the French mystic Antoinette Bourignon, 'who shared some of the principles of the Quakers and

Pietists', and of Madame Guyon, who taught the pre-eminent value of contemplation. Lord Deskford (d. 1698), son of the Earl of Findlater, had in his library the works of Kempis, Pascal and Scougal. George Garden (1649–1733), a professor at Aberdeen, edited the works of John Forbes, studied Pascal's *Thoughts* and wrote in support of Madame Bourignon, in whom he found 'the doctrines of the love of God and charity represented as the essentials of Christianity'. In Orkney, where church life was hardly affected by the troubles elsewhere, laymen owned devotional and theological works and one laird left 160 books 'for public use'. Possibly the whole north-east escaped a lot of the current 'distraction'. In the south anti-popery polemics attracted attention, for the Duchess of Hamilton purchased '100 books against popery', but the Duchess of Atholl turned to *A Rebuke to Backsliding or a Spur for Loiterers, The Soul's Preparation for Christ* and *Sermons of Acquaintance with God.*[68]

Responsibility for neither faith nor works lay solely with the established church, because, whatever influence it had over its faithful members, there were those who were not faithful members. There were Quakers and possibly a few other small splinter groups surviving from the divisions of the 1650s. There were also some Roman Catholics, whose history it is customary to trace from about 1580. It is an error to think too precisely of 'Roman Catholics' in the late sixteenth century and the early seventeenth, for there was rather 'a catholic "interest"', politically conservative, allergic to the ethos of the new religion, ... a politico-religious preference'.[69] There were few 'Roman Catholics' who did not conform outwardly. Wild rumours of plots in which Scottish noblemen and the Spanish government were involved had little substance, and visiting agents were apt to be too credulous.

What has been called the 'authoritarian conservatism' of James VI appealed to something in the ethos of the 'catholic "interest"'. He had one or two advisers who had sympathies with Rome, but neither they nor anyone else could be regularly practising Romanists, if only because of the shortage of priests. It was said in 1605 and again in 1613 that there was only one priest in Scotland.[70] That statistic may have been true occasionally, but there were usually some priests at work unobtrusively as private chaplains, in demand mainly by the female members of families.[71] (The greater zeal of womenfolk was noticeable also among the Covenanters. Scott's picture in *Old Mortality* of the conflict between Cuddie Headrigg and his mother reflects this, but it was usually a wife who got her husband into trouble for nonconformity. Scott himself remarked that 'William Scott of Harden ... suffered as much through the nonconformity of his Lady as Cuddie through that of his mother ... [and] was repeatedly called before the privy council and fined ... although he protested that he was totally unable to rule his wife'.[72] An associate of Scott observed, 'It is astonishing to consider how anxious the female zealots of that time were to make their husbands ... obtain the martyr's crown through the medium of a halter'.[73] Contemporaries had made similar observations from their divers points of view: 'Such a foolish generation of people in this country who are so influenced with their fanatic wives';[74] 'not many gentlemen of estates ventured to come to these field meetings, ... but their ladies ... were daily attenders'.[75])

It is often assumed that in the west Highlands and Islands protestant effort had been meagre, leaving a kind of vacuum. Not only does recent research disprove this,[76] but the reports of the Irish Franciscans who worked in Scotland between 1619 and 1637 testify to the energy of protestant bishops and ministers even in such small islands as Gigha and Eigg as well as in North Uist. The friars admitted that there had not been a priest in Eigg or South Uist or Arran for periods of up to a hundred years. They claimed 'conversions' on a scale not paralleled since the days of the early pioneers: 119 in Islay, 102 in Jura, 133 in Colonsay, 198 (in 8 days) in Eigg, 768 (in a fortnight) in North Uist and so on. There was sometimes direct conflict in reports: in 1615 Sir John Campbell of Calder stated that the inhabitants of Islay were Roman Catholics,[77] but in 1625 one of the Franciscans claimed to have converted 518 people there, including Campbell of Calder himself.[78] No doubt the missionaries did not want to understate their own achievement, but they admitted that their 'converts' had no enthusiasm for serving them without payment. It is hardly surprising that their claim of a total of nearly 10,000 'converts' was received at Rome with such scepticism that they received funds only irregularly. Perhaps the best comment on the mission was that of King James: when told that the missionaries had 'infected the whole of Kintyre with idolatry', he laughed and said that there was no need to be angry with those who were converting to Christianity people so wild as the natives of Kintyre.[79] The missionaries' report on Barra (where they claimed to have converted about 350 people), explodes the notion that that island was never protestant and has a flavour which anticipates Compton Mackenzie's *Rockets Galore*.

Enlightening information about the situation in the 1640s and 1650s comes from the *Minutes of the Synod of Argyll*. For a few years the synod seems to have been concerned entirely with an occasional stray priest or an isolated proselyte, but in the 1650s there are references to numbers of priests and their followers. The change may have come about partly because of renewed links with Ireland in the 1640s and then the general breakdown in ordered life consequent on the military operations from Montrose's campaigns onwards, and there may have been refugees from Ireland after the Cromwellian conquest. How far the Roman Catholicism was linked with various superstitions, some of them obviously of pagan origin, it is difficult to say, for the synod regarded both with equal disapproval.

An illuminating and highly entertaining picture of conditions in the 1680s is given by Martin Martin in his *Description of the Western Isles of Scotland*. He is quite specific as to which islands, or parts of islands, were protestant and which papist and indicates plainly that there had been an expansion of Roman Catholicism in the middle of the century, when Barra, for example, ceased to be Protestant. His tales about competitions in miracle-working, in which religion and superstition blended, recall St Columba and might be dismissed if they were not supported by the reports of the Franciscans.

In 1677 an envoy from Rome reported that there were only 12,000 Romanists in Scotland, 2000 of them between the Moray Firth and the Solway, chiefly in Dumfriesshire and the Highlands of Aberdeen and Banff.[80] Sustained Roman Catholic effort in Scotland did not begin until the 1690s.

Those who were not faithful members of the established church thus comprehended such diverse groups as Quakers, atheists and Roman Catholics. It can hardly be denied that they comprehended also those who had committed themselves to the power of evil by their involvement in witchcraft. Attention is usually drawn to Queen Mary's act of parliament of 1563 imposing the death penalty on those who practised or sought necromancy. It has somehow escaped notice that a few weeks earlier the English parliament had passed a similar act, imposing the death penalty for certain aggravations of the offence (5 Eliz. cap. xvi). Nor has it been noted that the same penalty of death was the penalty which Queen Mary's own proclamation had imposed for saying mass. The Old Testament was explicit that witches should be put to death (Exod. xxii, 18, Deut. xviii, 10), but the New Testament gave less guidance. The King James Version included what it called 'witchcraft' among the 'works of the flesh' (Galatians v, 20), but the term translates *pharmakeia* (whence 'pharmacy'), which commonly means also poisoning, and the same ambiguity attaches to the Latin *veneficia*. Yet one cannot doubt that the statute of 1563 reflected the thought of the Church, for at various points between 1573 and 1641 the general assembly urged action against witchcraft.

The theological context in contemporary thought is easily discerned. The stress of the reformation on the spiritual rather than the material took away some of the quasi-magical appearance of some medieval religious rites; this made people look for their magic elsewhere but also removed a kind of shelter from evil threats arising from sorcery. The cessation of auricular confession may have encouraged recourse to 'wise women' who were the repository of ancient spells. Even before the reformation Baptism, which after all was usually administered without the consent of the baptized, could presumably be renounced, but the reformers' emphasis on the individual's responsibility to God opened the way to the concept of a pact between the individual and the Devil; and in the early seventeenth century the frequent references to a covenant between man and God may have popularised the notion of a covenant with the Devil.

The incidence of witchcraft cases was not uniform or consistent in either space or time. It has been observed that the Highlands generally were almost exempt and that Fife, the Lothians and the Borders usually supplied most victims, but this may be an illusion arising from the distribution of the extant material, inevitably scarce in the Highlands. Such an explanation would not hold good of the temporal variations, with peaks in 1591, 1597, 1628–30, 1649–50, 1658–62. Although claims have been made that the bishops did something to temper the storm, it is hard to see a close correlation with the general ecclesiastical situation, for the 1590s and 1649 belong to periods of presbyterian ascendancy, 1628–30 to a point of settled episcopal rule, while 1660 was on the eve of the restoration of episcopacy. The possibility that popular resentment turned on witches in periods of high prices, bad harvests, plague or famine is not to be dismissed, though the correlation is not wholly convincing, and the geographical distribution, with the majority of known prosecutions in the more fertile and prosperous parts of the country, is hard to reconcile with that theory. Nor does one see a regular link between witch prosecution and periods of national crisis, though this would certainly apply to 1649–50 and 1658–62. Wildly differing estimates of the total number of convictions have been made, ranging up to an incredible 30,000, but the latest statistic is a total of no more than 1300 executions.

The rather startling suggestion that Scotland had more prosecutions of witches than England because the level of religion in Scotland was more intense looks wildly wrong, and it may be more likely that as Scottish religion was so largely a matter of intellectual conviction there was less sympathy with the irrational in witchcraft and consequently more readiness to prosecute. Similar reasoning might hold good of the lack of witchcraft cases in the Highlands, where religion had more of emotion (and more of lingering irrational superstition perhaps arising from a hostile physical environment) than in the Lowlands, and so was more sympathetic to witchcraft.

One thing that is clear is that the mania was on the way out before the end of the seventeenth century, partly because of a growth of scepticism about popular notions of the supernatural and partly because of a growing humanity. This is clear in the writings of Sir George Mackenzie (Lord Advocate 1677–86, 1688–9), who criticised the judiciary: 'Judges allow themselves too much liberty in condemning such as are accused of this crime because they conclude they cannot be severe enough to the enemies of God; and assizers [i.e., jurymen] are afraid to suffer such to escape as are remitted to them, lest they let loose an enraged wizard in their neighbourhood, and thus poor innocents die in multitudes by an unworthy martyrdom, and burning comes in fashion'.[81] In his *Pleadings in some Remarkable Cases* (1672) and his *Laws and Customs of Scotland in Matters Criminal* (1678), Mackenzie was as sceptical as he could be without laying himself open to the charge of atheism. It has been said that he was a key figure in stemming witch-hunting and his pronouncements coincided with a sharp decline in prosecutions and convictions.[82] He argued, exactly as many in the twentieth century would do, for a cautious attitude to the current beliefs and flatly denied the possibility of some of the deeds attributed to witches or the notion that people struck by some disease could be victims of witches: 'None now labour under any extraordinary disease but it is instantly said to come by witchcraft, and then the next old deformed or envied woman is presently charged with it'. Mackenzie won the day, to the extent that in 1684 the High Court of Justiciary determined that a death was not the result of witchcraft.[83] It appears that in England Lord Chief Justice Holt (1689–1710) had a similar influence in mitigating convictions for witchcraft.[84]

THE AGE OF REASON

Writers on Scottish history have shown more interest in human thought in the eighteenth century than in earlier periods, partly because in that century there was a great deal of intellectual activity, but partly perhaps for no better reason than to fill a vacuum. Eighteenth-century Scotland offers no focus of interest in international affairs, ecclesiastical revolutions or significant rebellions, while economic expansion had not yet come to the front of the stage. If thought is studied at all religion is involved, even if only in a negative way. One can, for example, learn a good deal about eighteenth-century attitudes to religion from *The Wealth of Nations*, by Adam Smith, a man who had no interest in Christian dogma. However, it is not too cynical to say that the attention given to religious belief in the eighteenth century may arise, rather paradoxically, because it was in that period that Christianity was for the first time challenged by men whose views attained not only notoriety but fame, in sharp contrast to the previous century, when at least formal acknowledgment of Christianity was made by nearly all men of standing.

A century is seldom a satisfactory unit for historical study of any kind, and to relate the history of thought to a century is as fatuous as believing that the days of the week determine the weather. There were, however, two events, a hundred years apart – the British Revolution of 1688–9 and the French Revolution of 1789 – which both had a bearing on religious as well as political thought in Scotland.

After abolishing the episcopal system in the established church in 1689, parliament restored presbyterian government in 1690. The Westminster Confession, now with statutory authority, became a standard from which men deviated if not to the peril of their immortal souls, at any rate (if they were ministers or teachers) to the peril of their livelihood.[1] An assembly act of 1708 laid down instructions for the visitation of every house in a parish by the minister, accompanied by an elder, in the course of which the family was catechised. How systematically this was carried out we hardly know, though some 'Examination Rolls' survive, mainly from the later years of the century.[2] However, the status of the Confession was such that anyone whose views diverged from the standards could easily be challenged. Possibly the reason why we now hear more of 'heresy' is simply because there was clearer definition of what constituted orthodoxy.

At the same time, the Revolution created a breeding-ground for discord on matters of doctrine. The ostensible reason for the establishment of presbytery was that it was 'agreeable to the inclinations of the generality of the people'. No referendum showed what the inclinations really were, and later debate has been inconclusive,[3] but the ministers were so heavily opposed to parliament's decision that almost exactly two thirds of them had to be deprived. The resultant composition of the ministry was so heterogeneous that disagreement on doctrine was almost inevitable. The direction of the Church's affairs was committed initially to sixty 'antediluvians', as they were called – aged ministers who had been deprived in the early 1660s for their refusal to accept episcopal oversight – along with a number of other presbyterians who had not conformed, at least in full, to the pre-revolution episcopalian establishment. The members of those groups mostly adhered rigidly to the dogmas of 'election' and 'reprobation' defined in the Confession. However, a number of ministers who had held office under the episcopal establishment but now elected to remain in their parishes under the presbyterian regime had more liberal views. Besides, the novelties in physics, chemistry and philosophy which came from Robert Boyle (1627–91), Isaac Newton (1642–1727), Thomas Hobbes (1588–1679) and John Locke (1632–1704) in Britain and René Descartes (1596–1650), Blaise Pascal (1623–62) and Baruch Spinoza (1632–77) on the continent had raised questionings about the structure of the universe and the nature of man and his mind, which all helped to loosen long-entrenched attitudes. In the late seventeenth century the 'Cambridge Platonists' amalgamated or reconciled the rational enquiry of the time with Christian theology, but it took time for this trend to have much influence in Scotland.

For over a generation obsession with the covenants had perhaps done as much to efface open atheism as to minimise true faith. However, in the very year when parliament prescribed presbyterian government, the general assembly complained 'there hath been in some a dreadful atheistical boldness against God, some have disputed the being of God and His providence, the divine authority of the Scriptures, the life to come and the immortality of the soul'. In a well known and frequently deplored incident in 1697 a youth of eighteen was hanged for blasphemy: he had said that theology was nonsense, Christ an impostor, the Trinity and the Incarnation worthy of ridicule. But within less than two generations much the same was being said – though no doubt in more guarded terms – by professors in the universities, whence were coming the newly trained ministers who were needed to fill the parishes being vacated as episcopalian incumbents were eliminated by deprivation or death.

It was said of William Hamilton, who became professor of divinity at Edinburgh in 1709, that he 'departs from the Calvinistic doctrine taught in the Church, though he has the wisdom to keep himself in the clouds'. More attention was attracted by John Simson, professor of divinity at Glasgow, who in 1714 was charged with heresy because he had been teaching Arminianism – the denial of predestination. In 1717 it was found that he had 'adopted some hypotheses different from what are commonly found among orthodox divines, that are not evidently founded on scripture and tend to attribute too much to natural reason'. Simson was merely told by the general assembly to be more cautious. He was in trouble again ten years later, this time for his teaching on the Trinity. His tendency towards Arianism (the denial of Christ's divinity) was evident, and he was condemned and suspended, but he escaped the deposition which most presbyteries thought he deserved.

The Arianism of which Simson had been accused was described as 'the too epidemic disease of our neighbours', and many Irish presbyterians (with whom Simson was in touch), as well as English, did adopt Arianism, otherwise Unitarianism, but in Scotland the central subject of debate settled on the relations of faith and works, an area which has often perplexed thoughtful Christians. Perhaps there is a narrow borderline between proclaiming that Christ died to save sinful men – an undeniable truth – and asserting that those who had made an act of commitment and believed themselves numbered among the Elect were assured of salvation irrespective of their way of life. There were traces of this problem in the seventeenth century,[4] but now extreme positions were adopted by – or at any rate attributed to – both sides. At one end of the scale were those who were disposed to eliminate divine action altogether and teach a mere moral code. At the other end justification by faith was distorted into antinomianism.

The controversy was sharpened by two events in 1717–18. In 1717 the presbytery of Auchterarder, alarmed by a tendency among candidates for ordination to lay undue stress on works, exacted from them a declaration that 'it is not sound and orthodox to teach that we must forsake sin in order to our coming to Christ and instating us in covenant with God'. This 'Auchterarder Creed' could mean no more than that Christianity is a religion not for saints but for sinners, but it could be interpreted as antinomian. In 1718 there appeared a reprint of *The Marrow of Modern Divinity*, a work on justification by faith originally published in England in 1646. The book belonged very much to the period of its composition and resembled Binning, Jaffray and Scougal in what it said about heartfelt conviction as opposed to formal observance or conventional church membership, but it sharpened the debate by adopting, somewhat in the manner of the *Pilgrim's Progress*, the structure of a discussion among a minister and three of his people – a neophyte or young Christian; a 'legalist' or formalist who held that the essence of the Christian life lies in obedience to God's laws and that, because he often repeated the Lord's Prayer, Creed and Commandments, sometimes went to Church and communicated at Easter, his 'condition was good'; and an antinomian who relied on grace, stood lightly to moral obligations and advised the neophyte 'to believe in Christ, to rejoice in the Lord and live merrily'. The minister urged the central place of faith in the Christian life: 'When a man comes to believe that all his sins, past, present and to come, are freely and fully pardoned, and God graciously reconciled to him in Christ', then his heart 'is at peace with God' and 'the devil hath not that hope to prevail against his soul as he had before'. Critics saw the book as propounding that the Atonement was for all men, that holiness was not essential for salvation, that love of God and neither fear of eternal punishment nor hope of rewards should be the true motives of Christian obedience. (This was at a time when there was still terrifying preaching about the torments of hell.[5]) Supporters, on the other hand, saw the book as a useful corrective to 'the growing humour of the times to turn religion into mere morality' (as 'legal' or legalist preachers did), and in so far as it was interpreted as an offer of salvation to all it encouraged evangelical preaching. One of the supporters was Thomas Boston (1676–1732), minister of Ettrick, who in the last days of the episcopalian establishment (1688) had undergone a conversion at a presbyterian meeting house. His autobiography shows that his faith was firmly based on confidence in the particular providence of

God, the closeness of man to Him, and a belief that all things fell out for men according as they did or did not follow the divine will. It was still usual to see misfortunes as punishments for sin, but Boston's point was that pure grace and faith, without the works of the law, sufficed for salvation.

The general assembly, by condemning both the 'Auchterarder Creed' and *The Marrow*, as well as by dealing leniently with Professor Simson, showed that it was prepared to go some way towards admitting new attitudes. Some professors continued to modify what had been thought orthodoxy. At Glasgow William Leechman, who was appointed in 1743 to the chair of divinity once held by Simson, stressed the life and teaching of Jesus rather than His divinity, and Francis Hutcheson, professor of moral philosophy from 1729, ignored the traditional themes of election and reprobation, encouraged his students to avoid 'high speculations', emphasised the dignity of human nature and taught that the standard of ethics was nothing more lofty than 'the greatest happiness of the greatest number'. Hutcheson went out of his way to popularise his views by giving Sunday evening public lectures. At Edinburgh William Wishart, principal from 1736, emphasised philosophy rather than theology and at St Andrews Archibald Campbell, professor of ecclesiastical history 1730-56, took a similar line and was criticised for teaching that the law of nature was sufficient to guide rational minds to happiness and that self-love was the motive of all virtuous and religious actions. He disparaged those who were always 'consulting at the Throne' and 'imploring light'. When accused, he made a good enough defence to escape with nothing more than a warning against shocking the simple.

Anxiety about the teaching which divinity students were receiving was nothing new, as acts of assembly in 1694, 1699, 1700 and 1714 show, and in 1724 the historian Wodrow wrote: 'I hear no good of the students of divinity. They very openly oppose the Confession of Faith'. That might have meant no more than the rejection of the doctrine of Election, but anxiety grew when it became evident that it was not a matter of deviating within the framework of Christian theology but of deviating from revealed religion and substituting the supremacy of reason or nature.

This trend had its roots in the works of some of the seventeenth-century writers on science and philosophy, but while their thought could lead away from religion it could also furnish a new approach to religion. Astronomy, physics, chemistry and botany revealed laws of nature which could tie in with the idea of God-given decrees. John Locke had written in *The Reasonableness of Christianity* (1695) that reason makes the existence of a God known to us, and the ordered marvels of the natural world, without supernatural revelation, suffice to convince that there is a Creator. John Ray (1627-1705), a botanist who aimed at a systematic description of the whole organic world, had written *The Wisdom of God manifested in works of creation* (1691). Newton, in the Preface to the second edition of his *Principia*, wrote 'We may now more clearly behold the beauties of nature and be thence incited the more profoundly to reverence and adore the Great Maker and Lord of all'. Alexander Monro *primus*, professor of anatomy at Edinburgh 1719-69, discoursed of the human body as one of the wonderful works of the Creator, and it was not only medical students who went to hear him. These strands went on through the century, and William Paley (1743-1805), in his *Evidences of Christianity* (1794) and *Natural Theology* (1802), summed up a lot of thought about the proof of the existence of God from nature. This could all lead to Deism rather than Christianity, which, while welcoming the revelation of God in His works, demanded also the revelation of God in His Word.

There were those who did not seek to balance or reconcile Reason and Revelation. John Simson had attributed 'too much to natural reason', and Archibald Campbell had taught that the law of nature was sufficient to guide rational minds to happiness. Matthew Tindal's *Christianity as old as creation: or The Gospel a Republication of the Religion of Nature* (1730) argued that belief must contain nothing not justified by nature and unassisted reason – a standpoint which denied the credibility of miracles – and that the end of religion was morality: the core of the Christian faith was thus dismissed and religion reduced to ethics or at best Deism. Next year the minister Robert Wallace wrote, 'The debates of our time are about the foundations of Christianity, and question is made whether the Christian church is to have a footing.' (Thirty years later he wrote, 'Scepticism is in a very flourishing condition; perhaps it has not abounded so much in any age since the commencement of Christianity, nor has it prevailed more in any country than Britain'.) It was not without good cause that the general assembly in 1735 urged ministers to preach revelation as well as reason and in 1736 to choose Gospel subjects, and not ethics, as their main theme.

The drift towards rationalism in the ordinary sense of that term had already gone some way before David Hume (1711–76) came on the scene with his writings, beginning with his *Treatise on Human Nature* (1739) and including a *Natural History of Religion*. By denying causation he cut at the ground of a main assumption lying behind much religious thought, and at the whole concept of Design. In retort to Locke, who held that miracles would infallibly direct us aright in the search for divine revelation,[6] Hume protested that no miracle, in the sense of a violation of the laws of nature, was sufficiently attested but that many bogus miracles had imposed on human credulity. By thus dismissing the possibility of a religion based on reason, Hume pointed away from Deism towards atheism.

The right of the period to be called The Age of Reason is not, however, based only on the spread of rationalism in the philosophical sense. There were growing doubts about long-held superstitions – the background to the abolition of the death penalty for witchcraft in 1736 – as well as an assumption of moderation and common sense and a distrust of the emotions. The whole idea of order in the universe, which for some pointed to Deism, could also produce a self-satisfied belief in progress which was not Christian. Eighteenth-century attitudes are reflected in much of the typical literature and architecture of the period: it is correct, formal, restrained, it does not soar, it is the antithesis of lofty speculation. The same is true of music: a reviewer in *The Scotsman* in March 1988 wrote that the *Eroica* has a 'hard-edged explosiveness' which makes it, 'when heard in suitable surroundings, seem to have burst its way out of the eighteenth century and into the nineteenth'.

In this context, 'enthusiasm', which Adam Smith bracketed with 'superstition',[7] was a 'dirty word' in that period, expecially undesirable in religion. Locke had used the word to mean 'the habit of giving unreasonable assent to religious propositions'[8] and Samuel Johnson defined it as 'vain belief of private revelation; a rash confidence of divine favour or communication'. When the diarist Ridpath heard of the appointment of new royal chaplains on the accession of George III, he wrote, 'Those who know the characters of this new set will be able to judge of the taste in religion which prevails at court, which I hope will be free of enthusiasm or fanaticism'. And a parish minister remarked in the 1790s that 'a tincture of enthusiasm or fanaticism, never before known, began of late years to infect a certain corner within the bounds of this presbytery; . . . but by every appearance it is now on the decline. The inhabitants are, in general, rational in their religion'. While such distrust of 'enthusiasm' was characteristic of the eighteenth century in other countries, it may have been especially potent in Scotland, where, at any rate from the reformation, intellectual apprehension – 'the head' – had dominated over devotion – 'the heart'. Sir Walter Scott, who grew to manhood in the years before eighteenth-century detachment was threatened by the fervour aroused by the French Revolution, was perceptive:

> The Scotch are more remarkable for the exercise of their intellectual powers than for the keenness of their feelings; they are, therefore, more moved by logic than by rhetoric and more attracted by acute and argumentative reasoning on doctrinal points than influenced by the enthusiastic appeals to the heart and the passions by which popular preachers in other countries win the favour of their hearers (*Rob Roy*, chapter xx).

Not everyone took a pejorative view of 'enthusiasm', and the fact that it was there to be condemned indicates that 'reason' was not all-pervasive. Yet the widespread belief was that revelation was superfluous and that religion consisted mainly of morality: a religion of nature, deprived of everything specifically Christian, armed with supreme confidence in man and the power of reason, and producing calm and sober principles of conduct.

Professor Campbell of St Andrews, in condemning 'enthusiasm', had declared that too much of it had survived from what he called the 'distracted times' of the Covenants. Enough of it, however, survived to give zeal to those who were dissatisfied that the 1690 statute prescribing presbyterianism said nothing about the Covenants. The Cameronians from the outset rejected that settlement, and the First or Original Secession, which broke away from the Church of Scotland in the 1730s, reinstated the Covenants among its standards. Although the Seceders were no less obsessed by ecclesiastical politics – 'Church-State relations' – than the Covenanters had been, their theological stance was conservative and they attached themselves to the defenders of *The Marrow* and the critics of Simson and of others who, although they signed the Confession of Faith, 'were very shy of preaching its truths, spoke of it as containing antiquated notions, hinted in quarters where they thought themselves safe that they did not believe some of its doctrines'.[9]

While the various challenges to orthodoxy drove some Christians to a diehard refusal to compromise, it led others to apply the light of nature and reason to traditional teaching with a view to rendering it acceptable to enquiring minds. As scepticism spread, religious observance, even on the part of those who would not have denied the basis of Christianity, became less strict. There was yet another important factor. Wodrow, who in one of his many jeremiads observed that 'A considerable party appear against everything that is serious, and some are open mockers of the ministry and the Gospel' and that there 'seems to be a growing opposition to discipline', remarked also that 'too great fondness upon trade' was weakening religion.

These were some of the roots of the 'Moderatism' for which the eighteenth century was noted and which was the antithesis of 'enthusiasm'. It prevailed in the church for about a century. Those who criticised the Moderates said that they 'flattered human nature as to its ability to obey the moral law' and that 'what the Apostles would have called sinful pleasures they called human weaknesses'.[10] On the other hand, those who approved of them said that they introduced 'better taste and greater liberality of sentiment'. Some of the characteristics of the ministers of the Moderate party were sketched by the perceptive Adam Smith in his *Wealth of Nations*:

> The clergy of an established and well-endowed religion frequently become men of learning and elegance, who possess all the virtues of gentlemen, or which can recommend them to the esteem of gentlemen; but they are apt gradually to lose the qualities, both good and bad, which gave them authority and influence with the inferior ranks of people and which had perhaps been the original causes of the success and establishment of their religion. Such a clergy, when attacked by a set of popular and bold, though perhaps stupid and ignorant enthusiasts, feel themselves as perfectly defenceless as the indolent, effeminate and full-fed nations of the southern parts of Asia when they were invaded by the active, hardy and hungry Tartars of the North.[11]

That was severe enough, but many of the anecdotes about Moderate ministers look so like caricatures as to suggest that their allegedly lax attitude to their duties was as much a standard target for jests as the illiteracy of medieval clerics had once been. A satirist put it thus:

> I do believe in stone and lime, a manse of large dimensions,
> Broad acres for a glebe and farm; that is my church extension.
> My folk may perish if they like – Christ's name I rarely mention;
> I take the stipend due by right to men of good intention.[12]

Reports of endless numbers of sermons based on single texts are not groundless, for a presbytery might intervene and order a minister to 'change his text';[13] two verses of a psalm (ix, 1–2) are said to have served for sermons for a year and a half, but the verses were 'I will praise thee, O Lord, with my whole heart; I will shew forth all thy marvellous works. I will be glad and rejoice in thee; I will sing praise to thy name, O thou most High', which, it must be admitted, offered plenty of scope. On the other hand, one minister, so it was said, had only two sermons, but he used a variety of texts for them. In one presbytery when any minister did write a new sermon it was passed round all his fellow-presbyters – a story which can be capped by a twentieth-century tale (told me as true) of a parishioner who thought that ministers met in presbytery to swop sermons and remarked ruefully, 'Our man must have done badly in the draw'. The classic picture of a Moderate minister owes a good deal to the *Autobiography* of Alexander Carlyle (1722–1805), minister of Inveresk, who emerges as a polished and handsome member of society. But it has been suggested that his pages represent the front he wished to show to the world and, while elaborating on what his left hand did, concealed what he was doing with his right. The records of his parish suggest that he was a faithful pastor and was much more among his people than his writings suggest: his interest in the poor seems to have been exemplary, he fought hard (ultimately with success) to get a church large enough to accommodate his hearers and in 1790 he opened a Sunday School, an institution then looked at with some suspicion. We can lay alongside our impression of the minister of Inveresk what we know about Hugh Cunningham, minister of the adjacent parish of Tranent; he was a conscientious and devoted pastor, systematically visiting and catechising his people.[14]

Very possibly some ministers, sceptical about the supernatural, preferred to give material assistance rather than attempt to make others better believers than they were themselves. We are told that John Thomson, the artist (1778–1840), minister of Duddingston, was asked by one of his people to 'put up a bit prayer' and replied by pressing a coin into her hand with the words 'Take that, Betty, my good woman, it's likely to do you more good than any prayer I'm likely to make'. No doubt such an action opened a minister to the charge of teaching that Christian conduct was more important than theology, but the area is one which has never ceased to be debatable. The Moderates may be seen as preaching some elements of Christianity, stripped of the theological verbiage and ecclesiastical politics which had so long obscured it. However, it is hard to acquit them of the charge of emphasising works at the expense of faith and of aiming at showing that Charles II had been wrong when he said that presbyterianism was no religion for gentlemen. Yet before the century was out there were complaints that they were not succeeding, for 'the higher orders are above the vulgar prejudice of believing it is necessary to worship the God of their fathers'.[15]

Infidelity and secularism went hand in hand with, if they did not stem from, a 'too great fondness upon trade' which became more attractive as it became increasingly profitable. The traditional condemnation of usury, which had in general ceased to have much force after the thirteenth century, had still been reflected when the Second Book Discipline included usury (with blasphemy, perjury, whoredom, drunkenness and dancing) among sins which, in a minister, deserved deposition from office, but it had finally become obsolete in the 1690s with the foundation of the Bank of England (by a Scotsman) and the Bank of Scotland. In a poor country where prosperity and even survival had hitherto depended more on the weather than anything else, man was now finding ways to master his environment and means of gain which owed more to human ingenuity than nature, and, in his growing sense of sufficiency, felt less need for God. 'Acquisitiveness, which had been regarded as a temptation or a sin, was now on the highway to being regarded as a virtue and its success as a mark of divine favour'.[16] Ralph Erskine, a leading Seceder, could write, 'If a man desires to be religious, God must have his whole heart, and he through grace must give it, and make a continual trade of religion; if a man desire to be rich, the world will oblige him to rise early and sit up late and eat the bread of carefulness . . . and therefore God and the world cannot be served by one and the same man'.[17] But, while earnest preachers could thus enlarge on the impossibility of serving both God and

Mammon, those who thought there was no harm in trying could quote Proverbs xxii, 29: 'Seest thou a man diligent in his business? He shall stand before kings'.

There were those who did try, and seemed to succeed, and it has been claimed that there were more Christians – measured by the standards of either faith or works – among the business men than among the philosophers. David Dale (1739–1806), who rose from humble beginnings to become a wealthy owner of some of the earliest and most successful cotton spinning factories in Scotland, had strong Christian convictions but took risks in speculation which might have involved others besides himself in heavy losses. Yet he was generous with his money, in time of scarcity he bought grain to sell cheaply to the poor and he gave great support to religious causes. An employer mainly of the unskilled labour of women and children, especially orphan children, by the standards of the time he was enlightened in his care for his workers, and his child labourers, if hard worked, were better fed, housed, clad and educated than most children of working-class homes at the time. Repelled by the chilly Moderatism of the Church of Scotland, Dale moved first to the more liberal-minded Relief Church and later became a Congregationalist.

Emphasis on works was matched by dilution of faith. Alexander Ferguson, minister of Kilwinning, who had been a student of the unorthodox John Simson, in 1767 published an article in *The Scots Magazine* in which he discarded the concepts of the Fall and the vicarious sacrifice of Christ and disputed the claim of the Confession of Faith to have full support in scripture. A complaint was raised against him in the presbytery, but the case was dismissed. In 1786 William MacGill, minister of the second charge at Ayr, published *A Practical Essay on the Death of Christ*, which indicated doubts about the depravity of man and obviously diverged far from the Confession. Even in this case the proceedings ended in a compromise and an acceptance of his explanation and apology.

Meantime, as ministers continued to subscribe the Confession of Faith and children to be taught the Catechism, the atmosphere can hardly have been one of sincerity. Robert Burns, who scoffed at predestination (chiefly because he thought it irrational), satirised hypocrisy. The Confession was indeed strictly upheld by the opponents of the Moderates and the founders of the Secession. These were styled 'Evangelicals', presumably because they professed to take their stance on the Gospels and on the interpretation of them which was embodied in Calvinist theology, but the terminology has caused misunderstanding, for these men were about as far as possible from evangelicals, or at any rate evangelists, as these terms are usually understood. The solemn declaration of the Seceders in 1754 that 'Our Lord Jesus Christ hath redeemed none others by his death but the Elect only' and the deposition of one of their number who maintained that Christ died 'for all and everyone of mankind and sinners' seemed poor foundations for preaching the Gospel to the unconverted. It is worth noting that the conservatism of Seceders appealed to some English dissenters: in 1731 some 'orthodox dissenters' at Kendal asked that Secession ministers should be sent from Edinburgh to preach the Gospel and combat the 'Socinian blight' [Unitarianism].[18]

Yet genuine evangelical movements were in the making which owed little to the Seceders but which had been foreshadowed in the seventeenth century, when, despite the general preoccupation with politics, there had been those who were able to focus their attention on the inner life of the soul and its relation to God. At the very beginning of the eighteenth century the 'damnable heresies' of Antoinette Bourignon were condemned, but some Scots had agreed with her in repudiating the doctrine of Election, representing 'the great end of Christianity' as bringing men 'to the love of God and charity' and asserting the possibility that any man might 'unite himself to God'. A sermon preached in 1697 by David Brown, a Paisley minister, to 'witches' sentenced to execution, centred on atonement and salvation, did not mention Election or suggest that the victims were destined to damnation, and instead made a plea to embrace Christ.[19] In the 1720s, amid the distractions of the 'Auchterarder Creed' and *The Marrow*, John Glas, minister of Tealing, was working his way towards an approximation to the Christian life of apostolic times. The sect which bore his name deviated from the main stream of Christian practice, but in his repudiation of any link with the government and his denial that the Covenants had a scriptural basis Glas implied the propriety of the 'gathered congregation' which in one way or another has been a mark of the evangelical approach. While there had not, it seems, been any bodies formally constituted as 'gathered congregations' since the 1650s, there had been informal and rather obscure 'Praying Societies', often short-lived, which had been condemned by the assembly as far back as 1640 and which, we can guess, stressed conversion, assurance of salvation and the guidance of the Holy Spirit. It is difficult to disentangle such societies from the 'societies' which maintained the Cameronian testimony between the loss of the Cameronian ministers to the establishment in 1690 and the acquisition by this sect of another minister in or about 1706.

The next influence helping to shape an evangelical movement in Scotland came, not for the first time, from England. John Wesley's Methodism, which after all itself began as a 'society', dates from the 1730s. Wesley visited Scotland no less than twenty-two times, but his rejection of predestinarianism made him suspect in official circles and he found that his preaching made less impression on the generally reserved Scots than it did on the English. He had little success in Scotland in founding separate congregations (which it had not been his original intention to do at all) and today there are only some 12,000 Methodists in Scotland, which puts them far behind Episcopalians, Congregationalists and Baptists. But Wesley's less direct influence extended far beyond the small numbers who named themselves his followers and reached those who did not leave their existing denominations. Methodism's emphasis on an itinerant ministry, outdoor preaching, work by the laity, 'cells' or 'classes' of faithful groups, hymn-singing and spiritual discipline all represented a flexibility which fitted with widening Christian influence but did not fit with presbyterianism. (In Ireland Methodism took roots mainly in areas with an existing Anglican population, most orthodox Presbyterians had little to do with it and in 1804 the Synod of Ulster condemned it.)

Wesley's decision to abandon Calvinism had estranged him from George Whitefield, whose experience, when he came to Scotland in 1741, was illuminating as to the state of Scottish religion. He not unnaturally thought that seceders from the Scottish establishment would look kindly on one who was critical of the

English establishment, and he expected that his allegiance to Calvinism would provide a strong bond. However, he overlooked the preoccupation of the Seceders with their ecclesiastical politics and their Covenants, about which he knew little and cared less. His hosts wanted him to confine his ministrations to their own congregations, whom they deemed 'the Lord's people', and pressed him to acknowledge that only presbyterian church government was scriptural. However, a man who declared that an archbishop did not necessarily know any more about Christianity than Mahomet did was not prepared to take Scottish Seceders at their own valuation. When he refused to disown the episcopal system (into which he himself had been ordained) and told his critics that it was the Devil's people, not the Lord's, who most needed his preaching, he was denounced as a dangerous 'enthusiast'. It is noteworthy that as Whitefield owed his own conversion to Scougal's *Life of God in the Soul of Man* he demonstrates continuity from seventeenth-century piety. Alienated from the Seceders, Whitefield preached in the open air and in some parish churches and probably had far more influence on members of the Church of Scotland than on the Seceders, who thought he had nothing to teach them.

The year after Whitefield's visit, though not as a consequence of it, at least directly, came 'The Cambuslang Revival', a phenomenon not unlike that at Shotts in 1630. In Cambuslang the praying societies had been active and they secured the appointment of a parish minister – William McCulloch – whose evangelical preaching produced a massive response. As the movement gathered momentum Whitefield joined in. Some 30,000 people are said to have turned up for a Communion service and a tenth of them received Communion. It seems that some praying societies maintained on a small scale some of the fervour of such a revival, but possibly an occasion like this created a kind of pattern for the mass Communions which now became customary. Occasional joint Communions, when people from several parishes gathered together, seem to have begun in the 1650s, when celebrations became rare – though it must be remembered that Johnston of Wariston had attended Communion outside his own parish in the 1630s.

Such mass Communions have attained notoriety, if only through the verses of Robert Burns in *The Holy Fair*. All the features which Burns satirised are amply substantiated from contemporary evidence, though it must be observed that the poet's emphasis was on a marathon of sermons delivered in the open air and not on what happened in church. The mass Communions have been roundly denounced as degenerating into 'jostling, promiscuous carnivals':

> It is difficult to describe the scandals of the Holy Fairs in moderate language. They had all the temptations of the old medieval pilgrimages. . . . In the tragi-comic welter of weeping, mocking, squeezing, cursing, lecherous humanity . . . it was impossible to be sure where genuine piety lay. Even in that coarse and by no means fastidious age the more serious minds had good reason to be disturbed and shocked. 'What must the consequence be when a whole countryside is thrown loose and young fellows and girls are going home together by night in the gayest season of the year? . . . When I was a young fellow at my apprenticeship I was a great frequenter of these

occasions and know them so well that I would not choose a wife that had often frequented them nor trust a daughter too much among those rambling saints'.[20]

To set against this, there is ample evidence that one reason why celebrations of Holy Communion were so infrequent was that a minister might not consider his people ready for it and that long and solemn preparation, extending over a year, was necessary.[21] In 1712 John Willison, a Brechin minister, attacked as an 'innovation' the idea that ability to repeat the Catechism was adequate preparation, though on the other hand he criticised Independents for demanding not only knowledge and a holy life but also signs of conversion and spiritual experience. Willison published *Sermons on the Lord's Supper* (1722) and a *Sacramental Catechism* (1737) – the latter translated into Gaelic – in which he emphasised communicating rather than preaching. Clearly there were those who took a very serious view of the danger of 'eating and drinking unworthily' and there were still those who thought of each Communion as the occasion of a fresh personal 'Covenant' with God. The 'fencing of the Tables', when wrongdoers were denounced, was a kind of successor to the medieval excommunication on Rogation Days.

It was neither in the 'Holy Fairs' nor in the politically obsessed Seceders nor in the cool intelligentsia of the Moderates that the most promising Christian commitment was to be found. It is not to be forgotten that it was in the 1750s and 1760s that Scottish Baptists built their first church and Scottish Congregationalists were organised. In the established Church itself the Moderates on the whole did not help Christianity, for to them the issue was not a matter of theological discussion between limited atonement and universal atonement but of disregard or even denial of an atonement altogether, and perhaps even rejection of any concept of the forgiveness of sins because sin itself was thought an outmoded idea. But the establishment comprehended evangelical preachers as well as Moderates. John Fraser, minister at Alness from 1726 to 1769, was a severe preacher, who likened his work to the discharge of arrows at the hearts of God's enemies and likened a neighbouring minister's work to the pouring of oil on the wounds of broken-hearted sinners.[22] His *The Scripture Doctrine of Sanctification*, published in 1774, based on Romans vi, 1 to viii, 4, represented evangelicalism. At St Giles' in Edinburgh the polished rhetorician Hugh Blair, unimpassioned and rather affected, had as a colleague Robert Walker, described by Alexander Carlyle as 'a rank enthusiast and nothing but heat without light', who preached sermons with a biblical and evangelical flavour and held prayer meetings which were not for the fashionable worshippers who crowded to hear Blair. Also in Edinburgh was the man who can claim to have been its most distinguished citizen – George Drummond (?1687–1766), the Lord Provost who had so much to do with the planning of the New Town and who kept a private diary in which he complained about 'the steps taken to undermine serious religion in the church, in Edinburgh especially', where affairs were thrown into the hands of 'men void of religion', but in which he also disclosed his own personal faith: after an evening with the Directors of the Royal Bank of Scotland he wrote, 'May the Lord pardon me the guilt of others. Closed the day with God.'[23] The diary of a humbler contemporary, a merchant named George Brown, details his prayer, Bible-reading and meditation.[24]

Literacy was all the time extending, partly through the increasing number of schools and partly through the growing availability of books through libraries. One of the first had been set up in Haddington during the Restoration period by the minister John Gray. In Kirkwall, William Baikie of Holland in 1683 left eight score of books to an already existing 'Publick Bibliothick'. Robert Leighton, who had been Bishop of Dunblane, left his books on his death in 1684 to be available for the clergy of the diocese. James Kirkwood, minister of Minto from 1679 to 1681, went to England when he was deprived for refusing to take the Test Act, but he raised money in England for Scottish parish libraries and the general assembly took up the idea. Between 1704 and 1708 no less than seventy-seven libraries were founded in the west highlands – contemporaneously with the beginning of the work of the Society in Scotland for Propagating Christian Knowledge (SSPCK). In 1691 Lord Madderty had founded Innerpeffray Library, where the borrower's book, beginning in 1747 and continuing until 1958, includes the names of a number of craftsmen, to whom was offered a wide range of history, philosophy, theology and devotional works, including writings of Richard Baxter, Binning and Robert Bruce. Allan Ramsay set up a lending library in Edinburgh in 1725. There was a library in Leadhills from 1743, set up by the local minister, schoolmaster and twenty-one miners, which had 1500 books by 1821, and one in the mining parish of Tranent during the ministry of Hugh Cunningham in the second half of the century. In Ayr, which (like Irvine and Kilmarnock) had a bookseller who did some publishing, a Library Society was founded in 1762, but its requirement of an entry fee and an annual subscription meant that its membership did not extend far down the social scale. Lending went on, as ever, among friends and neighbours: James Lawrie, minister of Kirkmichael in Ayrshire, lent books on theology and history, works in Latin, Greek and French and copies of plays. There were some burgh libraries, but they were endowed by individuals, and public libraries on the rates did not come until a statute of 1850 allowed them.[25] There was plenty of soul-searching literature in circulation, like Baxter's *Call to the Unconverted* (an English work translated into Gaelic in 1750); Pearse's *Preparation for Death*; and *The Christian's Great Interest*, by William Guthrie (1620–65), minister of Fenwick, based on Isaiah lv (originally published in 1658 but reprinted many times from 1695 until 1832, when there was a Gaelic translation).

There is something of a paradox about the eighteenth century. Unbelief then reached strengths which may have been unprecedented, but more people were touched by spiritual vitality of an intensity which, so far as we know, had been attained previously by only a few individuals or perhaps small groups. It was probably at this stage that there was for the first time a widespread appreciation that the 'national Church' comprised many nominal Christians who required not merely instruction and direction but conversion before enrolment among the true believers. Never before, except possibly by some of the first reformers, had there been systematic evangelistic campaigns like those of Wesley and Whitefield.

Meanwhile the so-called 'Evangelicals' among the Original Seceders were content to trudge the familiar but barren tracks of ecclesiastical politics. They split in 1745–7 over the oath required of burgesses in certain burghs to uphold 'the true religion presently professed within this realm', which some thought committed those who took it to uphold the establishment. At the end of the century each of these two factions split again, this time over the duty of the state to enforce ecclesiastical discipline. That was a purely academic question in an unestablished church, but it seems that the 'New Light' sections, who repudiated the state's powers and accepted the 'voluntary' principle that a church should not depend on the state, moved towards a generally more liberal theology.

The 'New Lights' thus came closer to the Second Secession or Relief Church, which originated in 1761 as a result of disputes over patronage but was not tied to conservative theology. Thomas Gillespie, founder of the 'presbytery for the relief of Christians oppressed in their Christian privileges', had spent some time with English nonconformists and had been ordained to an English Independent congregation before becoming minister of Carnock. He was thus another channel by which the more mellow air of the south came to temper the chill of Scotland. Gillespie could not accept the rigid theology and intolerance of the earlier Seceders and he retained the Confession and Catechisms only as 'collections of divine truths', the compilers of which had not been infallible. Gillespie himself was never very happy about separating from the establishment – any more than Wesley was – but his Relief Church continued, less strict in formal doctrine, critical of the association of church with state, less exclusive in its terms of membership and showing goodwill towards other Christian denominations by admitting their members to Communion.

The eighteenth century – 'The Age of Reason' – is thus also pre-eminently the Age of Secession, and no account of Scottish Christianity can pass over this without asking why Scottish presbyterianism became so divisive. The issues involved were far less profound than those which had separated Protestants and Papists in the sixteenth century or even those which had divided Presbyterians and Episcopalians in the seventeenth, and it would be an abuse of language to say that they touched the core of Christian faith. Yet there was a readiness, almost an alacrity, to secede, which contrasts sharply with the agonising which had gone on in the seventeenth century over 'separation' and the predominant willingness then to acquiesce in much of which one did not approve rather than secede. On the one hand, it is easy to say that a presbyterian system facilitates schism, to the extent that a group of disgruntled ministers can always form a presbytery, whereas in an episcopalian system schism is impossible unless the dissidents, like chess players, can capture a bishop; and one might go farther and say that, however sound Scottish theology was in other respects, it was so woefully weak in respect of the concept of the Church as the Body of Christ that the Church was thought of as no more divine than any man-made association. On the other hand, the epidemic of secessions was not the doing only of a handful of ministers. The issues were, or were thought to be, issues which affected every man and woman in the country – and, which is important, could be understood, if not by every one in the country, at any rate by a good many of them.

A century which on the whole played down faith, should have proliferated in good works. When Alexander Pope wrote

> In Faith and Hope the world will disagree
> For all mankind's concern is Charity

he was probably thinking of charity in the everyday sense of the word and not in the sense of 1 Corinthians xiii. One of the aims of the Moderates was to turn minds away from theological debates and from dogma to what were seen as the practical duties of a Christian life. Alexander Carlyle did his duty by the poor of his parish, and the story about John Thomson assessing pecuniary assistance as more likely to be helpful than prayer reflects such an outlook on the part of a rather worldly Moderate. But a sermon by a Seceder published in 1785 asserted that devotion which excluded attention to the state of Christ's kingdom outside a man and confined attention entirely to the kingdom of God within him 'must flow from another spirit than that of Christ'. That would have made a motto for any Christian philanthropist. If there was need for charity as well as faith – social commitment as well as evangelism – that need accelerated as a result of economic change.

It was churchgoers – mainly parish churchgoers – with their modest contributions to the collection ladles, who continued to provide the chief means for the relief of the poor. The direct responsibilities of the ecclesiastical authorities in the field of education continued. In 1724 the presbytery of Edinburgh, for example, was visiting, or as we should say inspecting, sixteen schools, eight of them in the towns of Edinburgh and Leith, the others mostly in what are now suburbs. The statutory parochial schools, financed by heritors, were increasingly being supplemented, especially in cities, by schools which, because they were boarding establishments, were usually called 'hospitals' and which owed their endowments to the munificence of private individuals. George Heriot's Hospital in Edinburgh had been established by James VI's jeweller in imitation of Christ's Hospital in London. In Glasgow George and Thomas Hutcheson (died 1639 and 1641) left money to establish a hospital for infirm men and a school for poor boys. Robert Gordon's College in Aberdeen, for the education of boys, followed a similar model in the eighteenth century. In Edinburgh the Merchant Maiden Hospital and the Trades Maiden Hospital developed from a bequest by Mary Erskine (d. 1707) for the education of the daughters of burgesses, and the equally well known George Watson's Hospital came in 1734.

The Edinburgh town council founded two charity schools, one in 1699 and the other in 1714; one of them received a bequest from Sir John McLurg of Vogrie in 1718. In 1743 the town council established the Charity Workhouse, which taught useful crafts as well as the usual rudiments, and in 1750 this institution received the revenues of a medieval establishment called St Paul's Work, where similar work had been done. There were two more charity workhouses by 1761.

The Society in Scotland for Propagating Christian Knowledge was founded in 1709, supported by private contributions and legacies. It had 25 schools by 1715 and 109 by 1732. It had a special eye to the need, particularly in the Highlands and Islands, to indoctrinate against popery and in favour of the protestant succession, but in terms of its second charter (1738) its schools were authorised to give instruction 'in some of the most necessary and useful arts of life'. In Edinburgh it co-operated with the town council, the presbytery and private benefactors in supporting the Orphan Hospital (1733), the charity workhouses and some 'English' (as distinct from 'Grammar') Schools.

Some of those educational developments were themselves indicative of the inadequacy now of the parochial system and also perhaps of the problems posed by the industrial areas in towns. But other eighteenth century developments reflected both some of those problems and a greater awareness of social responsibility. Some medieval models had still been followed in the seventeenth century. For instance, in Stirling a prosperous merchant called John Cowane (d. 1633) left 40,000 merks for an almshouse for twelve 'decayed guild brethren', but its residential character was not a great success and pensions were paid instead. However, disease and disabilities as well as old age demanded attention. Edinburgh's Royal Infirmary started in 1729, Glasgow's in 1791. The Royal Blind Asylum in Edinburgh, in 1793, reflected not so much the characteristics of the eighteenth century as those of the Awakening which will be the subject of the next chapter, for, besides some ministers, William Wilberforce was involved. It was followed in 1810 by the Edinburgh Institution for the Deaf and Dumb, set up by subscription. How far deep Christian commitment lay behind all of those foundations no one could say without an examination of the motives of all the individuals involved; it is hard to see them as other than a continuation of the tradition of all the 'hospitals' of the medieval centuries, and some of the founders may have thought that they were laying up treasure in heaven.

Many who benefited from charity may have profited less from either Christian preaching or the enlightening influence of reason. Superstition and naive beliefs persisted. William Aiton, in his *General View of the Agriculture of the county of Ayr* (1811), was not alone in mentioning the opposition incurred by artificial winnowing – the 'Deil's wind' instead of 'the Lord's' (to which Scott alluded, anachronistically, in *Old Mortality*); but he added that obsession with religion had retarded economic development: 'the road to heaven was too much talked about to admit of anything being done to those leading to the market town'.[26]

7

THE AWAKENING

If 'distraction' in the seventeenth century was followed by 'reason' in the eighteenth, did 'enthusiasm' come next? The term 'Awakening' has not become established in Scotland, possibly because it might challenge the claim of the eighteenth century to 'Enlightenment': could one awake after being 'enlightened'? In other countries there has been no hesitation about applying the term 'awakening' to a zest which replaced indifference, a reaction against restraint and a protest against classicism. Enthusiasm, despised in the eighteenth century, was transformed by a romantic movement into something respectable and fashionable. Wordsworth brought to the interpretation of nature a contemplation which drew the soul to God in a wonder unknown to the cool reasoning of the deist philosophers. The romanticism of Scott stirred up a kind of sympathy, partly aesthetic, for religious beliefs and practices laid aside for generations. The 'Gothic revival' in church design ran counter to the mainly intellectual appeal of Presbyterian churches and services, which some Scots (including Sir Walter) deserted. The Oxford or Tractarian Movement (or Catholic Revival), originating in England in the 1830s and in part an ecclesiological offshoot of the romantic movement, affected the Episcopal Church and as time went on had some influence on the worship of the Presbyterians.

One reason for dating The Awakening from the end of the eighteenth century is the influence of the French Revolution. Here was enthusiasm, to a degree and on a scale unimagined by the Moderates, aspiring to political and social liberation. The revolutionaries went on, however, to a Reign of Terror, they abolished Christian observance and deified Reason. Some Scottish observers thought that, as unbelief would lead to the collapse of morality and social order, the need was for religious renewal. In December 1795 *The Scots Magazine* carried a notice of a work called *An Alarm to Britain, or an Inquiry into the Causes of the rapid progress of Infidelity in the Present Age*. The author was that man of many parts, John Jamieson, and it was perhaps appropriate that a Secession minister who was also an historian and a lexicographer should attempt to assess the religious situation in some kind of context. (Anyone ready to jump to the conclusion that the prevalence of rationalism was the main cause of the situation which alarmed Jamieson need only look at *The Edinburgh Courant* for the fifth day of that same month of December and notice an advertisement for 'An illustration of the Occult Sciences or the Foretelling of future events'.) Others, however, thought evangelism suspect as an ally and saw the answer in repression of novelties in both political and church life.

It was characteristic that the members of Ayr Library Society burned the radical works of Thomas Paine in 1793, and in 1800 the general assembly alluded to the 'alarm' caused to 'the friends of order and peace' and gave an assurance that 'among the great body of the people committed to our care there prevails an unshaken attachment to our excellent constitution in church and state and a just abhorrence of that system of impiety and anarchy which hath spread misery and desolation through many parts of the earth'.[1]

From the religious point of view the main aspect of The Awakening was an evangelical revival, at least as notable in England and France[2] as in Scotland, continuing or renewing some elements which had appeared from time to time since the middle of the seventeenth century and which had taken shape in 'gathered congregations'. The continuing influence of Wesley and Whitefield was to some extent mediated through the work of two noble ladies – in England Selina, Countess of Huntingdon (1707–91), who set up 'tabernacles' from 1761 onwards for the use of preachers who were not necessarily ordained, and a training college in 1768; and in Scotland Willielma, Lady Glenorchy (1741–86), who founded chapels from about 1764 onwards.

The debt to England had other elements. The 'Clapham Sect', a group of wealthy Anglican evangelicals, though not politically radical, felt that their faith must be accompanied by good works. Among their activities were foreign missions (especially in India), opposition to the slave trade, the foundation of the Society for Bettering the Condition and Increasing the Comfort of the Poor, and Sunday Schools. William Wilberforce expounded such aims in his *Practical View of Christianity* (1797). Milestones in their progress were the establishment of the *Evangelical Magazine* (1793), the London Missionary Society (1795), the Church Missionary Society and the Religious Tract Society (both 1799) and the British and Foreign Bible Society (1804).

A direct personal link with England came about through David Bogue (1750–1825). Trained as a minister, he rejected appointment in the Church of Scotland under the existing system of patronage and became pastor of an independent chapel at Gosport near Portsmouth. One of the members was Adam Duncan (1731–1804), a native of Lundie in Perthshire who had been in the navy for many years but was yet to win the famous victory (1797) which made him Viscount Duncan of Camperdown. Duncan introduced to Bogue's chapel two young nephews who were in the navy – Robert Haldane of Airthrey (1764–1842) and his brother James (1773–1851). Robert left the navy at the end of the American War in 1783 and settled at Gosport with Bogue, who accompanied him on a visit to Paris in 1785. After touring the continent Robert went back to Airthrey and began to encourage evangelical preachers. His own spiritual life, he said, was strengthened by the excitement generated by the French Revolution, but he later renounced all connection with political agitation.

In 1796 a preaching mission was conducted in Perthshire by Charles Simeon (1759–1836), vice-provost of Trinity College, Cambridge, and one of the founders of the Church Missionary Society, and Rowland Hill (1744–1833). Hill, who had been rejected for ordination in the Church of England because he indulged in itinerant preaching, found fault with all the Presbyterian bodies except the Relief Church and was especially critical of ministers who subscribed the Confession but did not preach it. Simeon and Hill met James Haldane, who joined them in missionary tours, and Robert Haldane sold his property to obtain funds for evangelical work. In 1798 the Haldanes founded the Society for Propagating the Gospel at Home, pledged to undenominational evangelism. They encountered in Scotland the distrust of itinerant preaching which Hill had encountered in England: in 1799 the general assembly restricted preaching to ministers and criticised 'a set of men whose proceedings threaten no small disorder.... They assume the name of missionaries, as if they had some special commission from heaven, without any countenance from the presbytery of the bounds or the minister of the parish ... as if they were possessed of some secret and novel method of bringing men to heaven'. The Haldanes used their funds to build spacious 'tabernacles' in Edinburgh, Glasgow and Dundee. The Edinburgh Tabernacle, at Greenside, where the brothers had previously preached in the open to crowds of 10,000, could hold 3000 people. It remained in existence (though not as a preaching hall after 1864) until the 1920s, when it was demolished and replaced by the vast Playhouse Theatre – which gives some indication of its bulk. Other steps were to establish Sunday Schools and training colleges, and in 1805 the Haldanes claimed to have trained 200 lay preachers. Many Scottish Congregationalist and Baptist Churches derive from the activities of the Haldanes who in 1808 themselves became Baptists.

What the Royal Navy did for the Haldanes the British Army did for John Nicolson (1790–1828), a Shetlander who joined the Royal Artillery and saw action at Waterloo. In the ranks he met Edward McDermott, a devout Methodist, and under his influence 'broke league with Satan and sin' in 1810. When peace came in 1815 Nicolson became the apostle of Methodism in his native islands, where his work was followed up, with the result that Shetland has a higher proportion of Methodists than any other part of Scotland.[3]

It was characteristic of the aspirations of the time that Robert Haldane had first intended to imitate Robert Carey (1761–1834) and go to India, for it was among the evangelicals of the 1790s that a sustained concern for foreign missions began. This was not entirely a novelty, because from the earliest European colonisation one motive, at least ostensibly, had been the conversion of heathen peoples. The charter by James VI and I to Virginia alluded to the intention to propagate 'the Christian religion to such people as yet live in darkness'.[4] The Scottish ministers sent to Darien in the 1690s were expected to work among the natives, and in 1732 the Society in Scotland for the Propagation of Christian Knowledge engaged three missionaries to work among the American Indians. Now, in 1794, David Bogue pled that Christians who appreciated their own salvation had a duty to spread the Gospel among the half of the human race who had no knowledge of it, and Missionary Societies were soon founded in several Scottish towns. In 1797 the Glasgow Missionary Society sent out its first two missionaries – to Sierra Leone. The general assembly withheld support, in the belief that such societies were connected with radical political elements and with the agitation against the slave trade.

The assembly modified its attitude after panic about prospective revolution dwindled. It petitioned in 1813 that the East India Company's new charter should provide for missionary work, and in the 1820s collections for foreign missions were authorised. Ultimately, as a result of efforts by the Church of Scotland, other Presbyterian Churches and the Episcopal Church, Scottish missionary operations extended quite literally from China to Peru. The obligation to spread the Gospel throughout the world was constantly kept before church members, missionaries on furlough preached in pulpits and addressed rallies, and men of high calibre dedicated themselves to the mission field. The cause had a special appeal to Sunday School children, whose pennies generally went to this work, sometimes for a specific mission or even for a specific child, and there was no mistaking the pride that was generated in the doings of David Livingstone, Mary Slesser of Calabar and many others. Whatever may be thought of it now, it seemed to represent an outgoing and unselfish attitude.

The Scots might almost have been excused had they ignored foreign missions, because there was as much need for missionary work at home. In 1887 a writer in *The Scotsman* remarked cuttingly 'better send a deputation to Banff than to Beirut or Bombay'. Perhaps more appropriately, in the early 1820s this plea had been made:

> We have heard the cry of the... Hottentots, 'Come over and help us'; or rather we went uninvited, knowing their need of help and feeling in some measure our obligation to impart it; and shall the hills and glens of our native land, though actually re-echoing with the cry – 'Come – and help us' be unvisited?[5]

All the outlying parts of the country, Lowland as well as Highland, had often had less than justice from the established church, partly because of the physical difficulties of ministering in enormous parishes and partly because the prospects of social and geographical isolation deterred men of ability unless they were strongly committed.

It was in such areas that the early nineteenth-century evangelicals made much of their impact. Some parish ministers themselves underwent conversion: Roderick MacLeod, who for the first three years of his ministry had been 'an entire stranger to the Gospel scheme of salvation... for the staple theology of Skye preaching in those days was nothing better than scraps of Blair's sermons or of some other equally meagre stuff', changed his attitude to the extent of refusing to baptize the children of unconverted parents. From the late eighteenth century some missionaries were employed by the Relief Church and the United Secession, but most of the work was that of unordained men, some sent by organisations like the Haldanes' Society for Propagating the Gospel at Home. Partly as a consequence of their work there were a number of local revivals in the early nineteenth century. Some of the preachers worked within the establishment, but there was a trend to separation from it and its 'graceless ministers'. A considerable number of Baptist and Congregational churches were established, but they were mainly in Perthshire and Argyll or just within the Highland line and most of them were short-lived, partly because attention was distracted by the Disruption. Not surprisingly, the assembly condemned irregular actions like those of John MacDonald, minister of Urquhart, who preached outwith his parish, sometimes in dissenters' meeting-houses. There was local hostility too from ministers or heritors, and sometimes the apocalyptic teaching of missionaries (whose promise of a new heaven and a new earth appealed to a population which had outgrown the means of subsistence) led to charges of sedition.[6]

The advance of Christianity in Highland Scotland coincided more or less with its failure in industrial Scotland. Already during the eighteenth century various changes had directly or indirectly affected church life. Industrialisation was beginning, with textile factories and – though as yet on a very limited scale – some heavy industry. This meant migration. Between 1755 and 1831 the population of Lanarkshire grew from 82,000 to 317,000 and of Renfrewshire from 27,000 to 133,000. Rapidly growing numbers of people were concentrated in towns or villages hopelessly under-supplied with churches and ministers. Apart from pressure on buildings, there was an intolerable burden on the individual minister, who had to oversee various organisations and might have to marry thirty couples in a day. The existing parochial system, geared to the rural economy and society of the middle ages, was outworn. At one time most men died in the parish in which not only they but their forefathers had been born; now mobility and migration diminished the impression which minister or elder could hope to make by systematic visitation and catechising within a parish. It was in this context that the traditional system of public penance before the congregation had been abolished in 1763.[7]

The creation of new parishes was a cumbrous matter, involving procedure relating to civil as well as ecclesiastical affairs. The Secessions indeed multiplied church buildings, but it was the middle classes who could afford to be Seceders, while the parish church was left with those who had not the means for the hire of a carriage or the maintenance of a minister. The parish church tended to be crystallised round heritors and elders often drawn mainly from landed families; in the Secession, office and influence were open more widely, though hardly to the poor. The main point was that the established church, tied to a parish system governed by a whole code of laws, lacked flexibility, while other bodies, dependent on the giving of their members, sometimes lacked finance. Hitherto the average rural parish, the unit on which the whole pattern had been based, had seldom contained as many as 1000 people. Even so, the church could not have accommodated them all. In the coal-mining parish of Tranent there were 2732 parishioners and the church could hold only about 200, and when a new one was built in 1799 it was seated for only 446. Medieval structures, already inadequate in size, were collapsing, and both maintenance and replacement sometimes encountered difficulties from heritors, some of whom were episcopalian and few of whom were enthusiastic about using their means to finance church buildings. The *Statistical Account* of the 1790s has a lot to say about the poor state of churches. Some of the old churches were replaced in the years before and after 1800, but there were places where missionaries who were prepared to preach outside parish churches, sometimes in halls or in the open, filled a vacuum.

There were complaints that whole communities were not only churchless but were lapsing into paganism. At St John's in Glasgow in the 1820s, out of about 10,000 inhabitants only 3000 had even a nominal church connection and there were sittings for about 1640 of them, and in the Barony parish there was on average one church or chapel for 12,500 people; even taking into account the contribution made by Seceders, less than one-fifth of the people had any church connection, and in certain areas the proportion could be as little as one in 20. Hugh Miller, in *My Schools and Schoolmasters*, wrote of conditions in the Lothians: 'all the religion of our party was to be found among the Seceders. Our other workmen were really wild fellows, most of whom never entered a church'. He goes on to say that a reaction against the cold Moderatism had begun, but it was chiefly among the middle and upper classes, while the working men of Edinburgh and its neighbourhood were in large part either non-religious or included within the Independent or Secession pale; it was said that 'You might as well preach to them in Hebrew as in English'. It was not only the great cities that were affected. In the linen-weaving town of Dunfermline in 1844 around 17 per cent of the population had no known church connection and in 1849–50 one minister said that he had difficulty in introducing religious conversation among the weavers.[8]

The general assembly of 1835 admitted some guilt for the fact that 'in all the most populous districts of the kingdom multitudes are passing onwards to eternity in utter ignorance of the only way of salvation, and many thousands of children are growing up to manhood without being brought up in the nurture and admonition of the Lord' (a phrase taken from the undertaking exacted from parents at baptism). Sadder and more telling is David Stow's report in 1831 that among children in Glasgow 'one in six of those whom he questioned had never heard the name of Jesus but from the mouths of profane swearers'.[9]

Whatever may be said of faith, works were more measurable. Drunkenness increased sharply when in 1822 the duty on whisky was reduced to about a quarter of what it had been. There are statistics: in Glasgow a whisky shop for every fourteen families; in a Dundee parish eleven bakers' shops and 108 public houses; another parish had one church and 135 public houses. Such figures might be incredible if we did not have comparative figures for London, where retailers of spirits were numbered in many thousands and there were areas where the proportion of spirit-shops to houses was as high as 1:7.5 or even 1:5.[10] In Glasgow it was estimated in 1846 that nearly 30,000 persons were in a state of brutish intoxication every Saturday night, and on Sunday 1300 pubs were open in the city. Children were introduced to alcohol at an early age and there were innumerable customs which involved heavy drinking. Only in 1853 did the Forbes-Mackenzie Act close pubs on Sundays and from 11 p.m. to 8 a.m. on weekdays.

For towns there are figures for brothels, prostitution and illegitimacy, but the evils were not confined to the towns. In 1863 the figure for illegitimacy in Wigtownshire was nearly 17 per cent and about 1880 it was 25 per cent in Banffshire. The Free Church congratulated itself on having standards above the average – one minister remarked that although his congregation comprised half the population of the parish, they had been responsible for only two bastards out of the previous year's crop of nineteen. John Tulloch, who became principal of St Andrews University in 1854, had written when he was minister of Kettins, in Angus, 'I cannot say that real religion and morality are at all more prevalent in the country than in the towns. . . . Theological ideas are more current, but there seems a sad want of right religious apprehension. . . . Life and doctrine hang very loosely together. . . . The gravest practical offences . . . are . . . regarded as very trifling things'.

Consciences were stirred, and individual Christians were active in almost every field of social need. At a time when working men were accused of improvidence and the existing banks would not accept deposits of less than £10, Henry Duncan, minister of Ruthwell, who was influenced by Quaker teaching, in 1810 started the first Parish Savings Bank; by 1818 there were 130 of them. Some congregations continued to have 'Penny Banks' – and also their own friendly societies, which provided a form of insurance – well into the twentieth century, on the eve of an era when 'working men' flourish their cheque books and their credit cards. Stevenson MacGill, who had been a Methodist and became minister of the Tron in Glasgow, pioneered reform in prisons and in the care of the insane and founded the Glasgow Society for the Encouragement of Penitents, to help delinquents who wanted to mend their ways. James Begg, of the Free Church, who held that 'the physical circumstances of the people are matters with which we have much to do', made bad housing his target. He argued that the Commandments against murder and stealing enjoined 'sanitary and social reform', and he denounced one-roomed houses because Our Lord had said that when a man prays he should enter his closet and shut the door, which was impossible in a 'single end'. The same point was made by William Garden Blaikie, minister of Pilrig, and by his neighbour William Mackenzie in North Leith. Practical steps were taken by founding Co-operative Building Societies, which in those days really were building societies, for they built houses.

A less improbable target for Christian endeavour was drunkenness. John Dunlop, an elder in the Church of Scotland, seems to have been the pioneer of the temperance movement for Britain as a whole, and William Collins, also an elder, supported him. By 1830 there were about 100 temperance societies, and they multiplied as the advocates of temperance or abstinence won support in all denominations. Bands of Hope were attached to many congregations. As a child in the 1920s I attended one and used to recite the pledge every Friday evening, without being entirely clear about the meaning of either 'intoxicating drinks' or 'beverages'. The lessons gave me a lasting horror of the evils of drink and I have never entirely shaken off the feeling that a pub is not quite respectable; the fact that they did not make me a teetotaller should not detract from the effect which the temperance movement, encouraged by the churches, had on the country as a whole.

The social conscience found outlets in private munificence, on a scale hardly paralleled since the foundation of abbeys seven centuries before. Feudal nobles were replaced by industrial magnates, who had ample means when the Scottish economy was an important part of a Britain which was the workshop of the world. It may be that an important part in channelling money into religious and philanthropic causes was played by the Disruption. Never before, outside the Secessions and some minor sects, had individuals needed to dip their hands into their own pockets voluntarily for the erection of churches – heritors did it by compulsion – and individual charity had consisted mainly of bequests for the poor of the parish, but now the Free Church showed that private giving could produce massive results, and members of the Church of Scotland were moved to follow that path. The United Presbyterian Church (created in 1847 by a union of most of the

New Light Seceders with the Relief Church) also attracted a number of men of wealth, perhaps partly because its constitution gave its lay members more power than they had in other presbyterian churches, and their generosity produced 'the bonnie U.P. kirks' of R. L. Stevenson's lines.

James Baird of Gartsherrie, an ironmaster, gave half a million to found the Baird Trust for the work of the Church of Scotland. William Denny, a shipbuilder, who joined the U. P. Church, was very critical of the lack of Christian standards among professing Christians as well as throughout society generally and he set Christ's teaching that selfishness is death against the belief of economists that selfishness is salvation – or so he put it. John Campbell White, Lord Overtoun, an important figure in the chemical industry, became an enthusiast for evangelical work at home and abroad; he conducted a Bible class in his own congregation, he was chairman of the Free Church Glasgow United Evangelistic Society and gave generously to the Church. William Quarrier, who had started work in a pin-factory at the age of seven but became a successful business man, founded his Orphans' Homes at Bridge of Weir in 1876. Scotland's wealthiest benefactor, Andrew Carnegie, had no use for conventional religion, and the public libraries for which he is best known were as likely to spread rationalism, but he had a weakness for organs, which suddenly proliferated in Presbyterian churches, and Carnegie thus helped Christianity indirectly at a time when, as we shall see, hymns were coming into general use.

All up and down the country there are 'Memorial' Churches, immortalising the names of benefactors who were, all else apart, patrons of architects. Sometimes, however, the beneficence was more broadly based socially than the endowment of abbeys had been. At Govan a church which cost £27,000, all raised by voluntary subscriptions, was founded in 1884 to serve the whole parish, not just a congregation, with no seat-rents to deter the poor. As in the twelfth century there was an element of competition – this time among denominations rather than individuals – generating a degree of grandiosity which later generations, faced with problems of upkeep, were to regret.

How did individual enthusiasts relate to the churches? The founder of Savings Banks had come under Quaker influence, the prison reformer had been a Methodist, the founder of orphan homes was a Baptist and the first temperance leaders were elders. Outstanding among ministers was the eccentric James Begg, who prevailed on his Free Church to appoint a committee to examine working-class housing. In the temperance movement the Baptists and Congregationalists and some other smaller bodies made the best showing, while among Presbyterians the U. P. and Free Churches were first in the field with Temperance Societies. The comparative lethargy of the Church of Scotland suggests that it was not for nothing that it was called 'The Whisky Kirk' and that whisky, conversely, was known as 'The Auld Kirk'. By the beginning of the twentieth century the number of Scottish congregations which had recourse to grape juice at Communion was increasing rapidly, though they were still scarce in the establishment.[11]

If churches as institutions on the whole showed more detachment than individuals did, it was because there was division on the approach to social problems. Probably fewer people in the nineteenth century than in the eighteenth would have preached a purely social gospel, in the sense that concern with material needs should have priority over preaching a gospel related to the needs of the soul; and even fewer in the nineteenth century than in the seventeenth would have wished to take the puritan line of perfecting society by corporate action or by compulsion. The acceptance of the 'gathered congregation' can be seen as a retreat from a grand ideal; was it now acknowledged that the whole of society could not be perfected and that perfection was possible only for a limited few? There was still a question of emphasis. Should efforts be directed at working 'from the outside in' – changing the social and economic order either as an end in itself or with a view to making the individual's path to faith easier – or working 'from the inside out' – changing the hearts of individuals so that a healthier society would emerge? While most Christians assumed a society controlled by Christian standards, could those standards be expected outside the community of the faithful? There was an extreme view that Christian living was a part-time occupation little related to everyday work, but also a more moderate line that faith was a private matter and ethics personal, rather than matters of public policy. The general view probably was that churches should be concerned with the moral and spiritual lives of their members, and be involved in 'politics' not by making official pronouncements but by leaving it to their members to play their parts as citizens.

The one experiment in fusing religious and political involvement was in the Chartist movement in the 1840s. There were some Chartist churches, which aimed at a synthesis of Christianity with political demands which seem modest now – annual parliaments, manhood suffrage, secret ballots in voting, equal electoral districts, no property qualification for MPs, and payment of MPs. Patrick Brewster was the only Church of Scotland minister who associated himself with this cause and he was in trouble with his church courts on that account. If the Church stood aside from Chartism, it was more hostile to socialism. William Denny, who was critical enough of economic selfishness, was one of many who thought socialism was wrong in attempting to change the economic and social framework without changing men's hearts. And it was a commonplace that while Christianity preached that the rich should give to the poor, socialism incited the poor to take from the rich.

At any rate, all denominations did their best to influence men's hearts by providing not only additional churches but Sunday Schools. Starting only at the end of the eighteenth century, Sunday Schools became widespread by about 1840, and by 1861 the number of scholars was put at 292,549. Most congregations also had Bible Classes, Bands of Hope and latterly uniformed youth organisations, as well as associations for adults (including a choir with its weekly practices). A good-going congregation provided a focal point for a lot of activity, and some young people might be in the church premises two or three evenings a week as well as on Sundays.

While social and recreational activities were not overlooked, the period was revolutionary in regard to Christian training. A lady who had been young at the beginning of the century remarked later that in her youth there had been 'no religious instruction, no Sunday School, no church prayer meetings, no preparation for church membership'. She may have been unfortunate, because before her day some ministers had seen to the preparation of communicants and John Willison's *Sacramental Catechism* was still available.[12] Before the end of the nineteenth century the Young Communicants' Class had become usual. As the irregular celebrations of Communion familiar in the seventeenth century gradually gave way to a steady pattern of celebrations two or four times in the year, the routine of preparation was successively modified. Examination of members by minister and elders on visitations ceased to be a requirement before the issue of tokens or Communion Cards, which came to be handed out without any questions being asked. The pre-Communion 'fast day', associated with the Thursday before Communion, which had been usual for generations, degenerated into a mere public holiday and generally disappeared in the early years of the twentieth century. Its place was taken by a 'preparatory service' on the Friday evening before Communion, but this too declined and in many congregations was finally abandoned during World War II; a service of preparation may be held on the previous Sunday.

Some of the effort in the large cities was directed specifically at the slums, and it was common, not least in the Episcopal Church, for well-to-do congregations to devote some of their resources to slum missions which gave material as well as spiritual assistance to the needy – and which could welcome people who would not have felt at home in churches attended by the fashionable. There was inter-denominational missionary activity as well. Apart from the British and Foreign Bible Society (1804), there were local Societies in Glasgow, Port Glasgow and Greenock. The Scottish Bible Society was founded at Edinburgh in 1809 by the Church of Scotland, and the Edinburgh Bible Society by the other churches, the latter to send Bibles overseas.

Current theology was related, directly or indirectly, to missionary work, which, especially in foreign fields, seemed to challenge the concept of Election. Could a missionary do no more than preach that God loved not the whole world but a few men scattered here and there throughout it, for whom He gave His Son, and that there might be some of that favoured number among his hearers? Possibly an important part in bringing about a revulsion against predestination was played by James Hogg's *The Private Memoirs and Confessions of a Justified Sinner* (1824), a terrifying presentation of the mind of a fanatic who was convinced that as he was one of the 'Elect' no action he committed could make him guilty of sin. But evangelism demanded the modification of what had been standard ideas about predestination, and such modification was being advocated.

Thomas Erskine of Linlathen (1788–1870), an Episcopalian layman trained in the law, retired from professional business to live and write on his estate in Angus. He could not accept predestination and Election, he criticised the Church for substituting theological discussion for prayer and adoration and for stressing doctrinal conformity as against the Christian life; he thought the religion of his day was too much a theory or science and too little a matter of personal application.[13] Faith to Erskine was response to the love of God, belief in what Jesus Christ was and did and suffered. He went a long way to rejecting the legalistic view of the Atonement, which he called 'The humanly devised doctrine of substitution'. Christ, he explained, did not suffer the punishment of sin to dispense with our suffering it, but to change the character of our suffering from an unsanctified and unsanctifying suffering into a sanctified and sanctifying suffering. 'I believe', he said, 'that Christ is in every man and that it is His suffering voice which speaks in the conscience of every man. He is suffering for every man that he may bring us back to God'. Some of this, clearly, came close to the best piety of the seventeenth century.

Erskine became involved in meetings which included healing and speaking with tongues, and in this field he was associated with Edward Irving (1792–1834), who was a schoolmaster at Haddington and Kirkcaldy before becoming assistant to Thomas Chalmers at St John's in Glasgow. Irving moved to London, where he was able to strike out along original lines as a popular preacher in churches at Hatton Garden and Regent Square. His increasing detachment from mainstream Christian thought and his obsession with the Second Advent led to his deposition from the ministry (1833). His followers constituted the Catholic Apostolic Church, sometimes known as 'Irvingites', which gained a considerable following in both Scotland and England, partly because it offered an enriched liturgical worship beyond what even the Episcopal Church then offered, and a far more comprehensive Prayer Book, including a Blessing of a Ship, something previously known only in John Carswell's Gaelic translation of the Book of Common Order (1567).

Another well-known figure who, like Irving, repudiated the limited atonement was John MacLeod Campbell (1800–72), minister of Row in Dunbartonshire. He was deposed from his parish in 1831 but continued to preach outwith the Church of Scotland. In *The Nature of the Atonement* Campbell approached the position of Erskine of Linlathen. He held that what Christ suffered is not to be seen in physical pain alone but in the grief which holy love bore for the sins of men – a great grief which has power to work holiness in us and which, when it is received into the heart, punishes sin. This was an approach to the concept of Hell as a state of mind which had come to Robert Bruce about 1600.[14]

The liberal thought of the period produced one new sect which was less eccentric than the Irvingites. James Morison (1816–93), minister of Kilmarnock, was suspended in 1841 after he had written in support of the universal atonement – 'all that Jesus did on Calvary he did for you' – and, in association with other suspended ministers, formed in 1849 an 'Evangelical Union' which became in effect a new Congregational Church.

Fissiparous tendencies had clearly not vanished, and the greatest of all the secessions came with the Disruption of 1843. Accounts of the work of evangelical preachers, especially in the Highlands, in the early nineteenth century, are apt to be presented in the context of the conflict which preceded the Disruption. It is true that most of the leading preachers and many of their hearers did become members of the Free Church, the Highlands showed an overwhelming majority for it and more than a fifth of the ministers who left the established church in 1843 had been in the habit of conducting worship in Gaelic. But it is not easy to disentangle ecclesiastical politics from evangelical zeal. There is no doubt that the genesis of the Disruption is to be found partly in the democratic political tendency of the time, but it is equally true that the secessionists had not been originally concerned with politics: it was because they found that their aims to spread the Gospel at home and abroad were frustrated by conservatives in the courts of the Church that they were driven to attack its constitutional position. (It was noticeable, for example, that the erection of chapels of ease to supplement the parish churches had so little support from the Moderates that down to 1834 only about 63 were sanctioned, whereas thereafter, when the Moderates lost their domination, 222 were authorised in seven years.) Thomas Chalmers, who led the party of rebellion, had no sympathy with secular agitators or with those who proposed to build on the antagonisms of class against class. Like the general assembly in 1800 he feared for the stability of society and thought that sedition and infidelity went hand in hand. He admitted the appeal of foreign missions but pled for the millions in Britain who had never heard the Gospel, which he considered to be the only instrument for the betterment of society. His concentration on faith, in the manner of the sixteenth-century reformers, went to the length of declaring that even if he had persuaded all the sinners in his congregation to give up their sins, yet 'every soul of every hearer' would remain 'in full alienation from God . . . until the free offer of forgiveness through the blood of Christ was urged upon their acceptance, and the Holy Spirit given through the channel of Christ's mediatorship to all who ask Him'.

It is far from easy to evaluate the contribution of the Disruption to religious life. However great one's respect for the men who gave up so much when they left the establishment, it is impossible to avoid seeing the Disruption as a distraction which absorbed a lot of the fervour of the Awakening and diverted it, much as the Covenants had done with the religious vitality of the seventeenth century. At the lowest, thousands of pounds which went to maintain rival churches could have been better disbursed in serving churchless areas, and sometimes three ministers were employed in a parish where all the work could have been done by one.

It may be that, once the crisis of 1843 was over, the Church of Scotland could turn its mind more to the essentials of the faith, while the Free Church still had to harp on ecclesiastical politics to justify its existence. Yet within the infant Free Church there seems to have been a quickening of faith, possibly because of a feeling that the ministers who 'went out' for the sake of principle and at such material cost deserved to be taken seriously. Equally, the financial sacrifice needed to pay for buildings and ministers gave a sense of cohesion and mutual support, though it must be said that outside the north and west Highlands the poor, who found the Auld Kirk less expensive, had little use for the Free Church. The main stream of Free Church theology became liberal, partly through the influence of the evangelical movement in weakening adherence to old dogmas, but it contained a strand of Calvinism, especially in the Highlands.

While the Free Church stood for the principle of establishment, in the sense of state support for (without control over) the Church, in practice the Disruption made it undeniable that church and nation, church and community, could no longer be identified. The Free Church General Assembly had none of the trappings which implied recognition by the civil power, the Senators of the College of Justice could no longer process in unison from their court to the parish church, any more than a town council could be 'kirked' in the traditional manner. The Free Church, despite its pretensions, had something of the character of a gathered congregation and its existence encouraged the concept of the church as a private society, unrelated to the secular community. Possibly people who might have been happier as Baptists or as Plymouth Brethren could find no place for their corporate Christian life except in the Free Church.

The Disruption did little to help Christians to face two challenges which seemed to cut at the roots of their faith. One of them came from science and was far from novel, for earlier discoveries had in their time disturbed traditionalists. In 1785 James Hutton, in his *Theory of the Earth*, put forward geological facts irreconcilable with the opening verses of Genesis, and in the middle of the nineteenth century evolutionary theories created still greater difficulties. Some managed to close their eyes to science or at any rate to hold a kind of dual belief, while others preferred to take their stand on 'the words of Moses'. The versatile Dr Chalmers, while on the whole adhering to the latter view, maintained in 'Astronomical Discourses', which he delivered in the Tron Church in Glasgow on Thursday evenings to crowded audiences, that the vastness of the universe revealed by the telescope was more startling and more impressive than the older theory of the solar system on which scripture seemed to be based. Chalmers argued that the religion of Christ might not be for the dwellers on this planet only, but also for those on other planets; God was not limited, and to think of Him as limited was to reduce Him to human terms and lose sight of the essence of His divinity. James Clerk Maxwell, arguably the greatest British scientist of the nineteenth century, had a deep and orthodox Christian faith in which he saw no conflict with science but rather harmony within God's purposes. And Sir David Brewster, in the tradition of some eighteenth-century thinkers, considered it one of the objects of science to reveal the wonders of God's creation.

On top of the challenge from science came the application of scholarly criticism to the Bible. This was not a novelty either, to the extent at least that some passages in the Bible had been dismissed as absurdities by Origen in the third century,[15] and there had been a good deal of criticism of standard beliefs about the Incarnation and the Resurrection in the eighteenth century. One issue was, quite simply, whether the books of the Bible should be treated as historians treat other historical texts. The man in the street, who knew nothing of historical method and had never stopped to think what evidence he had for the existence of Robert Bruce or William Wallace, was shaken when he was told that the Gospels were not contemporary evidence. No one took the trouble to remind him - seldom does anyone even now take the trouble - that the Epistles, if not the Gospels, were closer to Our Lord's own day than Barbour's *Bruce* was to the lifetime of its hero.

But could the Bible still be 'the Word of God'? William Robertson Smith, Professor of Hebrew at the Free Church College in Aberdeen, wrote in the *Encyclopaedia Britannica* in 1875: 'The true idea of revelation is such an activity of God among and towards men as shall enable man to apprehend God in His holiness, justice and redemptive love, just by the same kind of experience as enables us to know our fellow men. It is the record of such revelation that lies before us in Holy Scriptures'. Smith was suspended in 1877 and deposed in 1881, but other views went far beyond his. Edward Caird (1825–1908), Master of Balliol, a brother of John Caird (1820–1898) and like him a Gifford Lecturer, had no place for Christ as God and Man or a member of a Trinity, but saw Him as no more than a symbol of the unity of God and Man, and the Incarnation as merely a kind of metaphor of what may happen in any man (a view to which Henry Scougal had approached). Others declared that Jesus became the Redeemer simply because he understood redemption in a moral sense, that Paul had derived his ideas not from what Christ had done but from his own mystical experience, and that he had borrowed the concept of sacraments from contemporary mystery religions. James Denney (1856–1917), a professor at the Free Church College in Glasgow, in his *Jesus and the Gospel*, wrote that few things in the history of Christian thinking 'are more extraordinary than the progeny of this ambiguous idea of satisfaction' [by Christ for the sins of men]. He thought that the Virgin Birth, the sharing of substance between the Son and the Father and the personality of the Holy Spirit were legitimate matters for speculation but should have no place in any formal profession of faith. Denney was echoing Erskine of Linlathen and MacLeod Campbell and might have spoken, like H. G. Wells, of 'the Miltonic fable of the offended Father and the sacrificial Son', but Wells did not profess to be a Christian. The dual challenge of science and criticism made adherence to the literal sense of the Confession untenable and one church after another, beginning with the United Presbyterians in 1879, passed a Declaratory Act qualifying the terms in which ministers subscribed it; when the Free Church did so in 1892 a party of conservatives left to found the Free Presbyterian Church, which, even more than the Free Church itself, had its strength in the west Highlands, where predestination may have made a special appeal to the fatalistic outlook of the natives.

Before the nineteenth century was out it was becoming commonplace in academic circles that the Fall was unhistorical, the concept of the Atonement an interpretation of Christ's importance as a moral teacher and neither the Virgin Birth nor the Resurrection a necessary article of faith. Some now seem to think that such ideas were invented by the Bishop of Durham within the last ten years. I heard them all – along with the notion of the Motherhood of God – in a Bible Class held by a Church of Scotland minister in the 1920s.

Many of the products of the parish schools and later the board schools knew enough to learn of the challenge presented by the scientists and the critics but not enough to know of the valid defences, and they surrendered too easily to the notion that the basis of the Christian faith had been cut away. While debates about science, criticism and the Atonement interested professionals, it may be that most ordinary worshippers or non-worshippers were more affected by the conflict between the Free Church and the Establishment. Yet on the whole the dogmatic content in the teaching which was disseminated was dwindling. A generation earlier a Scot who was asked about the faith might have tried to answer in terms of the Shorter Catechism, but by the early twentieth century he would have been more likely to reply that Jesus had taught a good way of life which would in time transform the world and that the Church was obscuring this simple message with complex doctrines.

The challenge of scientific disclosures and biblical criticism provoked – or stimulated, or inspired – evangelical preaching of an uncommon intensity. Cheaper printing and wider literacy took the preachers' message, in tract form, to those their voices did not reach, the train conveyed them and their hearers across countries, the steamship conveyed preachers from continent to continent. From one continent to another came Americans, who had not grown up among debates about ecclesiastical politics and ancient rivalries. Dwight Lyman Moody (1837–99) and Ira David Sankey (1840–1908) came together to England and

Scotland in 1872-5 and again in 1881-4. The Englishman Charles Haddon Spurgeon (1834-92) had less direct influence on Scotland, but the organisation which he built up in England for training preachers and distributing literature made its mark, and his name was revered for a couple of generations. A Scottish follower of Moody and Sankey was Henry Drummond (1851-97), a Free Churchman who explored in Africa, accepted the findings of science, held a chair of natural science in a Free Church College, expounded evangelical faith in *The Greatest Thing in the World*, conducted missions in universities and toured colleges in America and Australia. Probably most of the missionaries' converts were already nominally Christian, but the preaching did reach unbelievers and it penetrated to the roots of society in working-class areas in the towns, left its mark in some of the fishing ports of the east coast and had a more limited influence in some mining communities.

Important legacies from Moody and Sankey were those best-sellers *Sacred Songs and Solos* and *Redemption Songs* and the use of American organs to accompany their rousing tunes. The fervour of earlier periods had found no vocal expression save in metrical psalms, which, even when they were 'baptized' by the addition of the doxology (as they were from the reformation until the Covenanting ascendancy) were not Christian. The English nonconformist Richard Baxter (1615-91), author of *The Saint's Everlasting Rest* (1660), wrote hymns and was an enthusiast for hymn-singing, but his Scottish contemporaries spurned the 'hymns and spiritual songs' which should have accompanied the psalms (Ephesians v, 19; Colossians iii, 16). The 'Paraphrases' (half of them of passages from the New Testament) appeared in 1781 but received only a cool reception from the general assembly. Glassites had used hymns from the 1720s, Methodists from their early days and Episcopalians from the 1780s, and the Relief Church, liberal as always, authorised a Hymn Book in 1792. Presbyterians might compose hymns – as James Hogg did[16] – but the Church of Scotland did not authorise *The Scottish Hymnal* until 1870, followed by the Free Church in 1881; then the Free Church, the Church of Scotland and the United Presbyterians agreed on a *Scottish Church Hymnary* in 1898. The 'official' hymnaries were more restrained in their words and music than those prepared by evangelists, but they drew on a wide range of Christian hymnody representing the devotion of the centuries. The *Revised Church Hymnary*, which held the field for nearly fifty years in the twentieth century, had many items from both evangelicals and Tractarians in England – 30 from the Wesleys and 23 from J. M. Neale – but items from Scottish hands, except those of Horatio Bonar (1808-89), were hard to find, though they included some favourites. Mission-churches and halls tended to prefer *Redemption Songs*, and it was not unknown for a parish church to use that book on Sunday evenings, when the service had a 'gospel' flavour, intended for the less committed. It has been said that it is from hymns that worshippers get their theology, and the introduction and popularity of hymns gave the man in the pew something to add warmth to mere intellectual conviction and to replace the conservative theology of the Shorter Catechism. There was inevitably opposition. Begg thought the demand for hymns 'one of the most dangerous symptoms of the times', and the rump of the Free Church which survived after 1900 decided to adhere to the psalms.

Late nineteenth-century evangelism left its mark on a number of individuals in the main Presbyterian churches, but led many into the Baptist Church or one or other of the groups of Plymouth Brethren, who presented the most clearly recognisable re-creation (at least since the days of John Glas) of the primitive church of the days of the apostles – the gathered congregation *par excellence*. The movement contributed also to the growth of another English import, the Salvation Army. The 'Army' was unique in rejecting the sacraments and in combining concern for the individual soul with concern for the welfare of the needy and, with the visual and aural impression made by its bands and its military paraphernalia, had an ethos at the opposite pole from the withdrawn, self-contained piety of the Brethren.

The welfare work of the Army fitted into the growing emphasis on 'the social gospel' which affected most churches, but, except in the Army, this tended to lessen the significance attached to the traditional gospel message. Both Liberal and Conservative parties (wooing an electorate enlarged in 1867 and again in 1884) were passing legislation designed to benefit the 'working' class, and the emerging Labour party was proclaiming its dedication exclusively to the wellbeing of one section of society. Probably not for the first time, and assuredly not for the last, some churchmen were 'climbing on to the bandwagon' of fashionable political ideology and aligning themselves with one class.

In the earlier part of the century the imperfection of the parish system had led not only to a lack of Christian teaching and a dwindling of Christian faith but also to complications for such a traditional work of charity as the care of the poor. As late as 1818 the general assembly congratulated itself, with justifiable pride, on the work done for the relief of poverty by the unpaid labours of ministers and elders, but the system was hopelessly inadequate in the squalor of the slums. Thomas Chalmers, as minister of St John's in Glasgow, was determined to reactivate traditional local benevolence and show that even a congregation where only a handful of the people were other than 'working' class could be organised for its own poor and the education of its children. The scheme operated after a fashion, but only with some harshness in administration, and not long after Chalmers left the system was dismantled because voluntary charity proved insufficient. A little ironically, it was Chalmers' own action in founding the Free Church which was the last straw for the creaking old system, since parish church collections – already diminished as a result of earlier secessions – now fell disastrously. Two years after the Disruption poor relief was in effect secularised and the Church at last lost the prime place it had had in that field.

Despite the new Poor Law, there was still ample scope for voluntary effort. Little might be done for the hardened criminal or for the pauper who was the victim of his own improvidence or drunkenness, but children brought up in scarcity and squalor might be rescued. Sheriff Watson in Aberdeen and Dr Thomas Guthrie (a parish minister who 'went out' in 1843 and served in a Free Church at Castlehill in Edinburgh) started 'Ragged Schools' which attended to the physical as well as the mental development of children, at least to the extent of providing some food – 'soup-kitchen schools' they were sometimes called. As an organiser of non-sectarian schools for poor children Guthrie was famed throughout Britain, and it is an indication of the esteem which he won that a volume by him, with the unpromising title *The Gospel in Ezekiel*, sold 50,000 copies.

The education of the young, like the relief of the poor, was an age-old sphere of Christian activity, but, while the Church provided most of the poor's fund, the financing of parish schools had been laid on the heritors, and the Church's function was one mainly of supervision, partly to ensure orthodoxy. While there were various endowed schools, a number of schools founded by the SSPCK and other societies and many 'Adventure schools' – i.e., private ventures – the first major change came after the Disruption, when the Free Church, opposed to the establishment's privileges, set up its own schools, to the number of 712 by 1851. The Church of Scotland, Free Church, Roman Catholics and Episcopalians also established their own Training Colleges. All in all there may have been as many as 5000 schools in the country, educating probably four-fifths of the children, before the act of 1872 declared (not, as too often said, 'made', which it did not succeed in doing) schooling compulsory. It also transferred responsibility for oversight from the Church to elected school boards, superseded in 1918 by education authorities and in 1929 by committees of city and county councils. Supervision was carried out by Inspectors appointed by a national Education Department, but the Churches continued to have some voice through representatives on the school boards and their successors. Roman Catholic and Episcopalian Schools were brought into this system in 1918, with safeguards (which in the case of the latter proved illusory) to preserve their sectarian character. The denominational schools were important missionary agencies, but even in the non-denominational schools the tenets of the Westminster Assembly continued until about 1920 to be instilled through the medium of the Shorter Catechism (sometimes printed in convenient booklets which contained also the multiplication tables).

The bulk of material for the nineteenth century, and its variety and complexity, create difficulties about generalising as to whether Christianity was in a healthy state. Contemporaries took divergent views. Two ministers writing in the *New Statistical Account* in the 1840s were confident that there had been a decline in religion: 'A spirit of indifference prevails among the rising generation that painfully contrasts with that which... animated their fathers.... To be without the profession of religion was then a contemptible singularity; now it is very common, and little marked'. But Henry Cockburn, in *Memorials of his Time* (1856), was not so sure: 'Certain persons represent Scotland, particularly Edinburgh, as having been about the beginning of this century very irreligious, ... generally infidel. Religion is certainly more the fashion than it used to be... the general mass of the religious public has been enlarged. On the other hand, ... one half of some religious persons assure us religion is now almost extinct. My opinion is that the balance is in favour of the present time.... The very freedom... of conversation and views on sacred subjects [at the beginning of the century] would have excited the horror of those who give the tone on these matters at present'.

At the end of yet another century, we can see that the picture of the nineteenth bristles with paradoxes and contradictions. The facts and figures about behaviour suggest that moral standards may have been lower than in any earlier period. The effect of the challenge of science and biblical criticism led a writer in 1882 to observe that 'never, since the suppression of pagan philosophers, was Christianity attacked more than it is now'.[17] But he was discussing the views of J. S. Mill, who had argued for the paradox of what he called 'the enlivening influence of negation', and the fact that both in its early years and towards its end the century showed response to challenge, in two waves of powerful evangelism, the second of which may have spread warm Christian convictions more widely than ever before. Nor is it difficult to pick out illustrations of the extent to which Christian principles penetrated at all social levels. Anyone who is familiar – and who is not? – with the ideology of organised labour in the twentieth century can only look with something like admiring astonishment at what happened when the Bell Rock lighthouse was under construction between 1806 and 1811: the workers, with a good deal of reluctance, agreed to work on Sundays in such a good cause – *but only on condition that they did not receive extra payment*![18] How evangelical preaching made its mark is illustrated by John Galt in *The Entail* (1823):

> I hae sinned wi' my e'en open, and I thought to mak up for't by a strict observance o' church ordinances.... There are few shorter roads to the pit than through the kirk-door; and many a Christian has been brought nigh to the death, thinking himself cheered and guided by the sound o' gospel preaching, when a' the time his ear was tuned to the sough o' perdition.[19]

We learn of a working man who never left home in the morning without saying, as he went out of the front door,

> Forth in Thy name, O lord, I go,
> My daily labours to pursue,
> Thee, only thee, resolved to know,
> In all I think or speak or do.

Ideas about both church membership and church attendance are sometimes wildly adrift and often misleading. In the middle of the century, when Edinburgh's population was about 160,000, the numbers claiming a church connection were appreciably less, and attendance amounted to only about a fifth of the population. The census of church attendance over the whole country in 1851 showed the percentage of population attending church as 32.7 in the morning, 21.5 in the afternoon and 6.5 in the evening; how many attended more than once is not stated. In 1881, when enumerators took up their stances at church doors, only 16 per cent of the people of Glasgow were at church. Sunday labour had always been a problem, particularly in mills and salt works, but the development of the economy increased it, and the sense of the sanctity of the 'Sabbath' declined.

The one thing that was still abundantly clear in mid-century is that had everyone wanted to go to church there would not have been room for them all in the parish churches (which in theory everyone had a right to attend). In Edinburgh in mid-century the sittings would have accommodated only about one in three of the population. In larger towns, where different classes tended to live in different areas, the well-to-do could afford to be adequately churched and the poor might go without. However, intense ecclesiastical competition, allied to optimism, ambition and ostentation, added enormously to the capacity. At the opening assembly of the Free Church, Chalmers intimated that £232,000 had been raised or promised, and in less than two years £366,000 was raised. Within ten years the Free Church's stock had grown to about 859 churches, mostly with manses (of which by 1870 there were 719, at a cost of £467,000). By that time there were estimated to be seats for 63 per cent of the whole population of the country.

It was not long before it became evident that, despite the very real expansion of Christianity in the later part of the century, there were contrary elements which so added to indifference and infidelity that the supply of churches exceeded the demand. In 1872 it was reported that in a parish with 1850 people only 800 claimed a church connection. A report in the 1880s declared that in 706 parish churches there were 680,000 members and adherents but only 175,000 of them had communicated during the year. In the 1890s it was reported that in the presbytery of Haddington a third to a half of the Protestants did not attend church and 'indifference prevails to a large extent'; the minister of a rural parish in the north-east said 'there is scarcely one farm servant who attends church in my parish'; in a mining parish in Fife three quarters of the people were said to have lapsed; in one area of Glasgow five out of seven of the non-Roman population had no church connection. Other reports told of parishioners who were 'ignorant, licentious and profane' and there was much talk of 'heathenism', which was said to be 'as hard in the rural districts as in the lanes and closes of large towns'.[20] Farm labourers were often singled out for mention: one reason may have been that they moved from job to job at term time and lost touch with both church and community. One comment (from the Free Church side) was that most of them belonged nominally to the established church but their condition was slipping into that of the masses in the towns, and a United Presbyterian report declared them as non-churchgoing as the miners. It was not long before the supply of churches was seen to be excessive. In 1889 a church newspaper observed: 'In some of our large towns the actual church building accommodation provided... is much in excess of any reasonable needs';[21] and in 1893 the author of *The Churches and the Churchless in Scotland* remarked on 'the beggarly array of empty pews which chill the hearts of so many ministers and church members'.

8

INTO A SECULAR AGE?

'That which hath been is now; and that which is to be hath already been'
Ecclesiastes iii, 15

Before the twentieth century was far advanced many thought they could see the writing on the wall for Christianity, at least as their fathers had understood it or as evangelists presented it. The First World War, though a shattering blow to the optimism about progress which had prevailed before 1914 and, some thought, an argument for atheism, does not in itself seem to have had a very damaging effect, and indeed as it demonstrated the futility of human effort it encouraged an appeal to the Divine, resulting in a small increase in church membership. After the war there was a certain amount of local revivalism (without much encouragement from most churches) and some mission work continued which served some of the poor and the unemployed who could not afford church membership or appear in 'Sunday clothes'. (Seat rents, it should be recalled, were still general until the 1930s.) On the whole there was much anxiety, and a 'Recall to Religion', using the new medium of broadcasting, was a flop. The Union of 1929, which brought together the Church of Scotland and nearly all of the United Free Church, had little effect, probably because by that time few people in either denomination realised what was keeping them apart and fewer appreciated the enormous financial sacrifice which the Church of Scotland was making.

World War II, while it might fill churches for occasional 'Days of Prayer', was fought at a lower spiritual temperature than World War I and (despite the conventional blessings on British arms) with a certain amount of cynicism. There was a decline in church membership, it was obvious that there was a lowering of moral standards and it was noticed that chaplains in the forces seemed to be social welfare officers rather than spiritual guides. After the war there were various organised campaigns of evangelism: visits by American evangelists; a Tell Scotland campaign; Kirk Weeks; local efforts. And churches were not laggard in providing material resources: in a dozen years (1948–59) the Church of Scotland completed 129 buildings (some of them dual-purpose hall-churches, the dimensions of which were said to be determined by those of a badminton court) and other denominations expanded in proportion. The number of communicants in the Church of Scotland recovered its 1938 level in 1959 – only to resume almost at once a rapid decline. The general impression seems to have been that none of the campaigns led to sustained results, and some of the new buildings have found it hard to survive in the face of the epidemic of vandalism which has swept the country.

Curiously enough, in the period when committed church membership was falling, the Church was in demand as never before for family occasions. Burial services had crept back in the nineteenth century, and now they were increasingly held in churches or crematoria and not in homes; infants were far more frequently brought to church for baptism instead of being baptised at home; and marriages were more frequently in church than in a house or hotel. (The second and third of those changes were in accordance with the wishes of the reformers, the first contrary to them.) But between 1967 and 1982 there was a spectacular decline in baptisms in both the Church of Scotland and the Roman Catholic Church and it was noticeable that the proportion of marriages taking place in Registrars' Offices was consistently increasing – a testimony if nothing else to a growth in sincerity. In 1985 the Church of Scotland commented on 'secularisation and a continuing and significant decline in the membership of the Church'. Was Scotland becoming a secular society in which ideas of the supernatural and of revelation, miracles, redemption, eternal life, found no place?

Faith is not and never has been quantifiable. Church membership and attendance (which are far from being reliable thermometers of the spiritual temperature) are quantifiable and to some extent explicable. One minor factor in the decline, assuredly not a novel one though it may have operated on a wider and more organised scale in the twentieth century than ever before, was the movement of population consequent on re-housing. People who were pillars of the church when they lived in one of the older residential districts of a town gave up churchgoing on moving to a new housing area on the outskirts, though sometimes remaining nominal members of the church they now stayed away from.

A far more important factor, largely a novel one, is that in the complexities of modern life churchgoing has far more competitors than it used to have. There are competitors for time, in a range of activities now available as never before on Sundays as on other days – activities which mean leisure for some, but (it is too often overlooked) work for others. Churches themselves used to lead in the provision of facilities for leisure activities, but they cannot complete with organisations financed by local or central government, and in any event the focus of some leisure activities has moved from the parish to larger centres. Far from church attendance being in any way a matter of social conformity, it is now considered eccentric.

Further competition came from the media, especially television, that novel means of communication which uses all manner of gimmicks to capture the attention, even if for only about three minutes at a time, and never uses the spoken word without lavish illustrated matter. The moving picture is the chief means of spreading information in this post-literate age (comparable, as suggested in chapter 3, to the pre-literate middle ages). The nearest parallel in the past to the introduction of broadcasting was perhaps the invention of printing. But printing did not arrive in a partially secularised society; it was used by both the unreformed church and the reformed church (which abandoned symbolism for the printed word), and it did a lot to nourish religion. What was true of printing was at first true also of what we called 'the wireless' when it arrived in the 1920s, for religious material played a large part in it, the programmes were all set in the context of practising Christianity and it proved a valuable instrument for strengthening, if not extending, Christian belief. But sound radio and television alike have now largely ceased to be actively Christian and are sometimes positively anti-Christian and anti-moral. The revived importance of visual aids, often taking the form of plays, is indeed an opportunity for religious as well as secular drama, and there have been some impressive efforts, but it is hard to know how much influence they have on the unconverted, in the midst of so many rival programmes. A child can now hear the name of his Saviour 'on the lips of profane swearers' without leaving his own fireside, to which the profanity comes from the broadcasting agencies. The printed book is outdated, television is designed largely for the illiterate, and, all else apart, how can the average or even more than average preacher, like the average or more than average lecturer, compete with the professional communicators on the small screen with all the effects they have at their disposal? The Church is not accommodating itself to this. True, videos can be prepared, and have their use, but are not likely often to reach the eyes of the unconverted.

But supposing the Church was no mere suppliant for time 'on the air' and had free access to the media now available, what use would it make of them? All the signs are that the Church is unsure of itself, that it has somehow lost its way, so far at least as religious teaching is concerned. Nearly seventy years ago a Report framed by the principal of a Scottish divinity college spoke of 'a dim and instinctive theism which is the working faith of perhaps the majority of the youth of this nation'.[1] More recently someone wrote not of a dim theism but of a non-militant atheism, by which he presumably meant an atheism of indifference, an atheism which dismisses religion as merely irrelevant. However, if atheists no longer feel any need to be militant it may be because Christians on their side are less militant, less positive, whether in doctrine or in moral teaching, than they were say a hundred years ago, though the need to be positive is now so much greater.

The lack of positive affirmation of the faith takes different forms. There is, not only among church members, but among those to whom they might look for leadership, scepticism and more than scepticism about some central doctrines and about clauses of the Creed – no novelty, but more widespread. There was a time when those who were disturbed by the 'modernism' of the Church of Scotland could and did take refuge in the Episcopal Church, where – whatever eccentricities might from time to time issue from the pulpit – the Liturgy could be relied on to proclaim in unambiguous terms, Sunday by Sunday, the essentials of the Christian faith. But now the Prayer Book has been largely discarded and from the current 'Scottish Liturgy 1982' there was deliberately eliminated the whole concept of sacrifice. The faith of the saints has been set aside.

The discarding of the concept of sacrifice – which means of the Atonement – goes along with the discarding of the concept of sin, the lack of any differentiation between good and evil. In the past it was only too obvious that men so often knew the good and chose the evil, but they did know the difference. Now very often they do not, and, what is worse, they are sometimes taught that evil is good. It is some years since psychology was brought into service to explain – or explain away – human wrongdoing. I recall as a child hearing many times from the pulpit, 'The psychologists tell us that...', and in 1930 a leading divine, John White, saw 'the new psychology' along with 'an unquestioning rationalism and Hedonism' as the foundation of contemporary attitudes.[2] The Church has not only – and this would have been bad enough – done its best to accommodate fashionable 'permissiveness' but countenances what would not long ago have been regarded as deadly sins. There are those who think that ordinands should not be required to repent and renounce their sins before being commissioned as ministers, and a priest can write a newspaper article defending homosexual acts (*The Scotsman*, 9 March 1989). It appears, from an actual case, that a priest who rebukes a sinner is liable to be haled before a European Court for breaking the Human Rights Convention, which states that 'Everyone has the right to respect for his private life'.[3] It was startling one morning, listening to 'Thought for the Day' on Radio 4, to hear the speaker, an English divine, tell a story which started with a man going into a church: 'It must have been an old-fashioned church', said the speaker, 'for they read the Ten Commandments'. Anyone inclined to dismiss the Commandments as 'Old Testament stuff' would do well to look at Galatians v, study the list there of 'the works of the flesh' and lay alongside them modern ways of life – not only personal morals but the policies of political parties and other corporate bodies: 'hatred, variances, emulations, wrath, strife, envyings'. A sense of guilt, or at best inadequacy, going back to the Hebrew prophets, should remain embedded in Christian teaching. The prophets, when faced with doom, did not proclaim their righteousness, but asked, 'What are the sins of Israel?'

In the nineteenth century the Church was confronted not only with sin but with the findings of science, and reached an accommodation with them in which some saw the triumph of contemporary science over religion. Later scientific developments, however, seem capable of being used to gain a greater understanding of concepts which have been traditional among Christians. As matter is no longer thought indestructible (as it used to be), both the beginning and the end of Creation take on a novel shape and the Day of Doom looks not only less improbable but perhaps less remote. The idea that matter consists not of solid substance but of discrete particles offers a new interpretation of the concept of the Church as the Body of Christ. Other discoveries in physics offer, if not a new understanding of, at least a fresh field for speculation about, the Resurrection and the nature of Our Lord's Risen Body. Those who have digested modern physics and have also come to terms with the marvels of computers may have a fuller appreciation of what is meant by omniscience. Yet the Church seems to have done little to use modern science and it allows people to remain under the impression that our fathers' science demolished our grandfathers' religion.

Sin, scepticism and science are not new problems. But in the third quarter of the twentieth century Christianity encountered a quite new challenge. To the competition, already mentioned, for time and in communication, there was added competition from other faiths within Britain, especially Islam, Buddhism, Hinduism. This novelty is of more limited importance in Scotland than in some other parts of Britain, where Christians hardly dare proclaim their faith, while the followers of other religions enjoy protection and privileges: legislation designed to suppress discrimination on grounds of race has had the effect of denying freedom of speech to Christians. In England a chief constable was nearly hounded out of office because he dared to uphold Christian morality. The overall result, to some extent even in Scotland, has been to spread the notion that 'anything goes' in the religious field, to dilute – if there was much left to dilute – the Christian character of schools, and to pull the carpet from the feet of anyone proposing missionary work.

But if the Church, in relation to sin and science, has lost its way so far as religious and moral teaching is concerned, yet, by a curious paradox, some leading churchmen are supremely confident about everything else. They may regard the events of Our Lord's life and death as no more than metaphors, even to the extent of equating His Resurrection with a political revolution in some faraway country. Yet they dogmatise with easy assurance on what are often called political and social questions but which are usually really economic questions about which skilled economists are in dispute. Thus they ignore the warning given in the seventeenth century that although the Church had 'the keys of authority' she had not 'the keys of knowledge' and could 'in many ways err, especially when she meddleth with matters which are not within her horizon',[4] and the warning given in the eighteenth century by an English bishop – it was the Bishop of Durham curiously enough – that a Christian society should not 'meddle with things foreign to their proper business'.[5] And they speak confidently about secular events in any of the seven continents – ignoring the old aphorism *Ne sim curiosus in aliena republica,* which meant that one should mind one's own business so far as the internal affairs of a foreign country are concerned. 'Views and statements come thick and fast on every subject from poll tax to pit strike, from apartheid to Armageddon, from Mandela to multilateralism'.[6] Those who seek guidance on faith and morals feel betrayed, while left-wingers who seek ecclesiastical backing for their agitation find it readily. The Victorians, although there were centuries of Christian history against them, apparently felt that Christianity was compatible only with a society based on liberal democratic principles, but now Marxism or something like it has replaced liberal democracy.

Ecclesiastical spokesmen are ready with denunciations of any motes of selfishness and greed in right-wing policies or in the activities of capitalists, but fail to see the beams in the eyes of socialists whose creed is just as likely to promote the envy, hatred, malice and all uncharitableness from which, when we said the Litany, we used to pray to be delivered, or in the eyes of trade unionists whose slogan is 'a fair day's work for a fair day's pay' but whose incessant demands for less work and more pay look like the avarice and sloth which used to be reckoned among the seven deadly sins. Some said that the Conservative party was the Church of England at prayer; it would be truer now to say that the World Council of Churches looks like a revived Comintern at prayer. In 1988 the World Council of Churches, on the recommendation of the British Council of Churches, made a grant of £4200 to the families and supporters of persons convicted of the murder of a British police constable. Of course the fates of David Beaton and James Sharp, as well as similar crimes in other countries, show that it is no novelty for churchmen to approve assassination (which in this case the B.C.C. described weakly as 'a dreadful thing to happen'), but an attempt to protest against the grant was blocked on the ground that it might be 'construed as libellous'.[7] (It may be added that the Ayatollah Khomeini, in inciting the murder of Salman Rushdie, was following in the steps of sixteenth-century popes, including the one who declared that anyone assassinating Elizabeth Tudor would gain merit.)

Ecclesiastical approval of war has become as selective as approval of murder. During World War I and after it – as so many war memorials testify – few doubted that the sacrifice of life had been justified, and the pagan belief that it is honourable to die for one's country was fortified by the Gospel: 'Greater love hath no man than this, that a man lay down his life for his friends'. But that war had been 'a war to end wars', and after it both governments and individuals made various declarations renouncing war as an instrument of policy. Pacifism was less intense after World War II, and the distinction between 'conventional' and nuclear weapons led to an increase of nuclear disarmers rather than of out-and-out pacifists. More recently a fresh distinction has arisen. Jingoists used to be reproached for proclaiming 'My country, right or wrong', but there are now many who seem to believe 'My country always wrong' and would see neither Christian nor pagan justification for old-fashioned patriotism. Perhaps the selfish materialism of left-wing economics leaves no room for idealism or sacrifice.

The fashionable preoccupation of many church leaders can hardly be termed theology; it might better be termed geology, for it is terrestrial, it is about the world, not about God. It certainly amounts to an acceptance that, despite what Our Lord said, His kingdom is a kingdom of this world. C. S. Lewis remarked, 'If you read history, you will find that the Christians who did most for the present world were those who thought most of the next. . . . It is since Christians have largely ceased to think of the other world that they have become so ineffective in this.'[8] The tension is between the eternal and the temporal. Yet a divine of the 'geological' school went so far as to say that 'to place oneself in the perspective of the Kingdom means to participate in the struggle for liberation of those oppressed by others'.[9] This, it may be presumed, is 'liberation theology'. The 'this-worldly' approach was set forth in singularly brutal terms by Dr Ian Fraser, a 'research consultant with the Scottish Churches Council', in an article in *The Scotsman* on 7 March 1989. Controverting a writer who had remarked that Christianity 'sets out the path that mankind must take to get to Heaven', he proceeded: 'Who ever claimed that Christianity was a kind of manifesto or blueprint? It is light for living, in home, neighbourhood, nation, world'. Dr Fraser, scoffing at the idea of 'getting to Heaven', asked in 'what Victorian Sunday School' his opponent had been reared, and concluded that the Christian faith is 'about persons-in-community'. Thus the faith of the saints is discarded.

In different terms, the emphasis is on men's bodies, not on their souls. Like much else, tension between the two is nothing new, for it goes back to the beginnings of Christianity, perhaps to Our Lord's own temptations. One can certainly see the 'this worldly' as opposed to 'other worldly' in Judas, who thought that the costly ointment, instead of being used as a sign of love for God, should be sold for the benefit of the poor. Judas may be the patron of the 'geologists', but no amount of antiquity makes a heresy respectable. Perhaps the Church now concentrates on bodies because it has lost the ability to save souls. Christianity does not disapprove of the body, for God took human form – but in a body without sin, so that the Incarnation does not mean that Christianity approves of the sin in the body. The Incarnation, which meant that God experienced bodily needs, might indeed support James Begg's contention, in justifying his crusade against bad housing, that 'the physical circumstances of the people are matters with which we have much to do'. But concentration on bodies means concentration on the material, and this lies behind recent developments in worship, from which the numinous has been largely effaced and everything reduced to an ordinary, flat, everyday level. Even the Nativity narrative, if read from some modern version of the Bible, sounds just like a commonplace occurrence, stripped of the miraculous and the unique.

Should 'the Church' try to shape government policy through pronouncements by leading clerics or leave it to members, each according to his own judgment in the light of the Christian faith which the Church has nourished in him, to exert influence through the ballot box or other lawful means? If the Church cares for the souls of its members, they can care for the bodies of others. Individual Christians should not be denied their rights as citizens by self-appointed 'spokesmen' who resemble the 'presumptuous churchmen' who, as Drummond of Hawthornden put it, 'assume the power of kings to govern states'. Such 'spokesmen' take upon themselves to dictate that the policy of one particular political party has an exclusive right to the support of Christians, and their arrogance, far from unifying church members, is divisive and actually drives people away. If Christians have never been unanimous about theology, why should they be unanimous about economics?

On religious and moral issues the Church used to operate in its own sphere and could take direct action. It also operated in its own parts of the social and economic field, especially education and poor relief. Education was largely laicised at the reformation, it was nationalised in the nineteenth century, it has been largely secularised in the twentieth. Few would now contend that there should be ecclesiastical or theological control over all education and over the direction of the lives of the young, but a critic might now complain of the lack not only of ecclesiastical or theological control but of moral control. A church which has been ousted by the omnicompetent politicians from its functions in poor relief and education (through statutes) and from a lot of social activities (through financial pressure), and which has now abdicated some of its functions in its own field of faith and morals, has had to seek new roles. One role it has found has been that of an additional arm of social welfare (instead of insisting that the agencies paid by the state should be effective). It is hard to see a clear Christian motivation for the 'social welfare' activities of the Church nowadays, for the ideas on which they are based – justice, compassion and so forth – are not specifically Christian but could – and do – motivate pagans. 'Good works' are not performed now, as they were in the middle ages, for the good of the soul and as a way to salvation. The man who wrote 'It is practical religion, not theological disquisitions, that can fill the churches or keep them full'[10] did not, by 'practical religion', mean practising Christianity.

The other role the Church has adopted is that of a pressure group, offering advice and criticism. A church can of course lobby, like any other group: a former Secretary of State for Scotland said that the Roman Catholic Church was expert in lobbying, and credited it with considerable influence.[11] To offer advice and criticism is nothing new, in principle if not in practice. There was never any doubt about the Church's *concern* for the work of the government in serving godly ends:

the Book of Common Prayer's petition that the sovereign 'may truly and indifferently minister justice to the punishment of wickedness and vice and to the maintenance of God's true religion and virtue' was echoed in the Book of Common Order's prayer that the king 'may in such sort execute his office that Thy religion may be purely maintained, manners reformed and sin punished, according to the precise rule of Thy holy word'. Those who seek to justify the Church's meddling in 'politics' can recall that in the middle ages the Church was not merely a pressure group but was a partner in government and that after the reformation it made its voice heard, even on social and economic issues, in accordance with the dictum of the Second Book of Discipline that 'the ministers teach the magistrates how the civil jurisdiction should be exercised'. However, those who framed that clause never envisaged anything like the complications of twentieth-century economics and the ramifications of government activity. It will be observed, too, that they wrote of the ministers instructing the magistrates and said nothing about the activities of laymen other than the magistrates. One of the lessons of the nineteenth century was that individual Christians could achieve a lot on their own initiative, in the face of torpid churches. In the twentieth century, when many a layman is far better qualified than the average minister to adjudge current issues, 'The Church' can have a role other than the issue of pronouncements by clerical 'spokesmen'. If there is any hope now or in the future that the Church can so impress itself on the community that the gospel becomes the rule of society it is more likely to happen through the leavening influence of individual Christians than through such pronouncements.

As the mainstream churches are immersed in those new roles, 'the hungry sheep' who seek the Gospel but 'are not fed' tend to go elsewhere, and there have been developments in other organisations – some of them with long established traditions of their own, others of recent origin, some representing deviation from any previous norm, others concentrating on an evangelical message. Despair over the roles of the mainstream churches has not, however, led, as it might have, to a revival of the 'religious life', for monastic orders complain of a sharp decline in the number of vocations. What seems to be happening is that some who despair of organisations which subordinate the spiritual to the material withdraw into 'gathered congregations' which are neither given to assertion in the economic or political field nor satisfied with watered-down Christianity. Such bodies flourish, while many congregations of the Church of Scotland have been absorbed in 'unions', with the result that in Edinburgh, where that Church had 156 congregations in 1949, it has now only 95, and, as a feature of the landscape, becomes ever less conspicuous as buildings are secularised or demolished. The alignment of the Church's 'spokesmen' with a political party subjects the Church to the fluctuations of that party's fortunes, and if its policies are repeatedly rejected by the United Kingdom's electorate then the Church, already declining in its own sphere and now excluded from effective political influence, may slip into pessimism.

Some old questions remain. Is the Church to be an association of first-class Christians, purified by the exclusion of the imperfect, or are the wheat and tares to grow together until the harvest? Is the Church a school for sinners or an exclusive society of saints? It is not easy for a gathered congregation to avoid giving the impression that Christianity is only for the few – perhaps for The Elect. It may be that it is enthusiastic extremists who cannot distinguish between heavenly perfection and earthly imperfection who hive off into perfectionist sects whenever they think the Church is compromising. These questions recall thoughts which recur throughout the centuries of Scottish Christianity.

Christianity has done something to stimulate a belief in 'progress', embedded in thought about 'the coming of the Kingdom' and in that most familiar of all phrases, 'Thy kingdom come'. The individual certainly thinks that he is heading for a better place. Christianity sees a divine purpose creating in and through and out of suffering something of infinite value, something which will be found to justify all that has been endured on the way to it. The idea of the coming of the Kingdom may have given men a vision of something towards which they should work, a prospect of better times which they should help to shape. The Christian has his idea of perfection, but from his knowledge of human sin and limitations he does not expect to see it through mere human achievement on earth. Paul said, 'I can do all things through Christ which strengtheneth me', but secularists assume progress through liberal humanism, and hope is fixed on science – physical, social and economic.

The belief in progress has led to a belief that everything is for the best, and this notion has vitiated a lot of thinking, not least in the field of history. Historians have shown marked reluctance to admit that things have ever gone wrong, and the most catastrophic events have been labelled 'good things'. It is impossible to maintain such a facile belief in the face of the facts of history. Besides, belief in free will, belief that man is in a fallen state, belief that most men have so far rejected Christ, belief in an active force of evil, exclude the view that everything has been for the best. It is no part of the gospel to promise this (Mark xiii, 8, cf. Matthew xxiv). Uncomfortable though it may be to shed the idea of progress, the fact must be faced that disasters have occurred before and may occur again.

Ever since the first conversions, Scotland has contained a Christian community, but whether or not that community has ever been coextensive with the nation is simply not a realistic subject for debate, because there is such limited evidence about faith, which is largely imponderable. However, works, conduct – the fruits of faith – can be quantified, as can churchgoing, and they lend little support to the idea that Christianity ever permeated the nation. In chapter after chapter of this book the reader can find that criminal violence as well as disorders like drunkenness and, above all, profane language have been endemic over the centuries. While it could be said in the nineteenth century that 'life and conduct hang very loosely together' and profession and behaviour were in conflict, this is less true now, and to that extent there is probably less hypocrisy. There is also evidence almost age by age of scepticism and unbelief but also of testimony to evangelical truth, and each generation has had its committed Christians. Those who reject the mainstream churches today have ample precedents in the seventeenth century. Equally, attention has repeatedly been drawn to the way in which traditionalists and evangelicals may approximate, and at present they find themselves in something like an alliance against the ordination of women and other unscriptural practices favoured by the 'liberals' who occupy the middle ground.

No doubt there have been periods which were more religious and periods which were less religious. Certain patterns do recur and repeat themselves, if only because human nature does not change and men react to the same situation in different periods in the same way; Christianity, within historic times, does not seem to have led them to react in different ways and so break the cycle. The notion of 'the Kingdom' is fatal to a belief either that all will remain static or that human history proceeds in cycles and simply repeats itself. Sometimes there are positive somersaults. One of the features now distinguishing the Church of Scotland from the Church of Rome is that the former has women ministers; but in 1560 part of the case of the Church of Scotland against the Church of Rome was that the latter permitted women, 'whom the Holy Ghost will not suffer to teach in the congregation, to baptise'.[12] To take another example: until not long ago a 'high' Anglican reserved his most profound contempt for an evening celebration of Holy Communion, to which only the 'lowest' churchmen ever had recourse; but, when Rome introduced evening Mass, Anglicans made the Eucharist a service – almost the only service – for any hour of the day or night. At the same time, recurrence is so marked that sometimes the historian is tempted to say, rather wearily, 'This is where I came in' as one did when watching a continuous performance in a cinema.

In the eighteenth century there was scepticism about the Incarnation, but a metaphorical interpretation of that event had been hinted at by Scougal in the seventeenth century and was elaborated in the nineteenth. Already in the eighteenth century 'what the apostles would have called sinful pleasures they called human weakness', and in the nineteenth some doubted the Atonement. Those who remember the antics of Bishop Barnes of Birmingham (1924–53) are now less startled than their juniors are by Bishop Jenkins of Durham. The 'liberals' of today are less original than many think; and the amount of considered rejection of Christianity may be no greater now than it was in the eighteenth century. How close the 'dim theism' or 'non-militant atheism' spoken of in the twentieth century comes to the cool detachment of the Age of Reason is illustrated in the account of the Orkney island of Sanday in *The Third Statistical Account of Scotland* (1985): 'The popular feeling seems to be that good Christian living is not necessarily the same thing as regular attendance at Church. . . . In view of the fact that Sanday was subjected to a wave of fervent evangelisation during the latter part of the nineteenth century, surprise is often expressed that the descendants of such pious Church people should be so casual in the outward observance of religion. . . . The nineteenth century brand of religious belief was too austere and puritanical to make any lasting appeal. . . . The Orcadian abhors a strong display of emotional fervour, and . . . prefers an orderly service in which reason is more in evidence than deep emotion'.

A seventeenth-century writer remarked: 'The most strange accidents of our days have been already of old time before us. Persons who, after a long prosperity, are afflicted with a sudden calamity, when they find that nothing hath befallen them than what often before hath been, then in place of griefs, fears and amazements, patience, contentment and hope begin to possess the soul'. There we have the consolations of history and not least of religious history.

REFERENCES

Preface (pp. 13–14)
1 Coulton, *Friar's Lantern* (1948), 137.
2 *Expansion of Christianity*, i, 240.

Chapter 1 (pp. 15–24)
1 A. A. M. Duncan, *Scotland: The Shaping of the Kingdom*, 38; Alan Macquarrie in *RSCHS*, xxiii, 1–25.
2 *ES*, i, 411.
3 Socrates, *History of the Church* (1844), 509.
4 *MGH Epist.*, ii, 30–31; Mason, *The Mission of Augustine*, 44–5.
5 G. W. S. Barrow, 'The Childhood of Scottish Christianity', *Scottish Studies*, vol. 27.
6 Allan Maclean, *Telford's Highland Churches* (1989), note 17; *SHR*, lv, 29–40.
7 Latourette, i, 33.
8 R. B. K. Stevenson in *PSAS*, 113, pp. 469–77.
9 Barbara E. Crawford, *Scandinavian Scotland*, 215.
10 Museum Catalogue, *The French Connection*, no. 75.
11 Ian Finlay, *Columba*, 19.
12 Peter Godman, *Poetry of the Carolingian Renaissance*, 214–5.
13 Browne, *The Venerable Bede* (1919), 191–5, 280–81.

Chapter 2 (pp. 25–36)
1 *E.S.*, i, 445.
2 Ibid., i, 400 (cf. 425).
3 Ibid., i, 407.
4 *R.S.S.*, vi, 407.
5 Bulloch, *Adam of Dryburgh*, 158.
6 Robert Somerville, *Scotia Pontificia* (Clarendon Press, 1982), 19.
7 Cf. Donaldson, *Scottish Church History*, 220–4.
8 John M. Kemble, *Codex Diplomaticus aevi Saxonici*, ii, 209; R. H. Hodgkin, *History of the Anglo-Saxons* (3rd edn., 1952), ii, 604.
9 p. 25 supra.
10 *S.A.*, 179.
11 Walter Daniel, *Life of Ailred* (ed. Powicke, 1950), xxxii.
12 Alan Macquarrie, *Scotland and the Crusades*, 38–9.
13 Baillie, *L. & J.*, ii, 304.

Chapter 3 (pp. 37–60)

1 *TRHS*, ser. 5, vol. 38, pp. 131–46 passim.
2 *SR*, 15, 19 n. 5; Knox, ii, 233.
3 Patrick, 108.
4 Ibid., 266, n. 2.
5 John Durkan and Anthony Ross, 'Early Scottish Libraries', *IR*, ix; 'List of the books of John Grierson', *IR*, xxviii, 39–49; Duncan Shaw, 'A conserver of the Renaissance in Scotland', *The Renaissance and Reformation in Scotland* (ed. Cowan and Shaw), 41–69.
6 Beryl Smalley, *The Study of the Bible in the Middle Ages* (2nd edn., 1951), especially pp. 180–81.
7 Ed. Avril Henry, Scolar Press, 1987; cf. *Scot. Eccles. Soc. Trans.*, ii, 216–61.
8 EUL, La. III, 321, fos. 2–6; cf. *IR*, xvii.
9 *Aberdeen Eccles. Soc. Trans.*, 1889, pp. ix, 39–42; *Scot. Eccles. Soc. Trans.*, vi, 154–6, vii, 101. The great painting was probably above a rood screen and the lesser panels would fit a common pattern of reredos.
10 Allardyce Nicol, *British Drama* (1925), 21n and passim; Lucy Toulmin Smith, *York Plays* (1885); Alfred W. Pollard, *English Miracle Plays* (1890).
11 Anna Jean Mill, *Medieval Plays in Scotland* (1921).
12 Patrick, 40, 42, 55, 56, 77.
13 *TA*, i, pp. ccxxix, ccxl, ccxlv.
14 Knox, i, 62.
15 Calderwood, i, 141–3.
16 Donaldson, *James V to James VII*, 268.
17 M. L. Anderson, *The James Carmichaell Collection of Proverbs in Scots*, 920, 1076, 1259.
18 *SR*, 24 and n.
19 Ibid.; Moorman, 69.
20 *SR*, 25; *Wigtownshire Charters* (SHS), lvii–lviii.
21 *APS*, ii, 485; *SR*, 25; Patrick, lxiv, lxv.
22 *SR*, 20–23; *ER*, xvi, 65–6; *RSS*, iv, 641; *Public Affairs*, 359; *Wigtownshire Charters* (SHS), 131; *Paisley Register* (Maitland Soc.), 145–7, 152–6; PB John Crawford (MS), fo. 41a; *PB Thomas Johnson*, no. 345.
23 Moorman, 144–5, 210, 252.
24 *SR*, 25–6.
25 *LJV*, 162, 364.
26 Preface to First Prayer Book of Edward VI.
27 *St A. Formulare*, i, pp. xi–xii.
28 *Eccles. Hist.*, IV, xxi.
29 Kidd, *Documents of the Continental Reformation*, 12–3.
30 Patrick, 24–5; *Formulare*, nos. 60, 62, 510.
31 Patrick, 24–5.
32 *Bannatyne Misc.*, II, viii.
33 *Bannatyne Misc.*, III, v, vi.
34 Donaldson, 'The Dunbar Monument in its Historical Setting', *Dunbar Parish Church* (East Lothian Antiquarian and Field Naturalists' Society, 1987).
35 Steer and Bannerman – especially nos. 2, 19, 23, 26, 29, 44, 106.
36 *Robertus Richardinus* (SHS).
37 NLS MS 1746.
38 Cf. *P.B. of James Young* (SRS), no. 103.

39 Alasdair M. Stewart, 'Adam Abell's "Roit or Quheill of Tyme"', *Aberdeen Univ. Rev.*, vol. 44.

40 *Hamilton's Catechism*, ed. T. G. Law, xxxvi, 128, 171, 256.

41 *IR*, xv, 3–34.

42 Kennedy, *Two Eucharistic Tracts*, ed. Cornelis H. Kuipers, Nijmegen (1964), 162, 164, 183.

43 *The Poems of William Dunbar*, ed. Mackay Mackenzie, 154–5.

44 *Asloan MS* (STS n.s. 16), 162, 164, 183.

45 MacQueen, *Henryson*, 93, 100–1, 110–2.

46 STS 1966.

47 R. W. Pfaff, *New Liturgical Feasts in late Medieval England* (1920).

48 *IR*, xi.

49 *IR*, xix.

50 *IR*, vii, 25.

51 Macfarlane, *Elphinstone*, 222.

52 Patrick, 26–7, 63–4.

53 F. C. Eeles, *King's College Chapel, Aberdeen*, 139.

54 *APS*, ii, 485–8.

55 E.g. Wyntoun, ix, 2809; *TA*, i, Index, vii, 179.

56 *St A KS Reg.*, ii, 503–4 and n.

57 B. Ass i, 167; cf. *P.B. of James Young* (SRS), no. 338.

58 I. B. Cowan and D. E. Easson, *Medieval Religious Houses, Scotland*, 162.

59 *IR*, xvi, 199–216.

60 Ibid., xx, 80–106.

61 G. G. Coulton, *Friar's Lantern*, 137.

62 Gregory Dix, *The Shape of the Liturgy*, 596; Keith Thomas, *Religion and the Decline of Magic*, 189, 196–7.

63 *SHR*, xix, 305.

64 Patrick, c, ci, 4, 6, 26, 40, 75.

65 *St A F*, ii, 404, 438.

66 *St A KS Reg.*, ii, pp. lxxx–lxxxi and n.

67 Dix, *loc. cit.*

Chapter 4 (pp. 61–80)

1 *Devotional Pieces in Verse and Prose* (STS), 213, 264.

2 Donaldson, *All the Queen's Men*, 11; Margaret H. B. Sanderson, *Cardinal of Scotland*, App. iii.

3 *St A. F.*, ii, 225–7; *St A. K.S. Reg.*, i, 95–8.

4 The Thirty-nine Articles, no. xiv.

5 Calderwood, i, 141–3.

6 Cf. E. J. Cowan, *The People's Past: Scottish Folk in Scottish History* (Edinburgh 1980), 39–40.

7 Patrick, 127; *APS*, iii, 488–9.

8 R. G. Cant in *SHR*, xlv, 209.

9 *Rectorial Address at St Andrews* (1893), p. 45.

10 M. H. B. Sanderson, *Queen Mary's People*, 176.

11 Donaldson, 'The Dunbar Monument in its Historical Setting', *Dunbar Parish Church* (East Lothian Antiquarian and Field Naturalists' Society, 1987).

12 *Diary of the Short Parliament* (R. Hist. Soc.), III; *St A. K.S. Reg.*, see index s.v. 'Hammermen'.
13 Gregory Dix, *The Shape of the Liturgy*, 744.
14 Patrick, 188–90.
15 *Buik of the Kirk of the Canagait* (SRS), 38.
16 Pitcairn, I, i, *417.
17 David Knowles, *The Evolution of Medieval Thought* (1962), 274.
18 Michael Hunter, 'The problem of "Atheism" in early modern England', *TRHS*, 5th ser., 35, p. 145.
19 D. C. MacNicol, *Robert Bruce*, 301; Thomas, 198.
20 *St A. K.S. Reg.*, i, 135–6.
21 Ibid., 35–6, 85.
22 I. B. Cowan, *Blast and Counterblast*, 31.
23 Acts and Decreets (CS 7/305), fos. 50–51. I owe this important reference to Mr John Ballantyne.
24 Charles P. Finlayson, *Clement Litill and his Library* (Edin. Bibliog. Soc. and Friends of EUL).
25 J. N. King, *English Reformation Literature: The Tudor Origins of the Protestant Tradition*.
26 *St A. K.S. Reg.*, index s.v. Belief.
27 Archive and Record Centre, Dundee.
28 *Scottish Antiquary*, vii, 9, 111.
29 William Cowan, 'The Scottish Reformation Psalmody', *RSCHS*, i, 38–9.
30 *St A. K.S. Reg.*, ii, 913.
31 Ibid., p. lxxxii.
32 Calderwood, iii, 555.
33 Ibid., v, 410–11.
34 *Edinburgh Burgh Records*, iii, 145–6.
35 M. Lynch, *Edinburgh and the Reformation*, 103–4.
36 E.g., *RSS*, viii, 318, 1172, 1492, 1795, 2101, 2713.

Chapter 5 (pp. 81–102)

1 At the end of his life the Marquis of Argyll described himself as 'a distracted man, a distracted subject in a distracted time wherein I live' (*The Marquis of Argyle's Instructions to his Son* [1743], 5); an 18th century minister looked back on 'the distracted times of the Covenants' (p. 108).
2 Donaldson, *James V to James VII*, 273–4; Duncan Forrester and Douglas Murray, *Studies in the History of Worship in Scotland*, 47.
3 Donaldson, *Shetland Life under Earl Patrick*, 127–8; *Maitland Club Miscellany*, II, i, 129–30.
4 Lowther, *Our Journall into Scotland* (1894), 15, 16, 18, 23, 46.
5 *Archaeologia Scotica*, iv, 73–7.
6 Robert Hugh Macdonald, *The Library of Drummond of Hawthornden*.
7 Henry Scougal, *The Life of God in the Soul of Man*.
8 Calderwood, vii, 233 sqq.
9 *Scottish Liturgies of James VI* (Church Service Soc.), 79 sqq.
10 D. Macmillan, *The Aberdeen Doctors* (1909).
11 *SHR*, xxxiii, 171.
12 D. C. MacNicol, *Robert Bruce* (1907), 107, 116, 311–2.

13 *PCM*, 45.

14 Rutherford, *Letters*, i, 63–4, ii, 285.

15 *SHS* (1911, 1919, 1940).

16 *TRHS*, 5th ser. 36, p. 2; cf. Charles Bell, *Calvin and Scottish Theology – The Doctrine of Assurance.*

17 C. V. Wedgwood, *The King's Peace*, 185.

18 *TRHS*, 5th ser. 36, pp. 7–8; 37, pp. 7–8.

19 Copy (1687) of John Forbes' Diary in SRO CH/12/18/6; Hay of Craignethan published by SHS, Brodie by Spalding Club, Jaffray in various editions.

20 *Thomas Hope's Diary* (Bannatyne Club), 38–9; Rosaland K. Marshall, *Virgins and Viragoes*, 137.

21 *SHS Misc.*, iii.

22 *SHS Misc.*, vii.

23 W. Law Mathieson, i, 360.

24 Knox, ii, 3; Calderwood, iii, 554.

25 *Letters*, i, 102, 104, 111.

26 Donaldson, *Scotland; James V to James VII*, 315–6.

27 Wariston, 327–8.

28 Bannatyne Club, 78–9, 99, 106.

29 MacNicol, 309.

30 *PCM*, 103–4.

31 Donaldson, *Scottish Church History*, 208–12, 219.

32 George H. Gorman, *Introducing Quakers.*

33 E. J. Cowan, *The People's Past*, 42.

34 E. J. Cowan, *Montrose*, 167, 237, 259; John Buchan, *Montrose* (World's Classics), 312, 314 and n.

35 Baillie, 211–2; cf. Masson, *Drummond of Hawthornden*, 255.

36 *Ancram and Lothian*, i, 117.

37 *Protocol Book of James Young* (SRS), 492; *Original Letters*, 386; *Diurnal of Occurrents*, 21/4/1572; *RPC*, 3rd ser., ix, 66; Kirkton, 250–51.

38 Alexander Shields, *A Hind let loose*, 30, 138; Kirkton, 423n.

39 *Hind let loose*, 668, 675.

40 *Cambridge Modern History*, ii., 551

41 Alexander Peterkin, *Records of the Church of Scotland*, i (1838), 251.

42 Calderwood, iii, 384.

43 Ibid., 404.

44 Ibid., iv, 665–6, 689.

45 Ibid., v, 387.

46 Ibid., 376, 409–10.

47 J. Melville, *Diary*, 347 sqq.; Calderwood, v, 403.

48 St Andrews Presbytery Records, 4 Nov. 1596, 9 August 1600.

49 Kirkton, 48–9.

50 *Charles II and Scotland in 1650* (SHS), 134–40.

51 Brodie, 26, 190–1.

52 *Acts of the General Assembly* (Church Law Soc.), 125, 192.

53 *APS*, vi, 360–68, vii, 262, viii, 99; *RPC*, 3rd ser., i, 471–2, cf. ii, 111–2.

54 *Works*, 343.

55 G. B. Burnet, 122–3, 162, 175, 181, 184.

56 Butler, *Life and Letters of Robert Leighton*, 147.

57 Burnet, *Own Time* (Everyman), 106; my italics.

58 *Acts of the General Assembly*, 124.

59 *PCM*, 83; cf. Masson, 380–81.

60 *PCM, 87.*

61 Masson, 71, 212, 325–7, 369–74; *PCM*, 87.

62 *PCM*, 155–6.

63 Ibid., 82.

64 Ibid., 145.

65 Ibid., 147–8

66 David Stevenson, *The Origins of Freemasonry*, chap. 7.

67 NRA(S), Survey 885, 22/1, 27/12, 56/2, 66/5, 103/2; *Glamis Book of Record* (SHS).

68 GDH; Craven, 85, 91, 105; R. K. Marshall, op. cit., 138.

69 David Mathew, *Scotland under Charles I*, 20.

70 Cathaldus Giblin, *Irish Franciscan Mission to Scotland*, ix note.

71 Mathew, op. cit., 152, 161, 166, 174, 210–11, 216, 238.

72 Scott, *Letters*, iv, 342.

73 Kirkton, ix n.

74 *Lauderdale Papers* (Camden Soc.), i, 234.

75 Wodrow, i, 389.

76 James Kirk, 'The Kirk and the Highlands at the Reformation', *Northern Scotland*, vii; and 'The Jacobean Church in the Highlands 1567–1625', *The Seventeenth Century in the Highlands* (ed. Loraine Maclean).

77 *Highland Papers* (SHS), iii, 81.

78 Giblin, 79.

79 Ibid., 46.

80 D. Maclean in *RSCHS*, iii, 43–54.

81 Larner, vi.

82 Ibid., 32, 77.

83 Ibid., 12, 103, 189–90.

84 Keith Thomas, 547.

Chapter 6 (pp. 102–118)

1 Confessions of Faith from 1560 to the 1640s are discussed in chapter 5.

2 *Examination Roll of Arbroath* (SRS), p. ix.

3 Thomas Maxwell, 'Presbyterian and Episcopalian in 1688', *RSCHS*, xiii.

4 William Ferguson, *Scotland: 1689 to the Present*, 106.

5 Henry Grey Graham, ii, chapter x, gives a useful account.

6 *The Reasonableness of Christianity* (ed. Ramsey, 1958), 80.

7 *Wealth of Nations* (Everyman), ii, 275.

8 *Essay concerning Human Understanding*, Bk. iv, chap. 19, para. 10.

9 Andrew Thomson, *The Origin of the Secession Church*, 188.

10 Ibid.

11 *Wealth of Nations* (E.L.), ii, 270.

12 Quoted G. N. M. Collins, *Whose Faith Follow* (Edinburgh 1943), 26.

13 GDH 196.

14 T. Angus Kerr, 'Life and ministry of the Rev. Hugh Cunningham of Tranent', *RSCHS*, xv, 35–6.

15 *OSA*, xi, 165.

16 Drummond and Bulloch, 120.

17 Ibid.
18 A. P. F. Sell, *Church Planting* (Worthing, 1986), 42.
19 Summarised in Larner.
20 George B. Burnet, *The Holy Communion in the Reformed Church of Scotland*, 248–9; cf. H. Grey Graham, ii, 46–7.
21 Burnet, 212–3.
22 A. P. F. Sell, 'John Locke's Highland Critic', *RSCHS*, xxiii, 66.
23 An account of George Drummond, with quotations from his Diary (in EUL), is given in Alexander Grant, *The University of Edinburgh*, i, 363–74.
24 H. Grey Graham, ii, 53–4n.
25 *A Sense of Place* (ed. Graeme Cruickshank), 195–6; W. R. Aitken, *The Public Library Movement in Scotland*. I am indebted to Mr W. P. L. Thomson for information about the Kirkwall Library.
26 *A Sense of Place*, 192.

Chapter 7 (pp. 119–137)

1 *A Sense of Place*, 194–5; *Acts of the General Assembly* (Church Law Soc.), 878–9.
2 Alice Wemyss, *Histoire du Réveil*, 1790–1849 (Paris and Lausanne, 1977).
3 *Shetland Life*, no. 92 (June 1988).
4 Lucas, *Charters of the Old English Colonies in America*, 2; cf. Stock, *History of the Church Missionary Society*, i, 20.
5 Donald E. Meek, 'Evangelical Missionaries in the Early Nineteenth Century Highlands', *Scottish Studies*, vol. 28, p. 11.
6 Ibid., passim.
7 G. B. Burnet, 253.
8 Peter Chalmers, *History of Dunfermline*; Charles Rogers, *Leaves from my Autobiography* (1876).
9 Saunders, *Scottish Democracy*, 278–8.
10 *TRHS*, 5th ser., vol. 38, pp. 66, 68.
11 N. D. Denny, 'Temperance and The Scottish Churches', *RSCHS*, xxiii.
12 Burnet, 75n, 168, 277.
13 Erskine, *Letters* (ed. W. Hanna, Edinburgh 1877), i, 75.
14 p. 89 above.
15 W. H. C. Frend, *The Rise of Christianity*, 378–9.
16 'A Hymn for Sabbath Morning', in a Christmas Annual, *The Juvenile Forget-me-not*, for 1831, was reprinted in *Life and Work*, August 1986.
17 Alex. Bain, *J. S. Mill* (1882), 105.
18 R. L. Stevenson, *Records of a Family of Engineers* (Tusitala edn.), 265.
19 Galt, *The Entail* (1823), ii, 69.
20 Church of Scotland Commission on the Religious Condition of the People, 1890–96, 'Reports of The Commission on Non-church-going'; Drummond and Bulloch, 162, 170.
21 *Scottish Guardian*, 27 Jan. 1889.

Chapter 8 (pp. 138–147)

1 A. C. Cheyne, *The Transforming of the Kirk*, 177–8.
2 Ibid., 179.
3 It was on that ground that in 1988 David Norris, an 'Irish Gay Rights Champion', obtained a decree from the European Court of Human Rights ordering the Irish

government to pay him £12,000 because that government maintained laws against buggery and gross indecency.

4 Chapter v, n. 61.
5 *TRHS*, ser. 5, vol. 38, p. 74.
6 Joseph Kelly in *The Scotsman*, 18 August 1988.
7 BCC Community and Race Relations Unit, Issues Paper No. 5; letter to the author from the Editor of *Newscan*, 7 December 1988.
8 C. S. Lewis, *Christian Behaviour* (1943), 51.
9 Alison Eliot and Duncan B. Forrester, *The Scottish Churches and the Political Process Today* (Edinburgh 1986), 35.
10 D. J. Withrington, 'The Churches in Scotland c. 1870–1900', *RSCHS*, 19, p. 168 n. 21.
11 Eliot and Forrester, op. cit., 14.
12 Knox, ii, 269.

INDEX